# Arundhati Roy's *The God of Small Things*

On publication, Arundhati Roy's novel *The God of Small Things* (1997) rapidly became an international best-seller, winning the Booker Prize and creating a new space for Indian literature and culture within the arts, even as it courted controversy and divided critical opinion.

This guide to Roy's ground-breaking novel offers:

- an accessible introduction to the text and contexts of *The God of Small Things*;
- a critical history, surveying the many interpretations of the text from publication to the present;
- a selection of new essays and reprinted critical essays by Padmini Mongia, Aijaz Ahmad, Brinda Bose, Anna Clarke, Émilienne Baneth-Nouailhetas and Alex Tickell on *The God of Small Things*, providing a range of perspectives on the novel and extending the coverage of key critical approaches identified in the survey section;
- cross-references between sections of the guide, in order to suggest links between texts, contexts and criticism;
- suggestions for further reading.

Part of the *Routledge Guides to Literature* series, this volume is essential reading for all those beginning detailed study of *The God of Small Things* and seeking not only a guide to the novel, but also a way through the wealth of contextual and critical material that surrounds Roy's text.

**Alex Tickell** is a senior lecturer in English at the University of Portsmouth. He has published widely on South-Asian fiction and is the editor of *Selections from 'Bengaliana'* (2005), and co-editor of *Alternative Indias: Writing, Nation and Communalism* (2005).

# Routledge Guides to Literature

**Editorial Advisory Board:** Richard Bradford (University of Ulster at Coleraine), Shirley Chew (University of Leeds), Mick Gidley (University of Leeds), Jan Jedrzejewski (University of Ulster at Coleraine), Ed Larrissy (University of Leeds), Duncan Wu (St. Catherine's College, University of Oxford)

**Routledge Guides to Literature** offer clear introductions to the most widely studied authors and texts.

Each book engages with texts, contexts and criticism, highlighting the range of critical views and contextual factors that need to be taken into consideration in advanced studies of literary works. The series encourages informed but independent readings of texts by ranging as widely as possible across the contextual and critical issues relevant to the works examined, rather than presenting a single interpretation. Alongside general guides to texts and authors, the series includes 'Sourcebooks', which allow access to reprinted contextual and critical materials as well as annotated extracts of primary text.

**Already available:***

---

\* Some titles in this series were first published in the Routledge Literary Sourcebooks series, edited by Duncan Wu, or the Complete Critical Guide to Literature series, edited by Jan Jedrzejewski and Richard Bradford.

# Arundhati Roy's *The God of Small Things*

*Alex Tickell*

 Routledge
Taylor & Francis Group

LONDON AND NEW YORK

First published 2007
by Routledge
2 Park Square, Milton Park, Abingdon, Oxon OX14 4RN

Simultaneously published in the USA and Canada
by Routledge
270 Madison Ave, New York, NY 10016

*Routledge is an imprint of the Taylor & Francis Group, an informa business*

Typeset in Sabon and Gill Sans by RefineCatch Limited, Bungay, Suffolk
Printed and bound in Great Britain by
Antony Rowe Ltd, Chippenham, Wiltshire

*British Library Cataloguing in Publication Data*
A catalogue record for this book is available from the British Library.

*Library of Congress Cataloging in Publication Data*
Tickell, Alex.
 Arundhati Roy's The god of small things / Alex Tickell.
  p. cm. — (Routledge guides to literature)
 Includes bibliographical references and index.
 1. Roy, Arundhati. God of small things. I. Title.
 PR9499.3.R59G6338 2007
 823'.914—dc22

2006030863

ISBN 13: 978–0–415–35842–2 (hbk)
ISBN 13: 978–0–415–35843–9 (pbk)
ISBN 13: 978–0–203–00459–3 (ebk)

For Miles

# Contents

# Acknowledgements

First, special thanks to Shirley Chew, who has guided my studies in Indian litera-ture from the start, and Elleke Boehmer, for her valuable critical input. I would also like to thank Angelika Malinar, James Procter and Elodie Rousselot for their professional advice, and Maggie Bowers, Anna Clarke, Eugene McNulty, Padmini Mongia, Peter Morey, Stephen Morton and Amina Yaqin for their help. The University of Portsmouth assisted my research by providing some relief from teaching in spring 2005, and my colleagues at Portsmouth were encouraging and supportive and deserve many thanks. Discussions with Andrea Merrett and the students on my postcolonial literature course at the University of York generated numerous critical insights and shaped the foundations of this guide. Last, I want to thank Polly Dodson, Liz Thompson and Katherine Sheppard at Routledge and Liz O'Donnell for their assistance and, most of all, Rachel Goodyear, for her editorial help and faith in this project.

Brinda Bose, 'In Desire and Death: Eroticism as Politics in Arundhati Roy's *The God of Small Things*', *ARIEL: A Review of International English Literature*, 29 (2) (April 1998), pp. 59–72, is reprinted by kind permission of the Board of Governors, University of Calgary, Calgary, Alberta.

Émilienne Baneth-Nouailhetas, 'The Structures of Memory', in *The God of Small Things: Arundhati Roy* (Paris: Armand Colin/VUEF-CNED, 2002), pp. 49–60, 66–9, is reprinted by kind permission of the publisher.

While every effort has been made to trace and acknowledge ownership of copy-right material used in this volume, the publishers will be glad to make suitable arrangements with any copyright holders whom it has not been possible to contact.

# Notes and references

## Primary text

Unless otherwise stated, all references to the primary text are taken from *The God of Small Things*, Arundhati Roy (London: HarperCollins Flamingo, 1998). The initial reference will contain full bibliographic details and all subsequent references will be in parentheses in the body of the text, stating the chapter number and page number, e.g. (Ch. 1, p. 2).

## Secondary text

References to any secondary material can be found in the footnotes. The first reference will contain full bibliographic details, and each subsequent reference to the same text will contain the author's surname, title and page number.

## Footnotes

All footnotes that are not by the author of this volume will identify the source in square brackets, e.g. [Baldwin's note].

## Cross-referencing

Cross-referencing between sections is a feature of each volume in the Routledge Guides to Literature series. Cross-references appear in brackets and include section titles as well as the relevant page numbers in bold type, e.g. (see Texts and contexts, pp. 1–59).

# Introduction

Arundhati Roy's *The God of Small Things* generated controversy and encountered mixed critical opinion almost from the moment of its publication in 1997. It was not only professional reviewers and literary critics (not to mention publishers, lawyers and politicians) who differed in their judgement about the novel; Roy's wider readership also expressed strikingly varied opinions about its merits and, as this is a *reader's* guide to *The God of Small Things*, it is perhaps fitting to start our exploration of the novel by looking at some of these responses.

Reviews of any successful novel by its readers tend to divide naturally into distinctly positive or negative reactions – those who find a book mildly enjoyable or vaguely irritating are less likely to make the effort to record their feelings. But reading the 124 customer reviews of Arundhati Roy's *The God of Small Things* posted on the web site of a major online bookstore, we find opinions so opposed that it is sometimes difficult to believe that they refer to the same work. (Teaching *The God of Small Things* on university literature courses, this polarized response is also something I encounter in seminar discussions of the novel.) In their online reviews, a number of Roy's more admiring readers describe an almost mystical attachment to her fiction and regard the novel as 'magical', 'breathtakingly beautiful' and 'close to perfection'. Many also note the book's emotional impact and its lingering 'imprint' on the reader, and others talk perceptively about the fantastic, interlocking musical patterns of Roy's writing, its descriptive originality and the way key words and phrases evoke specific moods and events. In the opposite camp, Roy's less appreciative readers repeatedly attack the novel's unwarranted 'hype', its 'tediously' overwritten or needlessly embellished style and the difficulty of following the plot through its fragmented time scheme. Some readers even reflect on the passionate, contrasting reactions that Roy's novel often generates amongst friends to whom they have recommended the book, and one suggests, succinctly, that, without being able to anticipate which, readers of *The God of Small Things* will always be either 'lovers' or 'strugglers'.

This guide is designed for both groups, and has been written for students who have encountered *The God of Small Things* on college and university courses and readers who are simply interested in knowing more about this remarkable novel, its contexts and its critics. If you have enjoyed, or even fallen in love with, *The God of Small Things* then this guide will help you think about *how* Roy achieves her structural and stylistic effects and will introduce you to a range of the most significant literary criticism published on the novel, as well as outlining key approaches and significant biographical and historical details. If you have struggled with *The God of Small Things*, then this guide may not change your opinion of the work, but it will allow you to situate Roy's fiction in its cultural and political surroundings – from the structure of the Hindu caste system to the contemporary rise of Indian environmentalist activism – and will provide answers to questions about *why* Roy writes in the way she does. As the epigraph of *The God of Small Things* from the author, art critic and painter John Berger indicates, this is a novel that resists a 'single story' or a single exclusive perspective, and in writing this guide I have tried to preserve a sense of the different readings and sometimes conflicting critical views on *The God of Small Things*, in order to allow you, as much as possible, to come to your own conclusions about Roy's fiction. (Throughout this guide I refer extensively to Roy's essays and comments on her work, but we must remember that authorial perspectives are sometimes contradictory and changeable and do not exclude other interpretations or 'stand in' for the novel itself.)

Two further points need to be made here, both of which relate to Roy's own views. In recent interviews, Roy has drawn attention to the connection between knowledge and power and has criticized the role of education, especially 'specialists' in higher education, for using their knowledge to preserve, and justify, the actions of governments and financial institutions. For Roy, academic specialists of all kinds must be treated with suspicion because of their stake in protecting their own (overvalued) expertise, and their responsibility for 'trying to prevent people from understanding what is really being done to them'.[1] These are provocative claims, especially for teachers and students who encounter *The God of Small Things* (and read this guide) on special university courses devoted to women's writing, South-Asian fiction or postcolonial literature. However, the way specialist knowledge is used to support political systems (for instance, the strategic use of a knowledge of 'oriental' cultures in European colonialism) is a subject that also concerns academic critics working on literature from colonial and formerly colonized countries, and these debates will be explored as a matter of course in this guide. Moreover, Roy is not opposed to 'specialist knowledge' as such, as long as it is available to be shared and communicated and valued realistically – and one of the central aims of this guide is to make the academic discussions of *The God of Small Things* more accessible and understandable for the general reader.

Roy's self-proclaimed aim, as both author and political activist, is 'to never complicate what is simple, to never simplify what is complicated [and . . .] to be able to communicate to ordinary people what is happening in the world'.[2] If specialists maintain power by overcomplicating the simple then *The God of Small Thing* reveals, in its presentation of the traditional dance-drama of Kerala, *kathakali*, the dangers of simplifying the complicated. Stripped of its meaning and compressed into short pool-side performances for the benefit of Western tourists, the *kathakali* shows us what happens when cultural forms (such as oral narratives or even novels) are abbreviated and simplified. Guidebooks such as this one,

---

1 Arundhati Roy, *The Chequebook and the Cruise Missile*, London: HarperCollins, 2004, p. 120.
2 Arundhati Roy, *The Chequebook and the Cruise Missile*, p. 120.

especially when they introduce Western readers to literary works from non-Western cultures, risk the same kind of oversimplification, and for that reason I have provided a larger, more detailed cultural contexts section than is usual in the Routledge Guides to Twentieth-Century Literature series. However comprehensive a reader's guide is, its capacity to convey the complexity of a literary work is always limited – and in motifs such as the *kathakali* Roy hints that there are certain kinds of knowledge that are not easily summarized or condensed and implies that the task of understanding, especially across cultures, may involve both intuition and personal commitment. This guidebook will provide you with essential critical and contextual tools for reading *The God of Small Things*, but at the same time its aim is to encourage further reading and informed reflection and to provide a starting point, or a series of potential starting points, for your own ideas about this fascinating novel.

# 1

# Text and contexts

# The text

## Memory and identity

Set in the southern Indian state of Kerala and divided, chronologically, between the late 1960s and the early 1990s, the plot of Arundhati Roy's *The God of Small Things* pivots around a fated, forbidden relationship between a Syrian-Christian divorcee, Ammu, and a low-caste 'untouchable' carpenter, Velutha. Much of the narrative of *The God of Small Things* (cited hereafter as *TGST*) is presented from the perspective of Roy's twinned child-protagonists, Ammu's children Estha and Rahel, and the decisive events of the novel – the cross-caste affair, the subsequent beating and murder of Velutha by the police, and the death by drowning of the children's cousin, Sophie Mol – are revealed gradually as the adult twins meet more than twenty years later. Roy's complex doubled time scheme allows for a meditative, almost obsessive remembrance of these family tragedies, and it is through the close juxtaposition of past and present that Roy is able to develop the novel's other central concern, the delayed effect of these damaging events on Estha and Rahel, their traumatized return to the family home in the town of Ayemenem and their (incestuous) reconciliation in adulthood.

Like Ammu's deferred choice of a proper surname for her children, Roy's novel resists categorization and draws together elements of the fairy tale, psychological drama, pastoral lyric, tragedy and political fable. Roy's interest in the continuities between childhood and adulthood does, however, point to an important generic template in the *Bildungsroman* – a type of novel, usually narrated in the first person, in which the central character's growth from childhood to maturity and their developing self-awareness provide the main framework of the narrative. The enduring resonance of the past in Estha and Rahel's adult lives and their troubled return to Ayemenem suspends and almost reverses the genre's conventional progressive pattern, leading some reviewers to describe Roy's third-person narrative as an 'anti-*Bildungsroman*' in which the main protagonists 'never properly grow up'.[1]

---

1 Alice Traux, 'A Silver Thimble in her Fist', *New York Times*, 25 May 1997. See also Deepika Bahri, *Native Intelligence: Aesthetics, Politics and Postcolonial Literature*, Minneapolis, Minn.: University of Minnesota Press, 2003, p. 207.

In fact, the twins' 'arrested development' means that their story stretches both backwards and forwards: not only into the remembered/repressed past in a pattern of 'analepsis' (retrospection or flashback) but also towards its horrifying conclusion, which is anticipated, repeatedly, in a process of 'prolepsis' (a 'flashforward' in which future events are anticipated in the narrative 'present'). Roy succinctly describes the effect of these narrative devices when she states, 'the structure of the book ambushes the story – by that I mean the novel ends more or less in the middle of the story and it ends with Ammu and Velutha making love and it ends on the word tomorrow'.[2] As in the standard *Bildungsroman*, memory is central to both character development and plot in *TGST*, but the process of reminiscence is rarely ordered like a conventional narrative, tending instead to be repetitious, digressive and continually triggered by 'little events, ordinary things'.[3] Indeed, this sifting,[4] beachcombing return over the ground of memory shapes the structure of *TGST* as a whole, and the process through which 'remembered' small things become 'the bleached bones of a story',[5] is one of the triumphs of the novel.

Because of its close formal connection to biography and memoir, the *Bildungsroman* has often been used by postcolonial writers as a means of connecting the political with the individual and allegorizing the struggle for independence and the growth of the newly independent nation in the personal progress of a central protagonist.[6] In the 1920s and 1930s the highly popular memoirs of India's nationalist leaders, Mohandas K. Gandhi and Jawaharlal Nehru, fulfilled a similar function and seemed, in Nehru's words, to show how during the struggle against the British 'our prosaic existence [. . .] developed something of epic greatness in it'.[7] For many postcolonial writers and artists, however, the 'epic' experience of national independence was followed by a growing disillusionment with the tarnished ideals and unfulfilled promises of the independent nation-state. Thus, in contemporary Indian literature we are more likely to encounter ironic or satirical reworkings of the established convention of the national allegory. This is certainly the case in *TGST* where the tension between 'big and small things', and the obvious failure of political groups such as the communists to represent their constituents, serves to undermine the positive association of self and nation so evident in earlier nationalist fictions.

Postcolonial authors have also used the *Bildungsroman* to explore the problems of retaining roots and preserving a sense of cultural belonging in the aftermath of colonial rule. In *TGST*, these issues are registered in the uncanny linked consciousness of the twins, Estha and Rahel, who are 'physically separate, but

---

2    Roy, quoted in Julie Mullaney, *Arundhati Roy's The God of Small Things: A Reader's Guide*, London and New York: Continuum, 2002, p. 56.
3    Arundhati Roy, *The God of Small Things*, Ch. 1, p. 32.
4    In *TGST*, memory is compared to an eccentric woman whom Rahel encounters in a train carriage: 'Memory was like that woman on the train. Insane in the way she sifted through dark things in a closet and emerged with the most unlikely ones – a fleeting look, a feeling' (Ch. 2, p. 72).
5    Arundhati Roy, *The God of Small Things*, London: HarperCollins Flamingo, 1998, Ch. 1, pp. 32–3. All subsequent references will be given in the body of the text.
6    See Fredric Jameson, 'Third-World Literature in the Era of Multinational Capitalism', *Social Text*, 15, 1986, pp. 65–88, and Aijaz Ahmad, *In Theory: Classes, Nations, Literatures*, London: Verso, 1992.
7    Jawaharlal Nehru quoted in Arvind Krishna Mehrotra (ed.), *A History of Indian Literature in English*, London: Hurst, 2003, p. 153.

with joint identities' (Ch. 1, p. 2) and who seem to embody, in their compound subjectivity, the dislocated or split cultural identity of the colonized.[8] In addition, the desire to recapture childhood or to reconcile oneself with a lost homeland has been a rich theme for 'diasporic' South-Asian writers, who have been forced to negotiate their sense of identity and 'translate' themselves after experiencing personal or familial migration. This is something that we will return to in comparisons between *TGST* and Salman Rushdie's writing (see Text and contexts, **pp. 46–8**), and while Roy is not part of India's literary diaspora herself, *TGST* relates numerous journeys and points towards the dislocating effects of migrancy and dispossession in the multiple returns of the story: Ammu's shameful return after her divorce, Rahel's return from America, Estha's 're-return' and the unhappy homecomings of South Indian migrant workers from the gulf states. Haunted, as adults, by a past that *cannot* be physically returned to, or changed, Estha and Rahel also experience the quintessentially 'migrant' predicament of an enduring sense of exile and loss, even as they are reunited in the familiar surroundings of their family home.

In common with other postcolonial novelists, Roy's sense of her own identity demands an awareness of the continuing, damaging effects of colonial rule. As she explains: 'Fifty years after independence, India is still struggling with the legacy of colonialism, still flinching from the cultural insult [and . . .] we're still caught up in the business of "disproving" the white world's definition of us.'[9] This issue is most evident in her sensitivity to language use and the force of 'History' in *TGST*, and we will see in the following pages that Roy recycles and challenges the linguistic inheritance of British colonialism in various ways. The dense patterns of quotation and literary reference that she weaves through *TGST* not only reveal the intermixtures and cross-fertilizations of contemporary South-Asian culture but also throw hidden or disturbing aspects of this history into relief. In keeping with her two-way time scheme, Roy does not confine herself to redressing the 'insults' of a colonial past, but is also keenly aware of the shadow of an older pre-colonial history. In this sense, 'the postcolonial' (as a belated 'disproving' critical response to colonialism) is just one aspect of *TGST*, and the novel also considers the enduring effects of India's ancient Vedic and Hindu history and traditions, as well as looking forward to its fully industrialized, globally integrated present.[10]

## Melodrama and romance

In some of its European language translations, *TGST* has appeared with a subtitle defining it as 'a romance', and while this is clearly a marketing decision by Roy's publishers it also highlights another generic feature of her fiction. Much older than the novel, the romance, and popular subgenre variants such as the fairy tale, tend to be non-realist and deal in archetypes or emblematic figures, and, as a story of thwarted love, *TGST* inherits Indian folk-tale and romance traditions from

---

8 See Alex Tickell, '*The God of Small Things*: Arundhati Roy's Postcolonial Cosmopolitanism', *Journal of Commonwealth Literature*, 38(1), 2003, pp. 73–89, at p. 79.
9 Arundhati Roy, *Power Politics*, 2nd edn, Cambridge, Mass.: South End Press, 2001, p. 13.
10 Roy, *Power Politics*, p. 12.

devotional *bhakti* literature as well as repeating some conventions of the European 'tragic' romance.[11] The recent success of another (historical, non-fiction) Indian romance, William Dalrymple's *White Mughals* (2002), which deals with a 'forbidden' love affair between a colonial official and an Indian princess, suggests that *TGST*'s popularity may owe something to enduring Western fantasies of India as a setting for interracial or – in this case – intercaste romance. As Saadia Toor points out, transgressive sexuality haunts the novel in the same way as it overshadows some famous English fictions about colonial India such as E. M. Forster's *A Passage to India* (1924).[12] Forbidden love that breaks religious or social boundaries (albeit between partners who often, ultimately, gain social acceptance) is also a staple of the Indian film industry and, whilst Roy herself is scathing about mainstream cinema in India, *TGST* can be read as a clever reworking and reinterpretation of this established popular-cultural theme.

Roy's debt to popular romance is also evident in the more melodramatic aspects of her novel. Indeed, Roy's moral vision is so uncompromising that complex characters are often presented in terms of their own overshadowing fates, or 'emblematic' character traits such as greed or jealousy, something that also echoes the dramatic conventions of *kathakali* (discussed in more detail on **pp. 40–2**). These techniques result in a novel that sets up melodramatic situations and relationships but then structures and nuances them in increasingly subtle ways.[13] In a process of internal mirroring, *TGST* includes a number of unhappy subromances that counterpoint Ammu and Velutha's affair. The twins' great-aunt, Baby Kochamma, is disappointed in her unrequited love for an Irish priest, which is sublimated in the 'fierce, bitter garden' she raises, and their uncle Chacko's undergraduate marriage to an Englishwoman ends in divorce. Ammu herself is haunted by an exploitative marriage to the alcoholic manager of an Assam tea estate, and Rahel too inherits this pattern of doomed cross-cultural love in her marriage to an American architect. Significantly, all these 'romances' cross the boundaries of the Syrian-Christian community and threaten its 'caste' identity, but none is proscribed as severely as Ammu's 'unthinkable' affair with Velutha.

Romance and sexuality are both overshadowed by death in *TGST*, either figuratively, as a marital death-in-life (which Mammachi and Ammu, for a time, share), or as the brutal, often symbolic consequence of actual liaisons. In the latter category, Ammu, Velutha and Sophie Mol's deaths all occur as a darkly ironic, interminable working-out of the biblical warning about the wages of sin.[14] The use of heightened melodramatic effect and the thematic proximity of love/desire and death also point towards Gothic romance influences in *TGST*, and these mesh with the novel's colonial antecedents in images of ghosts (most clearly in Kari Saipu as a spectral figure of paedophiliac desire), the haunting persistence of the past and the uncanny doublings and premonitions generated by Roy's narrative technique. In the conclusion of *TGST*, the moment of incestuous love

11  See Gillian Beer, *The Romance*, London: Methuen, 1970.
12  Saadia Toor, 'Indo-Chic: The Cultural Politics of Consumption in Post-Liberalisation India', *SOAS Literary Review* 2, 2000. Online. Available HTTP: <http://www.soas.ac.uk/soaslit/2000_index.htm>.
13  Michiko Kakutani, 'Melodrama as Structure for Subtlety', *The New York Times*, 3 June 1997.
14  Romans 6:23.

between the 'returned' twins re-establishes the romance theme on the level of mythical archetype, providing an unsettling but also potentially redemptive counterpart to the sexual taboo-breaking of inter-caste love at the heart of the narrative.

## Language and play

Roy's use of language, with its ability to disconcert, convey subtle tonal change and challenge received ideas, is an unmistakable characteristic of her fiction. In a much-quoted phrase, Roy has described language as 'the skin of my thought',[15] and a sensual pleasure in wordplay, puns and rhymes infuses the novel. TGST works as an interesting postcolonial example of narrative as a 'word hoard', into which incidental phrases, songs, proverbs, road signs, quotes from Shakespeare, Kipling, The Sound of Music and fragments of Hindu epic are all intertextually gathered. Like its more fabular or fairy-tale aspects, a pleasure in collection, arrangement and hoarding mirrors the preoccupations of Roy's child-protagonists in the very form and patterning of TGST. Furthermore, with its non-standard spellings, reversed words, neologisms, repetitions and emphatic capitalizations, Roy's novel often tests the limits of prose; it frequently resembles blank verse, lingering, like an imagist poem or haiku, over an isolated detail or emotional state. In some instances the use of playful child-centred language to represent the cruelty of the adult world gives Roy's writing a tangible capacity to shock (as in Estha's encounter with the Orangedrink Lemondrink Man),[16] but Roy herself has also suggested, conversely, that some of her linguistic effects, such as repetition, work as a form of insulation against the horrifying events in the narrative. As she states: 'Repetition [was] used because it made me feel safe. Repeated words and phrases have a rocking feeling, like a lullaby. They help take away the shock of the plot.'[17] As we shall see in the course of this guide, several critics have discussed Roy's linguistic effects, but her ability to capture the idiosyncrasies of children's language acquisition, which also forms an extended, subversive 'play' with language, is an aspect of the novel that deserves further study.

Because of its stylistic virtuosity, TGST has been criticized as sentimental, flawed by a 'facetious whimsicality' and 'inescapably and fatally compromised by the self-indulgence of its style'.[18] Whether or not Roy's arch asides, repetitive phrasing and sometimes clumsy symbolism are major defects, or simply the inevitable weaknesses of a first novel,[19] is a matter of opinion, but we should keep in mind that, as an Indian-English author, her experiments with language indicate some very specific cultural and political concerns. Indian novelists writing in English have frequently drawn attention to the problems involved in making an 'alien', colonially-imposed language the medium of Indian literary

---

15 Taisha Abraham, 'An Interview with Arundhati Roy', ARIEL, 29(1), 1998 p. 91.
16 See Elleke Boehmer, 'East is East and South is South: The Cases of Sarojini Naidu and Arundhati Roy', Women, 11 (1 and 2), 2000, pp. 61–70, at p. 70.
17 See Arundhati Roy, 'Winds, Rivers and Rain', The Salon Interview. Online. Accessible HTTP: <http://www.salon.com/sept97/00roy.htm> (accessed 28 November 2005).
18 Tom Deveson, 'Much Ado about Small Things', Sunday Times, 15 June 1997.
19 Shirley Chew, 'The House in Kerala', Times Literary Supplement, 30 May 1997.

expression,[20] and in Roy's novel, the cultural dislocations inherent in the twins' education are underlined in Chacko's lecture on their incurable Anglophilia (Ch. 2, p. 52). However, while the early pioneers of the Indian-English novel tried to infuse their English with the idiomatic tone of an Indian mother tongue or capture the texture of 'Indian English', Roy is more interested in presenting contemporary India as a multilingual society in which Indian English operates as just one (privileged) language amongst many. In *TGST*, the proximity of English and Malayalam reveals Kerala's multiple local linguistic cross-currents, and the fact that Roy's protagonists switch between different registers and languages, rather than speaking a generic Indian English, sensitizes us to the politics and petty snobberies that underlie postcolonial language use and, through this, the status of English as India's semi-official elite *lingua franca*.

Again, like many postcolonial Indian authors who transcribe words from India's state languages into their English prose, Roy assumes the role of interpreter for her non-Malayalam-speaking readers when she glosses and explains words: 'In Malayalam, Mol is Little Girl and Mon is Little Boy' (Ch. 2, p. 60). But, in a technique that reflects her unease over other forms of cultural interpretation, she also asserts the power relations of this act of cultural mediation by sometimes refusing to explain: 'Estha and Rahel couldn't call [Chacko] Chachen because when they did, he called them Chetan and Cheduthi. If they called him Ammaven he called them Appoi and Ammai [. . .] So they called him Chacko' (Ch. 2, p. 37). As well as emphasizing her interest in names and naming (and the power of language to construct meaning and identity), the passage quoted above partially alienates Roy's non-Malayalam readers and underlines the fact that cultural differences cannot, and should not, always be easily translated or explained.[21] Roy's decisions about the level of cultural mediation she is willing to provide in *TGST* pose important questions about her intended audience, and the assumption that she anticipates the tastes and cultural preconceptions of a predominantly Western readership is something we will return to in the Critical history and Critical readings sections of this guide.

## History, order and transgression

While Roy's use of English marks an awareness of how language shapes identity and reveals the lingering residue of colonialism in contemporary Indian English, her novel is more immediately political in some of its other themes. The oppression of women is a key subject and provides the catalyst for the novel's pivotal, caste-breaking affair: Ammu's rage at her lack of legal status or 'Locusts Stand I', Mammachi's experience of domestic violence at the hands of Pappachi, and Baby Kochamma's humiliation by the men on the trade-union march all condense in

---

20  See Raja Rao, Foreword to *Kanthapura*, 2nd edn, 1938; New Delhi: Oxford University Press, 1993.

21  See Gayatri Spivak, 'The Burden of English' in C. A. Breckenridge and P. van der Veer (eds), *Orientalism and the Postcolonial Predicament*, Philadelphia, Pa.: University of Philadelphia Press, 1993, pp. 134–57. In a different context Roy has argued that 'The Western notion of thinking that you must understand everything can also be destructive. Why can't we just be satisfied with not understanding something? [. . .] There ought to be a balance between curiosity, grace, humility and letting things be' (Arundhati Roy, *The Chequebook and the Cruise Missile*, p. 19).

their differing reactions to the forbidden liaison. Furthermore, in placing the cross-caste relationship at the centre of the narrative, the oppression of women in the novel is associated with (but not necessarily made equivalent to) other entrenched social inequities in Kerala such as untouchability (see Text and contexts, **pp. 27–8**). Roy's technique, in *TGST*, is to present these socially sanctioned oppressions under the umbrella term, 'history'. In one of her early interviews she states that *TGST* is 'not about history but biology and transgression',[22] but she later revised this definition, arguing that 'the theme of much of what I write, fiction as well as non-fiction, is the relationship between power and powerlessness and the endless circular conflict they're engaged in'.[23] Her equivocation is revealing because it shows us how the term 'history' can signify a number of related things in *TGST* including, variously, an 'inchoate past', or the ordering of past events or, alternatively, 'the weight that tradition imposes on the present, pre-determining actions and interpretations'.[24]

If we concentrate on the last of these definitions we realize that the weight of tradition on the present is always intimately bound up with power, since to perpetuate a particular cultural-historical custom also means selecting and authorizing events in a certain way. The Hindu legal texts which determine caste intermixture are a prime example of this kind of historically naturalized order, and the evocative passage in which the 'origins' of the events in *TGST* are discussed underlines their continuing relevance: 'It really began [. . .] when the Love Laws were made. The laws that lay down who should be loved, and how. And how much' (Ch. 1, p. 33). As history reinforces social convention and separation in Roy's fiction, it also, paradoxically, absorbs new 'traditions', such as Syrian Christianity and Marxism, into itself. However revolutionary or liberating these religious or political belief systems promise to be, once they are absorbed into 'history' in *TGST* they become associated with the power of orthodoxy, order and separation.

In its depiction of history as a powerful force of order and classification, *TGST* thus appears to celebrate its opposite in images of mixedness and hybridity, concepts which have been highly influential in postcolonial theory (see Critical history, **pp. 72–5**). Not only are the twins a type of transgressive two-egg hybrid, in numerous instances in the novel – from Mammachi's illegal jam-jelly mixtures to the unclassifiable moth that haunts Pappachi's dreams of entomological discovery – hybridity 'blurs' laws and transgresses rules.[25] However, the distinction between making and breaking rules in *TGST* is far from clear. In fact, all the members of the Ipe family 'transgress' in different ways: 'They all broke the rules. They all crossed into forbidden territory' (Ch. 1, p. 31), and, as Baneth-Nouailhetas suggests: 'Rather than present[ing] us with a definite separation between the world of power that makes the laws, and the world of the transgressors, the narrative uncovers a multiplicity of intersecting, sometimes contradictory, sets of rules, and [. . .] ways they are tampered with.'[26] These contradictions are most noticeable in

22  Arundhati Roy, quoted in <http://website.lineone.net/~jon.simmons/roy/tgost6.htm>.
23  Arundhati Roy, *The Ordinary Person's Guide to Empire*, London: HarperCollins, 2004, p. 13.
24  Émilienne Baneth-Nouailhetas, *The God of Small Things: Arundhati Roy*, Paris, Armand Colin/ VUEF-ONED, 2002, p. 118.
25  Tickell, 'Arundhati Roy's Postcolonial Cosmopolitanism', p. 78.
26  Baneth-Nouailhetas, *The God of Small Things: Arundhati Roy*, pp. 117–18.

Ammu's fierce concern for her children's cleanliness, and her strictures about dirt and hand-washing echo the ancient fear of caste pollution encoded in the 'love laws', which she herself will eventually transgress.[27] Even Estha and Rahel participate in forms of arrangement in their desire to list and account for things and events, suggesting that order is, on some deep level, an innate human need.

Significantly, patterns of order and transgression also shape the structural arrangement of *TGST*, when the novel's regular alternation between present and past (in odd- and even-numbered chapters) suddenly changes in the final sections, confining events to the past. This effectively 'breaks the chain of the narrative',[28] creating a 'dissonance [that] compels an extra degree of attention' in the last stages of the novel.[29] But, in the midst of its interwoven thematic network of regulation and transgression, Roy still distinguishes between characters who negotiate order and rules generally and more negative, authoritarian figures such as Comrade Pillai and the police inspector Thomas Mathew. Described as 'mechanics who serviced different parts of the same machine' (Ch. 13, p. 262), these figures are wholly cynical and, in a novel that invests so much in the moral clarity of child perspectives, it is telling that they are the most 'truly terrifyingly adult' (Ch. 13, p. 262) characters. Their 'exploiter' roles in the narrative are epitomized in Roy's description of Comrade Pillai putting his hand into 'History's waiting glove' (Ch. 14, p. 281), an image that emphasizes his covert manipulation of the existing order and presents history as a political resource for those who know how to use it. More accurately, then, the fictional world of *TGST* is divided between characters like Pillai and Baby Kochamma who misuse and (fearfully) enforce the status quo, and those, like Ammu and Velutha, who are part of the social order but also have the potential to 'wrong-foot' or transgress history (Ch. 8, p. 176).

## Big and small things: making connections

If there is a principle that links *TGST* with Roy's later essays and journalism, it is the power of the writer to make connections and to challenge the boundaries that are set up (and, continually, 'historically' reinforced) between the powerful and the powerless. The ability to make connections – and envisage the world from multiple perspectives *across* these boundaries – is implied in the title of Roy's novel. To imagine that 'small things' might have, or deserve, a deity immediately poses questions about priorities and reminds us that godlike authority, when it manifests itself on a large 'monolithic' scale in religious, governmental or social forms, rarely allows power to be shared evenly among everyone and often maintains control by marginalizing particular groups. To counteract this tyranny of 'big things', Roy's strategy in *TGST* is to develop an 'aesthetic of connection' – in other words an artistic process of forging meanings and tracing the reach of power that has, at its heart, the creative potential of dissent.

---

27  For an influential study of the social taboo of dirt as 'matter out of place', see Mary Douglas, *Purity and Danger: An Analysis of Concepts of Pollution and Taboo*, London: Routledge and Kegan Paul, 1966.
28  Mullaney, *Arundhati Roy's The God of Small Things*, p. 44.
29  Michael Gorra, 'Living in the Aftermath', *London Review of Books*, 19 June 1997.

As we might expect from our discussion of the formal and linguistic playfulness of Roy's writing, these ideas are rarely presented to us directly in *TGST*. Instead, Roy prefers to convey her moral and political messages more obliquely, so that the whole novel becomes a subtle meditation on the interconnectedness of the world:

> *The God of Small Things* is a book which connects the very smallest things to the very biggest. Whether it's the dent that a baby spider makes on the surface of water in a pond or the quality of the moonlight on a river or how history and politics intrude into your life, your house, your bedroom, your bed, into the most intimate relationships between people – parents and children and siblings and so on.[30]

For Roy, the process of connecting 'the very smallest things to the very biggest' is politically significant in two related ways. The first of these depends on the revelatory power of connecting cause and effect and is hinted at strongly in the passage quoted above. In a globalized world where governments and multinational companies operate at increasing distances from the people they affect, Roy's 'aesthetic of connection' forces power to remain accountable, drawing attention to its hidden political alliances and profit motives. This investigative mandate is apparent in the sharp unflinching eye for injustice and poverty that characterizes *TGST* and is underlined in Roy's beliefs about her authorial role as someone who 'ask[s] [. . .] very uncomfortable questions'.[31] (Roy's claims about the author are reminiscent of a statement made by the French existentialist philosopher and novelist, Jean-Paul Sartre, that 'the function of the writer is to act in such a way that nobody can be ignorant of the world and that nobody may say that he is innocent of what it is about'.)[32] This first type of connection-making is also very clearly apparent in essays such as 'The Greater Common Good', with its aim to dig deep in the files of the Indian government and 'spill a few State Secrets'.[33]

Less obvious, but equally important, is a second pattern of connection, which tends to be holistic rather than investigative. This mode is most evident in Roy's literary focus on the value of 'smallness' and 'small things' and their vital place in larger political formations in *TGST* – a strategy that questions the perspectives of our received world view and represents an attempt to find new 'ways of seeing'. Related closely to an emphasis on ecosystems and the interdependence of humanity and nature in environmentalist thought, but also evoking some of the philosophical foundations of Jainism,[34] Roy's constant privileging of the small refuses the conventional ordering of politics in its public or national guises and replaces it

---

30  Roy, *The Chequebook and the Cruise Missile*, p. 11.
31  Arundhati Roy, *The Algebra of Infinite Justice*, London: HarperCollins, 2002, p. 177.
32  Jean-Paul Sartre, *What is Literature?*, trans. B. Frechtman, London: Methuen, 1978, p. 13.
33  Arundhati Roy, *The Cost of Living*, London: HarperCollins, 1999, p. 26.
34  Alongside Buddhism, Jainism was one of the heterodox religions that flourished in northern India between the seventh and fifth centuries BCE. Jainism survives in India to the present day and is known for its deep respect for all forms of life. Some of its central tenets – especially hylozoism, or the belief that all matter has a soul, and the epistemological relativism of *anekāntavāda* or 'the Doctrine of Manysidedness' – have an interesting resonance in Roy's work. For a useful overview see Ainslie T. Embree (ed.), *Sources of Indian Tradition*, Vol. I, New York: Columbia University Press, 1988.

with a radical *equivalence* in which a sense of community, personal relationships and an individual's imaginative response to his/her surroundings become as momentous as paying taxes and supporting particular parties.[35] For Roy, this almost spiritual awareness of the relatedness of the world, in which 'small things' dance on the edges of larger tragedies, does not rule out collective forms of activism; instead it becomes the very basis for a political and imaginative perspective which is grounded in local concerns.

These different expressions of an 'aesthetic of connection' merge in Roy's writing and must be seen as part of a combined strategy that constantly emphasizes the dignity of the powerless and denies those in power the exclusive right to define (and justify) their own actions. Symbolically, the presiding example of interconnection in *TGST* is, of course, Ammu and Velutha's affair, an act that denies the dehumanizing, exploitative separations of caste, class or ethnic difference and becomes, in the process, a symbol of future change.

## The author

A brief review of Arundhati Roy's life, and especially her early childhood, seems to confirm the truism that most first novels are strongly autobiographical. We should beware, however, of making simplistic connections between author and novel, as some reviewers have done, or using Roy's personal experiences as a model for what is essentially an imaginative work of fiction. In fact, Roy's biography is ultimately more useful as a way of charting her political concerns and her development as a writer than as a template for *TGST*.

Suzanna Arundhati Roy was born on 24 November 1961 in the north-eastern Indian state of Assam to a Syrian-Christian mother, the activist and teacher Mary Roy, and a Bengali Hindu father. Roy's parents divorced when she and her brother were still very young, and Mary Roy was forced to return with the children to her family home in the small town of Ayemenem (or Aymanam), in the southern Indian state of Kerala. A memorable feature of *TGST* is its evocation of the rural world of Ayemenem, and Roy ascribes her deep sense of place to her childhood surroundings: 'The kind of landscape that you [grow] up in, it lives in you [. . .] if you spent your very early childhood catching fish and just learning to be quiet, the landscape just seeps into you.'[36] The idyllic natural environment of South India is also tempered, in Roy's fiction and prose, by memories of vulnerability and social stigma. Because of her divorce, Roy's mother was never fully accepted back into the conservative world of rural Kerala, and in *TGST* Ammu's humiliation as a divorcee may reflect the emotional texture of Mary Roy's 'shameful' return after her failed marriage.

The political awareness and the sensitivity to social injustice in *TGST* can also be traced back to Roy's childhood, and the example of her mother's uncompromising feminism and social activism. After her return, Mary Roy founded a small

---

35  Although she disagrees with the village-centred 'traditionalism' of Gandhian thought, Roy's views bear comparison here with Gandhi's emphasis on the local in his concept of *swaraj*. See M. K. Gandhi, *Hind Swaraj* (ed.), Anthony J. Parel, Cambridge: Cambridge University Press, 1997.
36  Quoted in <http://website.lineone.net/~jon.simmons/roy/tgost2.htm>.

but successful independent school in Ayemenem and achieved notoriety when she became involved in a high-profile public-interest litigation case in which she disputed Syrian-Christian succession laws that limited the amount a daughter could inherit to a quarter of the amount a son could inherit (or 5,000 rupees, whichever was less). In 1986 Mary Roy eventually won her legal battle at the Indian Supreme Court, getting the law backdated to 1956, but found that institutional resistance from the Syrian-Christian church and an ingrained local sense of tradition and family duty meant that few women claimed their inheritance rights under the new law. (Some years later, however, church leaders tried to reinstate the old law but were defeated by a Syrian-Christian women's rights group.) Arundhati Roy would later become involved in various legal battles herself, amongst them a short-lived obscenity case over the allegedly 'corrupting' content of *TGST*, and, more famously, a contempt-of-court charge for demonstrating outside the Supreme Court against government dam-building projects.

Mary Roy's dissatisfaction with her children's education and her subsequent plan to set up her own informal primary school continued a family involvement in education which had started with Arundhati Roy's great-grandfather, who had founded a school in Ayemenem for the education of untouchable children. With only a few students, Arundhati and her brother became, in Roy's words, the guinea pigs of their mother's unconventional 'sliding, folding school', which would be held during the day in some rooms owned by a local Rotary Club.[37] In 1967, Mary Roy started a larger school, Corpus Christi (now known as Pallikoodam) on a campus in the nearby town of Kottayam, and Roy praises the institution for its coeducational remit and unconventional approach: 'People know that the education children get from my mother's school is invaluable [. . .] yet it makes them uncomfortable because she's not amenable to all the rules and regulations of their society.'[38] In interviews, both Arundhati and her mother credit her unconventional education as the basis of Roy's stylistic 'freedom', and the seedbed of her rebellious attitude towards authority:[39] 'My childhood's greatest gift was a lack of indoctrination [. . .] it's not that I'm somebody who's remarkable because I've learned to think outside the box. The fact is that the box was never imposed on me.'[40] Perhaps because of their similarity and the pressures of being parented and taught by the same person, Roy's association with her mother became increasingly 'complex', and, 'desperate to escape' the stifling conventionality of Ayemenem, she left when she was sixteen to attend the Lawrence boarding school at Lovedale in Tamil Nadu.

After finishing her secondary schooling, Roy moved to Delhi, where she eventually joined the Delhi School of Architecture, and, even at this early stage, her politics were apparent in the subject of her undergraduate thesis, a plan for housing the urban poor.[41] In a novel as biographically involved as *TGST*, it is tempting to make comparisons between Roy's undergraduate experience and Rahel's aimless studies at her architecture college, where the 'careless reckless lines' of her

37  Roy, *The Chequebook and The Cruise Missile*, p. 8.
38  Roy, *The Chequebook and The Cruise Missile*, p. 8.
39  See R. Krishnakumar, 'Ayemenem and Aymanam', *Frontline*, 8 August 1997, p. 111.
40  Roy, *The Chequebook and The Cruise Missile*, p. 106.
41  Maya Jaggi, 'An Unsuitable Girl', *The Guardian Weekend*, 24 May 1997.

drawings are 'mistaken for artistic confidence, though in truth, their creator was no artist' (Ch. 1, p. 17). A similar autobiographical resonance can be found, if we care to look for it, in the student character of Radha in Roy's 1988 screenplay *In Which Annie Gives It Those Ones*, which is set in a Delhi architecture college. Certainly, both Rahel's and Radha's fierce lack of professional aspiration, which disconcerts peers and professors alike, echoes Roy's personal views on success, which tend to equate excessive ambition with an 'unimaginative' materialism.[42] (She has stated that her fiction centres much more clearly on 'loss, grief, brokenness and failure, the ability to find happiness in the saddest things'.)[43] But while her six years as an architecture student were financially 'precarious' and fraught with more family conflict, there is also little evidence that her undergraduate life, which included a sojourn in a squatter's colony in Ferozeshah Kotla, where she rented cheap lodgings, was negative or unhappy.

Roy's architectural training deserves close attention, because of her comments, in several interviews and in the preface to *In Which Annie Gives It Those Ones*, that her writing is shaped by her knowledge of architectural design: 'Studying architecture taught me to apply my understanding of structure, of design and of minute observation of detail to things other than buildings. To novels, to screenplays, to essays. It was an invaluable training.'[44] Prompted by Roy's statements about her famously non-linear writing method, some critics have discussed the 'structural ambiguity' and 'design' of Roy's fiction,[45] and Roy develops the metaphor herself in her comments on the formal construction of *TGST*, which she likens to working on an architectural plan: 'I would start somewhere and I'd colour in a bit and then I would [. . .] stretch back and stretch forward. It was like designing an intricately balanced structure.'[46] In fact, the sequential structure, which shuffles the novel's two time schemes, is one of the most complex aspects of *The God of Small Things*, and, during the five years it took Roy to write the novel, the meticulous positioning of these (largely unedited) sections took the place of closer redrafting. Roy has also used architectural metaphors in theorizing the politics of globalization, and, more literally, an awareness of the environmental impact of industrial engineering has been central to her activism against large-scale dam schemes in India.

At the College of Architecture Roy met a fellow student, Gerard Da Cunha, who would become her first husband. After growing disillusioned with the work they were doing for architectural firms in Delhi, both Roy and Da Cunha decided to drop out and become 'flower children', moving to Goa to join the hippy community. Roy survived for seven months, selling cake to people on the beach and trying to 'choose between a career [. . .] smuggling hashish and cutting up old Benares saris and turning them into silk beach shirts'.[47] Eventually, she decided against both and growing 'tired of the tourists' moved back to Delhi, separating

42  Roy, *The Cost of Living*, p. 134.
43  Roy, *The Chequebook and The Cruise Missile*, p. 66.
44  Arundhati Roy, *In Which Annie Gives It Those Ones*, New Delhi: Penguin India, 2003, p. xii.
45  See R. K. Dhawan (ed.), *Arundhati Roy: The Novelist Extraordinary*, New Delhi: Sangam, 1999, pp. 328–41.
46  Arundhati Roy, quoted in <http://website.lineone.net/~jon.simmons/roy/tgost4.htm>.
47  Arundhati Roy, Personal CV, HarperCollins Publishers.

from Da Cunha after four years of marriage. In Delhi she worked for a short time as a research assistant at the National Institute of Urban Affairs. She was also talent-spotted in the street by the film-maker and environmentalist Pradeep Krishen, who gave her a small role in the film *Massey Saab* – allegedly based on Joyce Cary's novel of colonial Africa, *Mister Johnson* (1939) – in which she played 'the tribal bimbo'. After becoming increasingly involved with Krishen, Roy unexpectedly won an eight-month scholarship to study the restoration of ancient monuments in Italy. During her stay in Italy Roy realized, writing letters to Krishen, that she wanted to become a writer.

Roy and Krishen married after her return to India, and she started working on documentary film commentaries and television screenplays, the first of which was a commentary for Ashish Chandola's wildlife conservation film *How the Rhinocerous Returned*, which traced the attempted reintroduction of a group of rhinos to their former habitat in Uttar Pradesh. Later she and Krishen embarked on a collaborative project entitled *Bargad* (*The Banyan Tree*), which Roy wrote and Krishen directed. A twenty-six-episode epic set in Allahabad that traced the fates of four college graduates in the turbulent years of the Indian freedom struggle, *Bargad* was conceived, in Roy's words, as an alternative to both 'the-Jewel-in-the-Crown school of absurd colonial nostalgia [and] our home-grown brand of moustache-quivering, chest-thumping nationalism'.[48] The serial was commissioned for the Indian state television company Doordarshan, and funded by ITV, but was axed, disappointingly, after just a few episodes had been filmed. With the agreement of Doordarshan's director general, Bhaskar Ghose, Roy wrote a screenplay of her own based on her student experiences, which became the film *In Which Annie Gives It Those Ones* (1988). The film got mixed reviews and was screened only once but won two awards at the Indian National Film Festival in 1989, including Best Screenplay. Roy also wrote the screenplay and was production designer for a Channel 4 film, *Electric Moon*, in 1992.

These productions are important because, in Roy's view, they were 'limited' apprentice pieces for her novel, and the screenplay of *In Which Annie Gives It Those Ones* is particularly interesting when compared with *TGST*. In her loosely plotted vision of undergraduate life, a rough, incipient version of the themes of Roy's later work is reflected in the social consciousness of characters such as Radha, whom Roy played in the original film and who tells a tutor that 'every Indian city consists of a "City" and a "Non-city". And they are at war with one another. The city consists of a number of [designed] institutions [. . .] the non-citizen has no institutions. He lives and works in the gaps between institutions.'[49] Roy's interest in language is also prefigured in *In Which Annie Gives It Those Ones*, although in the more dramatic medium of the screenplay it is the auditory realism of undergraduate speech and 'the idea of accurately reproducing the idiom and the rhythm of [. . .] language', rather than the stylistic manipulation of prose, which fascinates her. As Roy states in the preface to *In Which Annie Gives It Those Ones*: 'English as she is spoken by students in Delhi university [became] one of the main characters in the film. English as an alloy – melted down and then

48  Roy, *In Which Annie Gives It Those Ones*, p. vi.
49  Roy, *In Which Annie Gives It Those Ones*, p. 91.

refashioned, soldered together with Hindi (occasionally even a little Punjabi) to suit our specific communication requirements.'[50] Roy was less pleased with her subsequent venture, *Electric Moon*, which she now sees as a technical failure and a work marred by her lack of knowledge about film-making.[51]

In addition to her screenwriting, Roy started publishing newspaper articles in the early 1990s, most notably three damning reviews of Shekhar Kapur's controversial 1994 film *Bandit Queen*: 'The Great Indian Rape Trick', which appeared in two parts, and a further essay entitled 'The Naughty Lady of Shady Lane'. Kapur's *Bandit Queen* is based on the life of Phoolan Devi, a low-caste woman who became the leader of a band of outlaws after being gang-raped by high-caste men from her village, and draws on a biography by Mala Sen titled *India's Bandit Queen: The True Story of Phoolan Devi* (1991). Roy objected to the film because it purported to be a truthful account of Devi's life but was filmed without her consent. It was also released while Devi's jail sentence was still under appeal and could, therefore, have biased the legal process. Roy was particularly worried that, in spite of the suspect 'truth claims' of Kapur's representation of Devi, the film would eventually *become* the truth. However, since the release of *Bandit Queen*, a number of biographical accounts of Devi's life have appeared, leading some critics to suggest that Devi was 'in more control of the production of her own story than Roy's intervention implies'.[52] Perhaps more important are the related questions that Roy's *Bandit Queen* essays raise about the responsibilities of artistic representation: in Roy's view Kapur reduced Devi's life to the fact of her rape and her quest for revenge, whereas the biography he drew on took account of a wider set of circumstances and motives. Roy's anger at the gratuitous representation of rape[53] in Kapur's *Bandit Queen* may have been sharpened by memories of the Malayalam films she watched in childhood, in which rape was a staple theme. As Roy comments in an interview: 'Until I was about fifteen, I believed that every woman gets raped. It was just a question of waiting for yours to happen. That was the kind of terror [these films] inculcated in young girls.'[54]

By the mid-1990s, Roy had already been working on the manuscript of *The God of Small Things* for several years. The book had apparently grown out of writing Roy had done when she had acquired a computer and started 'finding out what it could do'.[55] Because of the novel's idiosyncratic structure, she was unwilling (and effectively unable) to show anyone drafts of her work in progress. When the manuscript was complete she gave a copy to the writer and literary agent Pankaj Mishra, who subsequently managed the purchase of the Indian rights

---

50  Roy, *In Which Annie Gives It Those Ones*, pp. viii–ix.
51  Vir Sanghvi, 'The Rediff Special Interview'. Online. Accessible HTTP: <http:/www.rediff.com/news/apr/05roy2.htm>. (Accessed 19 June 2006.)
52  Mullaney, *Arundhati Roy's The God of Small Things*, p. 12.
53  Of the film, she claims, 'Rape is the main dish. Caste is the sauce that it swims in.' See Roy, 'The Great Indian Rape Trick'. Online. Accessible HTTP: <http://www.umiacs.umd.edu/users/sawweb/sawnet/roy_bq1.html>. (Accessed 19 June 2006.)
54  Roy, *The Chequebook and The Cruise Missile*, p. 4.
55  Quoted in <http://website.lineone.net/~jon.simmons/roy/tgost2.htm>. Roy corrects this version of events in her *Frontline* interview: 'Of course, it's true I bought a computer and wrote on it, but that's not how novels happen! Writing *The God of Small Things* was a fictional way of making sense of the world I lived in, and the novel was the technical key with which I did it' ('When You Have Written a Book, You Lay Your Weapons Down', *Frontline*, 8 August 1997).

and alerted publishers overseas to what he described as 'the most important Indian English novel since Salman Rushdie's *Midnight's Children*'. Published in April 1997, and coinciding fortuitously with the fiftieth anniversary of Indian independence that year, *TGST* won the Booker Prize the following October and became a global best-seller, subsequently translated into over forty languages. The success of *TGST* ensured Roy a very high media profile and raised critical questions about the promotion of both the novel and its author (see Critical readings, **pp. 103–9**). In India, the response to *TGST* was generally positive, although soon after publication Roy was embroiled in a short-lived court case, involving a charge of obscenity against the novel's sex scenes, brought by Sabu Thomas, a lawyer from Kerala. Roy herself was unprepared for the demands of celebrity and, although aware of the positive power of 'recognition', the experience of literary fame forced her to reassess her own values in an impromptu manifesto reproduced in her essay 'The End of Imagination', in *The Cost of Living*.

For Roy, these fundamentals are:

> To love. To be loved. To never forget your own insignificance. To never get used to the unspeakable violence and the vulgar disparity of life around you. To seek joy in the saddest places. To pursue beauty to its lair. To never simplify what is complicated or complicate what is simple. To respect strength, never power. Above all to watch. To try and understand. To never look away. And never, never to forget. [56]

Roy's 'manifesto' differentiates her from many contemporary authors, whose sense of irony prevents them from making such candid and, some would say, naïve statements of their views. Certainly, Roy herself recognizes that for 'a writer of the twenty-first century', her willingness to 'have a point of view [and ...] make it clear that I think it's right and moral to take that position' is considered 'a pretty uncool, unsophisticated thing to do'. [57] Roy is quick to admit that political allegiances do not rule out the subtleties of literary ambiguity, but she does ask questions about the present role of Indian authors and artists and suggests that 'there are times in the life of a people or nation when the political climate demands that we – even the most sophisticated of us – overtly take sides'. [58]

Since the publication of *TGST*, a second fictional work has been eagerly anticipated, but instead Roy has turned her attention to journalism and political/ environmental activism, most notably in her support for the Narmada Bachao Andolan (NBA) or Save the Narmada movement, a group that campaigns against the building of large dams on the Narmada river in Maharashtra. (In 2001 Roy was charged with criminal contempt of court for demonstrating with the leaders of the NBA outside the Indian Supreme Court. The following year she was sentenced to three months imprisonment or a fine and, after a 'symbolic' night in jail, Roy paid the fine.) [59] When she won the Booker Prize, Roy donated her prize

---

56  Roy, *The Cost of Living*, pp. 134–5; italics in the original.
57  Roy, *Power Politics*, p. 11.
58  Roy, *Power Politics*, p. 12.
59  See Roy, *Power Politics*, p. 87.

money to the NBA, and her literary celebrity has subsequently allowed her to reach a large audience with her prose essays. Since *TGST*, Roy has published *The Cost of Living* (1999), which includes her essay on India's dam projects on the Narmada river: 'The Greater Common Good', and her scathing indictment of the Indo-Pakistani nuclear-arms race, 'The End of Imagination'. These pieces, along with a number of more recent essays that document Roy's increasing concern over the damaging impact of trans-national capital in India were recently republished, with additional essays on the political role of the writer and the 'War on Terror', in *The Algebra of Infinite Justice* (2003). Challenging labels such as 'writer-activist' and defending her decision to concentrate on prose essays, Roy has repeatedly stated that: 'Good fiction is the truest thing that ever there was. Facts are not necessarily the only truths. Facts can be fiddled with by economists and bankers. There are other kinds of truth.'[60] This view has led Roy to question the very distinction between fiction and non-fiction and to argue that the two are simply 'different techniques of story telling'.[61]

Certainly, there are a number of strong continuities between *TGST* and Roy's subsequent prose pieces, not least a 'morally strenuous'[62] need to debunk received ideas and expose the injustices that underlie 'normality'.[63] Since the second Gulf war in 2003, Roy's attention has turned increasingly to issues of public dissent and 'Empire', a term that now encompasses US-led foreign policy, 'instant-mix imperial democracy'[64] and corporate globalization. In her opposition to the war, she has supported, and become increasingly associated with, an older generation of dissenting American intellectuals, such as Noam Chomsky and Howard Zinn. She has also praised the work of global justice movements such as the World Social Forum, which campaigns under the slogan 'Another World is Possible' and represents itself as an ethical alternative to the powerful World Economic Forum (an annual meeting of politicians and business leaders). On these terms, Roy sees dissent as 'the only thing worth globalising' and warns of a global future that will have to face the massive inequalities and 'humiliations' that the new 'Empire' perpetuates:

> As the rift between the rich and the poor grows, as the need to appropriate and control the world's resources to feed the great capitalist machine becomes more urgent, the unrest will only escalate [. . .] The urge for hegemony and preponderance by some will be matched with greater intensity by the longing for dignity and justice by others.
>
> Exactly what form that battle takes, whether it's beautiful or bloodthirsty, depends on us.[65]

60  Roy, *The Chequebook and The Cruise Missile*, p. 68.
61  Roy, *The Ordinary Person's Guide to Empire*, p. 13.
62  Traux, 'A Silver Thimble in her Fist'.
63  Arundhati Roy, *Public Power in the Age of Empire*, New York: Seven Stories Press, 2004, p. 39.
64  Roy, *The Ordinary Person's Guide to Empire*, p. 104.
65  Roy, *Public Power in the Age of Empire*, pp. 57–9.

# Cultural contexts

## Syrian Christianity in South India

Arundhati Roy's novel is unusual compared with other South-Asian fictions in English because it deals with one of India's smallest religious minorities, the Syrian Christians. References to the ancient history of the Syrian-Christian community are made throughout *TGST*, and the complex intermixture of their faith with local Hindu social structures (especially the Hindu caste system) is integral to the plot of Roy's work.

Resident in the south-western state of Kerala, the Syrian-Christian community dates its origins to 52 CE, when the apostle St. Thomas allegedly arrived in India near the port of Cranganore, converted a number of Hindu and Jewish families and founded seven churches along the Malabar coast. The basis of this story is a fourth-century church text, *The Acts of St. Thomas*, which tells us that St. Thomas was purchased as a slave by the Indian king Gundaphorus, who commissioned him to build a palace. He promptly gave the King's money to the poor, explaining to Gundaphorus that he had constructed a residence for him in Heaven, rather than one on Earth. The King threw St. Thomas into prison but relented when his dead brother returned to life to assure him of the existence of his heavenly palace, after which he and his brother were baptized by St. Thomas. With such limited evidence, it is difficult to judge the historical accuracy of the story of St. Thomas's arrival in Malabar, although the well-established trade routes between India and the eastern Mediterranean at the time of Christ make the expedition quite possible.[66] In the absence of a direct apostolic link, Syrian traders and immigrants under the leadership of Thomas Kinayi (Thomas Cana) may have carried their religion to South India later on, in the fourth century, when Hindu rajahs granted them settlement rights in the area.

Whatever its historical basis, the legend of St. Thomas remains an integral part of Syrian-Christian identity and is often used to explain and justify the high status of the community. According to legend, St. Thomas's first Hindu converts were thirty-two *brahmin* families – the highest rank in the Hindu social hierarchy of the caste system (see Text and contexts, **pp. 22–7**) – who retained certain social privileges, even though they had changed their faith. In addition, some of the oldest Syrian-Christian families share their names with *brahmin* families,[67] and outside their churches Syrian Christians still practise many ritual aspects of Hinduism, including ceremonial baths, astrology and the rite of *annaprasanam*, the first feeding of rice to a child.[68] Traditionally, the community has preserved its high social standing by a custom of strict endogamy (marriage within the community) and a careful observance of many of the social restrictions of upper-caste Hindus. Operating rather like a caste organization, the Syrian-Christian church council has also exerted close control over the community through its informal authority and

---

66  Leslie Brown, *The Indian Christians of St. Thomas*, Cambridge: Cambridge University Press, 1956, p. 59.
67  Brown, *The Indian Christians of St. Thomas*, p. 172.
68  Ken Parry, Dimitri Brady, Sidney H. Griffith, David J. Melling and John Healey, *The Blackwell Dictionary of Eastern Christianity*, Oxford: Blackwell, 1999, p. 249.

its powers of ostracism and its ability to excommunicate or expel individuals from its Church.[69] It is this power of spiritual sanction, and its wider implications, that Mammachi fears when she learns of Ammu's affair with Velutha.

Accepted by the local Hindu rulers and fulfilling important social roles in trade and banking prohibited to upper-caste *brahmins*, Malabar Syrian Christians lived amicably alongside their Hindu neighbours for over 1,000 years before the arrival of the Portuguese. The successful integration of the Syrian Christians in south-west India was due, partly, to the fact that they made no attempt to spread the Gospel, as this would have threatened their own privileged position.[70] Indeed, the unwillingness of the Syrian-Christian community to accept new converts, espe-cially if they came from the lower castes, proved a particularly difficult issue for European missionaries who wanted to spread the faith in the nineteenth century. By the time the Portuguese adventurer Vasco da Gama landed on the Malabar coast in 1498, there were over 100,000 Syrian Christians in the region (some historians estimate a much higher number) and numerous churches. Until this point, the Syrian-Christian church maintained Syriac as the language of worship and recognized the Eastern Nestorian church tradition and its head, the Patriarch of Antioch, as their supreme authority. This tradition is part of the Eastern 'Orthodox' faith that includes Greek, Russian and Middle Eastern churches, which distanced itself from Western 'Roman' Catholicism after the 'East–West Schism' of 1054. Even today, the central theological beliefs of Syrian Christianity derive almost entirely from the Eastern church although the Syriac words of the liturgy are now written in Malayalam.

The organized suppression of the Syrian-Christian faith by the Catholic Portuguese started in the mid-sixteenth century, after Portugal had gained a terri-torial foothold in the subcontinent at Goa. Acting on the authority of the Roman Catholic Church, the Portuguese pressured the Syrian Christians to recognize the Pope, and not an Eastern patriarch, as God's intermediary on Earth. These devel-opments culminated in a forced show of allegiance to Roman Catholicism, planned by the autocratic Archbishop of Goa, Alexio de Menezes. Backed by a large army, de Menezes landed at Cochin in January 1599 and compelled the Syrian-Christian Archdeacon to accept the Pope's supremacy.[71] A few months later, he presided over a church meeting or synod at Diamper (Udiamperer), attended by 153 priests and 660 lay people, which passed decrees reforming the Syrian church, 'correcting' liturgical and ecclesiastical elements derived from the Eastern Nestorian tradition and banning rituals that were deemed Hindu in origin. De Menezes also ordered the burning of what he regarded as heretical religious texts and concluded the synod, which would become an infamous turning point in the history of the Syrian-Christian community, by making Syrian-Christian priests sign a declaration in Portuguese (a language few of them knew), under the terms of which they would be excommunicated if they remained loyal to the Syrian Church.

---

69  Parry et al., *The Blackwell Dictionary of Eastern Christianity*, p. 250.
70  Benedict Vadakkekara, *Origins of India's St. Thomas Christians: A Historiographical Critique*, Delhi: Media House, 1995. Vadakkekara argues that 'the St. Thomas Christians never undertook a policy of proselytization [as this] would have automatically upset the social equilibrium' (p. 30).
71  Charlie Pye-Smith, *Rebels and Outcasts: A Journey through Christian India*, Harmondsworth: Penguin, 1998, p. 160.

Under Roman Catholicism, many Syrian Christians became increasingly frustrated by their lack of religious freedom, and in 1653 they rebelled against the Pope, reaffirming their allegiance to the Eastern Church and swearing an oath (known as the Coonan Cross Oath) in which they pledged to expel the Portuguese. The rebellion was sparked by rumours that Mar Ahattalla, a Syrian bishop sent to preside over the Indian Syrian Church, had been captured by the Portuguese and drowned. In *TGST* this legend resurfaces in the embellished image of 'three purple-robed Syrian Bishops murdered by the Portuguese [. . .] floating in the sea, with coiled sea serpents riding on their chests and oysters knotted in their tangled beards' (Ch. 1, p. 33). Another Eastern bishop, Mar Gregorios of Jerusalem, reached Malabar in 1665 and was welcomed by the Syrian Christians. The arrival of Mar Gregorios returned the Syrian church to the authority of the Patriarch of Antioch, but a large group of Syrian Christians, the so-called Romo-Christians (now known as the Syro-Malabar church), remained in communion with the Catholic Church in Rome.

The Syrian Christians who kept their independence from Roman Catholicism were ruled throughout the eighteenth century by a succession of bishops who adhered to West Syrian rites and who all took the name Mar Thoma (after the first bishop ordained by Mar Gregorios). They soon faced another European colonial influence, however, when the British consolidated their political presence in the region in the early nineteenth century. The British appointed a resident to oversee the districts of Travancore and Cochin and subsequently sent missionaries from the Church of England's Church Missionary Society to India in 1816, with orders to assist the Syrian church but not to interfere with its rites.[72] In fact, these missionaries did attempt to reform some practices such as ordination (the rite that confers holy orders on priests) and, in 1836, as a response to this perceived threat, the church reasserted its adherence to the Eastern Patriarch. The Anglicans also tried to attract converts from lower-caste groups and offered small incentives such as food and money. Indeed, in *TGST* it is the Anglican church that admits Velutha's grandfather, who converts to escape untouchability but finds he is still stigmatized as a 'Rice-Christian' (Ch. 2, p. 74). In spite of their reaffirmation of faith, some Syrian Christians, who had been influenced by the Anglican missionaries in the 1830s, broke away to start a church reform movement. Led by a seminary teacher Palakunnathu Abraham Malpan, the movement combined aspects of the Protestant reformation – such as a return to the written word of the Bible and ecclesiastical and liturgical changes – with elements of the Eastern church. It was eventually recognized as a separate church tradition, the Mar Thoma Church, in 1889, and it is this most Protestant wing of the Syrian-Christian community that the Ipe family are associated with in *TGST*. As we are told in the first chapter of the novel, Estha and Rahel's great-grandfather, the Reverend E. John Ipe, is a priest of the Mar Thoma Church, and this point has some relevance when we recall Chacko's self-mocking statements about the family's Anglophilia.

Further disagreements about the extent of the authority of the patriarch at Antioch have led to more divisions, and at present the Syrian-Christian community in Kerala is divided into at least seven different churches, from the largest,

---

72 Parry et al., *The Blackwell Dictionary of Eastern Christianity*, p. 253.

romanized Syro-Malabar group, with 3 million adherents, to the tiny Malabar Independent Syrian Church which has just one diocese and only 25,000 members. The convoluted development of Kerala's ancient Christian faith is complicated further by a broad division between 'northists' and 'southists', the former group tracing themselves from the families converted by St. Thomas, and the latter, smaller group claiming descent from seventy-two Syrian families who emigrated to India under the leadership of Thomas Kinayi (Thomas Cana) in 345 CE. (Some Syrian Christians claim, alternatively, that the two groups are descended from Thomas Cana's two wives.)

If we try to summarize some of the main points of this long and involved history, we might locate a dual process of cultural accommodation and exclusion as the central feature of the Syrian-Christian community. One historian describes this as the 'two worlds' of church and wider Indian society, in which the Syrian Christians have lived 'with no consciousness of tension between them or disharmony within themselves'. In other words, members of the community have always been 'Christians of Mesopotamia in faith and worship and ethic [and] Indians in all else'.[73] In many ways, this ability to 'blend in' culturally and yet maintain control over their own faith and religious traditions has been essential to the survival of the Syrian Christians in South India. Local Hindu expectations that early Syrian Christians would conform to the existing caste system would have reinforced their strategy of selective, partial assimilation, and it is the unusual social balance of caste groups that developed in Kerala, favouring non-Hindu communities such as the Syrian Christians, that we will turn to now.

## Hinduism, untouchability and the caste system

The caste system or *caturvarna* (literally, four colours) is an ancient four-part division of Hindu society that arranges the human world in the context of a socio-cosmic order (*dharma*) that existed from the time of creation. The concept of *varna* or caste appears in some of the earliest creation myths of Hinduism. In the *Rig Veda*, a sacred hymn composed between 1200 and 1000 BCE (and the earliest text of the Vedic religion, which forms a major foundation of modern Hinduism), caste is associated with the creation myth of *Purusa*, the primeval cosmic man out of whom the universe is formed. The creation of humankind and its differentiation into four different castes relate to the sacrificial dismemberment of this cosmic being:

> When [the gods] divided the Man, into how many parts did they disperse him? What became of his mouth, what of his arms, what were his two thighs and his two feet called? His mouth was the *brahmin* [the priest class], his arms were made into the nobles [*ksatriyas*], his two thighs were the populace [*vaisyas*], and from his feet the servants [*sudras*] were born. The moon was born from his mind; the sun was born from his eye.[74]

73  Brown, *The Indian Christians of St. Thomas*, p. 4.
74  Wendy O'Flaherty, ed. and trans., *Hindu Myths*, Harmondsworth: Penguin, 1975, p. 28.

As we can see from this creation myth of caste, the fourfold division of *varna* entailed different duties and obligations for each of its groups: *brahmins*, as the revered priest caste, officiated at temples and religious ceremonies and were authorized to learn and recite holy scriptures. The *ksatriya* caste group traditionally associated itself with warfare and military service and the *vaisya* group involved itself in trade, business and agriculture. The low-caste *sudra* group was designated as a 'service' caste and performed agricultural labour and menial tasks. These broad caste groupings do not represent the whole of Hindu society, however, and 'outcaste' or 'untouchable' communities exist at the bottom of the *sudra* group, on the margins of the caste system. Always economically and socially dependent on higher castes, these untouchable communities traditionally perform dirty, spiritually polluting activities such as leatherwork, street-sweeping, rubbish collection and disposing of the dead. As a *paravan*, Velutha in *TGST* belongs to this stigmatized 'untouchable' group, and it is this fact that makes his affair with Ammu – and their mutual erotic 'touching' – such a transgressive act.

The outline of caste divisions in the *Rig Veda* should not lead us to assume, automatically, that excluded or stigmatized outcaste groups existed in the society of the early Vedic period. Some historians of caste have argued that, in fact, neither the *Rig Veda* nor later Vedic texts indicate that any group was tabooed or socially restricted and chart untouchability as a gradual social development that started in the first (Christian) millennium and reached its peak in the thirteenth century CE. Others have claimed that, although caste is clearly an ancient social division within Hinduism, its observance has fluctuated over time and argue that the concept of rigorous, exclusive caste hierarchies can be dated from relatively recent reassertions of Brahminical power in central India in the eighteenth century. In these models, caste observance could vary across different regions and gain or decrease in political importance in relation to numerous other factors.[75]

What most historians and theorists of caste agree on, however, is the importance of caste identification with different occupations in ancient India, and the consequent multiplication of numerous sub-castes to cater to the growing complexity of Hindu society. As K. M. Sen states,

> The division of the society into four castes has, in all probability, always been theoretical, for, from the earliest times, we find references to a much more complicated caste structure [. . .] the occupational divisions with which castes were associated give us a better view of the role of castes in the working of society.[76]

These *jati*, or occupational sub-castes (which number more than 3,000), are arranged hierarchically within the fourfold divisions of *varna* and usually encompass hereditary professions and occupations, although regionally various *jati* may be arranged differently. In modern India the association of caste

---

75  Mary Searle-Chatterjee and Ursula Sharma, *Contextualising Caste: Post-Dumontian Approaches*, Oxford: Blackwell, 1994, pp. 1–24.
76  K. M. Sen, *Hinduism*, Harmondsworth: Penguin, 1961, pp. 28–9.

sub-groups with specific types of work has become much less rigid although, as a famine in 1992 that only affected the weaver caste of Andhra Pradesh showed, the link between *jati* and profession still limits occupational mobility – and ties certain communities to their professions, even in times of economic hardship – in some parts of rural India.[77] A review of any of the 'matrimonial' pages of the major Indian newspapers, in which prospective marriage partners are advertised, shows that when it comes to marriage, caste identity, alongside other considerations such as occupation, age, appearance and educational status,[78] is still a significant social marker. Thus, while it is a constitutional offence in India to discriminate against low-caste groups, 'within political parties, professional groups, municipalities, in social and economic life, in education, and in government service, caste has remained an important fact of life'.[79]

While caste solidified as a social hierarchy in the proliferation of occupational *jati* in the last centuries BCE, it was also codified as a set of social rules in one of the most influential books of the Hindu legal system, the *Manava Dharmashastra*, compiled in the first two centuries CE, and attributed to the sage Manu. As a response to the increasing complexity and mobility of Hindu society, the law code of Manu (also known as the *Manusmriti*) reinforces the superior status of the *brahmin* or priest caste, and delineates, in meticulous detail, the rules of caste conduct and punishments for their infraction.[80] In Roy's novel, references to the 'Love Laws' which 'lay down who should be loved, and how. And how much' (Ch. 1, p. 33) can be associated most clearly with the regulation of inter-caste marriage in the *Manusmriti*. It is in this legal text that we also find the first differentiation within the lowest *sudra* caste between servants and 'untouchables', and in the 1920s the book was burnt as a symbol of caste oppression during some of the earliest demonstrations against untouchability.

In order to understand the significance and social stigma of untouchability fully, we must remember that the caste system is linked to the Hindu cycle of reincarnation and the regulatory workings of *karma* accrued in past lives. The three upper or 'twice-born' castes, so named because the process of caste initiation involves a second, ritualized 'birth' into the caste community, are eligible for religious rites and represent different levels of spiritual purity in the cycle of karmic rebirth (rituals of caste initiation are the precondition of ritual purity). The lowest *sudra* caste is destined to serve the other castes and is designated as such because its members have to atone for sins committed in past lives. The gradual progress towards *moksha* (a transcendent escape from the cycle of reincarnation) is also, then, a process of increasing spiritual purification, a progression that is threatened by the unclean nature of the outside world and the innate impurities of the body itself. Higher castes can alleviate the temporary pollution of bodily products such as blood, sweat, semen, urine and faeces, with

77  Gail Omvedt, *Dalits and the Democratic Revolution*, New Delhi: Sage, 1994, p. 334.
78  Searle-Chatterjee and Sharma, *Contextualising Caste*, p. 17.
79  Klaus K. Klostermaier, *A Survey of Hinduism*, 2nd edn, Albany, NY: State University of New York Press, 1994, p. 335.
80  One such punishment, cited by Roy as evidence of the Brahminical 'colonization of knowledge', states that if an untouchable hears the recital of a *shloka* or sacred verse he must have molten lead poured in to his ears. See Roy, *Power Politics*, p. 25.

baths and ritual purifications.[81] Untouchables, on the other hand, are born polluted and cannot purify themselves except through death and rebirth.

In modern India, accounts of the caste system are filtered, like many other historical archives, through the translations of colonial European 'Orientalist' scholars who saw in caste a way of understanding Hinduism and explaining 'both the cause and effect of India's low level of political and economic development' and 'its repeated failure to prevent its conquest by outsiders'.[82] Some European scholars also 'racialized' caste in their widespread assumption that caste divisions had developed after advanced Aryan races had invaded northern India in the pre-Vedic period and subjugated darker-skinned native Dravidian peoples, excluding them from 'twice-born' caste status. There was an obvious bias in this view of Indian history, which reflected nineteenth-century European theories about racial evolution and made the further conquest of India by the British seem inevitable and beneficial. Even so, the 'invasion' model became highly influential and later formed the basis for Hindu nationalist readings of history.[83] It would be challenged by the brilliant leader and spokesman of the untouchables, B. R. Ambedkar, in his argument that early Indian history involved a series of civilizational changes that started in the Buddhist period and that caste was a later social development imposed by a resurgent Hinduism.[84]

The word 'caste' derives from the Portuguese *casta*, meaning pure or unadulterated (sharing a Latin root with the word 'chaste'), and its European etymology should immediately make us suspicious of definitions of 'caste' that rely exclusively on ideas of purity and defilement.[85] This is not to deny that concepts of pollution are used to justify untouchability, and one of the defining studies of caste, Louis Dumont's *Homo Hierarchicus* (1967), sees the opposition between purity and pollution as a central feature of caste hierarchies. However, more recently sociologists have criticized Dumont's model, arguing that it repeats forms of colonial thought that 'essentialized' and fixed Indian society around a specific, historically static concept, thus presenting India as the reverse mirror image of a 'rational', progressive and enlightened Europe. It is useful to quote a 'post-Dumontian' definition of caste at this point:

> We can think [. . .] of caste in terms of a system of action [. . .] To look at caste as something which people 'do' rather than something which they 'are' appears to go against the grain of modern interest in identity, but the two perspectives are complementary if we regard identity as something which emerges in certain situations.[86]

81  See Alan Dundes, *Two Tales of Crow and Sparrow: A Freudian Folkloristic Essay on Caste and Untouchability*, Lanham, Md.: Rowman and Littlefield, 1997, p. 7.
82  Ronald Inden, quoted in Klostermaier, *A Survey of Hinduism*, p. 334. See also B. S. Cohn, *Colonialism and its Forms of Knowledge: The British in India*, Princeton, NJ: Princeton University Press, 1996.
83  See Chetan Bhatt, *Hindu Nationalism: Origins, Ideologies and Modern Myths*, Oxford: Berg, 2001.
84  B. R. Ambedkar, *The Untouchables: Who Are They? And Why They Became Untouchables*, New Delhi: Amrit Book Co., 1948.
85  See Declan Quigley, *The Interpretation of Caste*, Oxford: Oxford University Press, 1993.
86  Searle-Chatterjee and Sharma, *Contextualising Caste*, p. 9.

In a model like this, caste, like 'racial' identity, is not so much an inherent essence as the result of dynamic social interactions that produce meaning. For many untouchables, caste is experienced not as a sense of self, but as 'something [. . .] which is "done to you" by other (high caste) people'.[87] And yet the process of this oppression may also provide an identity through which low-caste groups can organize and represent themselves.[88] Accordingly, in *TGST*, we might read Velutha's defining characteristic as a dangerous unwillingness to agree to the 'performance' of his own low-caste status in 'the quiet way he offered suggestions without being asked [and] disregarded suggestions without appearing to rebel' (Ch. 2, p. 76). Similarly, when news of Ammu and Velutha's affair becomes public, both Vellya Paapan and Mammachi give the event meaning and construct it as a transgression, through their fearful and disgusted responses.

During the struggle for independence, M. K. Gandhi, the spiritual leader of the Congress Party, took up the cause of the untouchables, renaming them *harijans* (Children of God), lobbying for their access to temples and encouraging his followers to perform duties associated with untouchability, such as sweeping and latrine-cleaning. However, while condemning 'the curse of untouchability',[89] Gandhi did not reject caste entirely, and many lower-caste groups were dissatisfied with the paternalism of his message. Indeed, Gandhi's '*Harijan* programme' could only appear as authoritarian and hypocritical to radical anti-caste groups.[90] Until the early 1930s, B. R. Ambedkar, in his fight for India's lower castes, remained a pragmatic supporter of Gandhi's methods, but he clashed with the Mahatma over the latter's decision to represent the untouchables in political negotiations with the British. After independence, Ambedkar entered a four-year period of cooperation with the ruling Congress Party and became Nehru's Minister for Law. During this time he chaired the drafting committee of the Indian constitution, and defended constitutional minority safeguards and the policy of reserving quotas of educational places and government jobs for 'scheduled' castes, as a necessary stage on the road to social equality.[91] This policy was reaffirmed in 1980 by the controversial Mandal Commission report which recommended an increase in reservation quotas for lower castes.

Ambedkar publicly converted to Buddhism shortly before his death in 1956, a decision that reflected his historical reading of caste, and made 'a non-Hindu [religious] identity a collective material and radicalizing force in India'.[92] He also initiated the short-lived Republican Party, which he hoped would represent all India's dispossessed peoples. While widespread in the subcontinent, Ambedkar's legacy was strongest in his home state of Maharashtra, where disaffected untouchable groups, taking their name from the Marathi word for 'downtrodden' and the radical African-American separatist group the Black Panthers, organized themselves in 1972 as the Dalit Panthers, and also started a *dalit* literary movement. (*Dalit* has now become the preferred self-designation for India's

---

87  Searle-Chatterjee and Sharma, *Contextualising Caste*, p. 9.
88  Searle-Chatterjee and Sharma, *Contextualising Caste*, p. 9.
89  Stanley Wolpert, *A New History of India*, 5th edn, Oxford: Oxford University Press, 1997, p. 311.
90  Omvedt, *Dalits and the Democratic Revolution*, p. 341.
91  Stephen Hay (ed.), *Sources of Indian Tradition*, Vol. II: *Modern India and Pakistan*, New York: Columbia University Press, 1988, p. 342.
92  Omvedt, *Dalits and the Democratic Revolution*, p. 249.

untouchable groups.) Like many other radical *dalit* groups, the Dalit Panthers took inspiration from the 1967 Maoist-Leninist 'Naxalite' uprising (mentioned in *TGST*, and discussed in Text and contexts, **pp. 32–5**), and their anger was exacerbated by an upper-caste backlash against government reservation policies and the perceived failure of mainstream political groups to represent them. After economic liberalization in the early 1990s and the subsequent decline of Congress power, caste (and the vote banks represented by lower-caste groups) has become an increasingly visible feature of Indian democratic politics. More troubling in recent years has been the increase in brutal violence between armed upper-caste militias and left-wing *dalit* revolutionaries in states such as Bihar – clashes that have ensured that caste remains a live social and political issue.

## Velutha's inheritance: caste regulations in Kerala

In *TGST* Roy explains the crushing sense of caste inferiority felt by older untouchables such as Velutha's father, Vellya Paapen, as a product of Kerala's ancient, ingrained rules of caste, epitomized in the 'Crawling Backwards Days' of the pre-independence period, when *paravans* 'were not allowed to walk on public roads, not allowed to cover their upper bodies, not allowed to carry umbrellas' (Ch. 2, p. 74). Roy's list of caste proscriptions is no exaggeration, and at the start of the twentieth century the region had one of the most complex, restrictive caste systems in the Indian subcontinent. Described by the Hindu reformer Swami Vivekananda as 'a mad-house of caste',[93] the social structure of south-west India comprised more than 500 sub-categories of caste and included exceptionally strict regulations on caste interaction. Among Kerala's highest caste group, the *namboodiri brahmins*, the fear of pollution was so great that when walking in public they were often preceded by a *nayar* servant who would warn all untouchables to hide in case the sight of them, or even contact with their shadows, defiled the approaching *brahmin*.

This level of caste regulation can partly be explained by the distinctive imbalance of the four main caste groups in Kerala. In contrast to other regions of India (and indeed, to the 'ideal' model of a fourfold system of *varna*), the two intermediate caste groups, the nobles or 'warrior' *ksatriya* caste and the merchant *vaisya* community, were always rare or absent in the region. The *namboodiri brahmins* settled in the area from the eighth century CE and became major landowners, priests and temple administrators. Below them, the traditional military and landowning duties of the *ksatriya* caste were fulfilled by a comparatively high-status *sudra* group, the *nayars*. Without a specific merchant caste, and hampered by the reluctance of upper-caste groups such as the *namboodiris* to engage in the polluting work of commerce,[94] Kerala's pepper trade and other businesses such as money-lending were managed by outsiders such as Gujaratis, Tamils and Europeans. Traditionally, the Syrian Christians, the second richest community in the state after the *brahmins*, were employed in business and banking, but they are

93  T. J. Nossiter, *Communism in Kerala: A Study in Political Adaptation*, London: Hurst, 1982, p. 26.
94  Nossiter, *Communism in Kerala*, p. 26.

also associated with plantation-agriculture, a business that the Ipe family falls back on after the closure of their pickle factory.

The *nayar* caste group established themselves as small-scale landowners but also worked as servants of *namboodiri* households and provided soldiers and retainers for local rulers. As the caste associated with military expertise, *nayars* trained in Kerala's martial art of *kalarippayattu* and were the first performers of *Ramanattam* and *kathakali*.[95] (Actors had always been designated as low-caste in the classical law-texts.) In places where *namboodiri brahmins* and *nayars* were the principal landowners, rural society took the form of numerous feudatory hierarchies of caste that depended on a base of untouchable *pulayas* or *parayas* for the heavy work of rice cultivation and agricultural labour.[96] These groups were kept in virtual slavery, and, until the nineteenth century, *pulayas* who polluted a member of a higher caste risked death. As comparatively recently as 1901 there are reports of untouchables being murdered by higher-caste land-holding *nayars* because they had accidentally broken caste restrictions or failed to abase themselves in the appropriate manner.[97]

A central theme in *TGST* is the continuation of these inequalities – in more covert forms – in post-independence (Marxist) Kerala, and, because of its focus on caste oppression and betrayal, Roy's novel has been welcomed by *dalit* cultural organizations in Kerala, especially the Dalit Sahitya Akademi (the Academy of Untouchable Literature), which is aligned with the Dalit Panthers. In January 1999, at a meeting in Calicut, Roy pledged the royalties of the Malayalam translation of *TGST* to the Akademi 'in memory of Velutha'.[98] Speaking to the audience in Malayalam, she stated: 'I know that you share the anger [. . .] at the heart of *The God of Small Things*. It is an anger that the "modern" metropolitan world, the Other India (the one in which I now live), tends to overlook, because for them it is something distant, something unreal.' Roy went on to assure her *dalit* audience that 'you better than anyone else know that there is nothing unreal about barbarism' and concluded by 'enlisting' in the *dalit* struggle, claiming that the eradication of caste inequality was 'going to be, and indeed ought to be [India's] biggest challenge' in the twenty-first century.[99]

## Communism in Kerala

In March 1957 Kerala became the first Indian state – and indeed the first government anywhere in the world – to bring a democratically elected communist party to power. Rather than espousing violent revolution, the party leader, E. M. S. Namboodiripad, proposed a 'peaceful' transition to communism, and in *TGST* Roy engages with the political legacy of communism in Kerala in her satirical

95  Phillip B. Zarrilli, *Kathakali Dance-Drama: Where Gods and Demons Come to Play*, London: Routledge, 2000, p. 21.
96  Zarrilli, *Kathakali Dance-Drama*, p. 7.
97  Dilip M. Menon, *Caste, Nationalism and Communism in South India: Malabar, 1900–1948*, Cambridge: Cambridge University Press, 1994, p. 20.
98  R. Madhavan Nair, 'In Solidarity', *Frontline*, 16(3), 30 January–12 February 1999. Online. Available HTTP: <http://www.flonnet.com/fl1603/16030810.htm>. (Accessed 21 January 2002.)
99  Roy quoted in Peter Popham, 'The God Comes Home', *Independent on Sunday*, 11 April 1999, pp. 10–16, at p. 16.

portrayal of Namboodiripad himself and his party followers. Marxism, the economic and political theory devised by Karl Marx and Friedrich Engels in the mid-nineteenth century, which would form the ideological basis of communism, had been a feature of Indian politics since the 1920s, and after independence the Congress government adopted recognizably socialist economic policies. But in contrast to revolutionary liberation movements elsewhere in the world, Marxism never provided the ideological motor for the Indian freedom struggle and was overshadowed by the village-based utopianism of Gandhi's civil-disobedience campaigns, associated with the dominant Congress Party. The Congress had its own socialist wing, the Congress Socialist Party (CSP), founded in 1934, which elaborated an 'Indian Marxism'. The leaders of what would later become the elected Communist administration in Kerala, P. Krishna Pillai,[100] and, more famously, E. M. S. Namboodiripad, came to left-wing politics through Congress socialism, founding the Kerala unit of the CSP in 1937 and only later breaking away to form a regional wing of the Communist Party.

Under the direction of M. N. Roy and P. C. Joshi, the Communist Party of India (CPI), which was banned by the British and operated from outside India for much of the pre-independence period, distanced itself from the Congress and 'never assimilated nationalism into its anti-colonial cause, refusing to put the colonial conflict above that of internal class conflict'.[101] This meant that the CPI, although it later became a powerful force in regions such as Bengal and Kerala, lost significant national support to the CSP during the independence struggle. The CPI's comparative inability to appeal to the masses was hardly surprising given its numerous confusing shifts in policy and its failure to formulate a culturally recognizable, truly Indianized form of Marxism. Its position on the Second World War was indicative of this: in 1939 the party opposed the war; by 1942, they supported the British as 'anti-fascists', and by 1946 they had turned their attention to re-educating the rural masses and promoting agrarian (rural) revolution.[102]

As Roy outlines in *TGST*, the first period of communist rule in Kerala, during which 'the communists found themselves in the extraordinary – critics said absurd – position of having to govern a people and foment revolution simultaneously' (Ch. 2, p. 67), came to a swift end after they introduced unpopular bills, such as the ending of concessionary fares for students, and faced strikes and civil unrest. The past came back to haunt the CPI in 1964, when the party was riven over allegations that their chairman had offered to turn informer for the British during the 1920s in exchange for his own release from prison. A split had already formed due to divided allegiances during the war between China and India in 1962, and the leadership scandal prompted a number of CPI members to leave and form the Communist Party of India (Marxist) or CPI(M).[103] The CPI(M), under the direction of E. M. S. Namboodiripad, saw itself as the 'real inheritor of [the communist values of] the undivided CPI',[104] and concentrated on

---

100 There is no specific connection between P. Krishna Pillai and Comrade Pillai in *TGST*.
101 Robert J. C. Young, *Postcolonialism: An Historical Introduction*, Oxford: Blackwell, 2001, p. 315.
102 Young, *Postcolonialism*, p. 315.
103 Nossiter, *Communism in Kerala*, p. 20.
104 E. M. S. Namboodiripad, *Selected Writings*, Vol. I, Calcutta: National Book Agency, 1982, p. 178.

developing rural power bases at a regional rather than national level, gaining a surprise victory in the 1967 elections in Kerala as part of a seven-party anti-Congress coalition with the older CPI. This second communist administration lasted for thirty-one months before succumbing to internal conflict,[105] but the communists stayed in office as part of various coalition groupings and remain an active presence in the politics of the state.

If the CPI historically played such a limited role in national politics, why did it become a successful force in Bengal and Kerala? In *TGST* this is a question 'even Chacko [has] no really complete explanation for', but which Roy tries to answer in an interestingly detailed aside. The main points of her argument are worth revisiting here:

> There were several competing theories. One was that it had to do with the large population of Christians in the state. Twenty per cent of Kerala's population were Syrian Christians [. . .] Structurally – this somewhat rudimentary argument went – Marxism was a simple substitute for Christianity. Replace God with Marx, Satan with the bourgeoisie, Heaven with a classless society, the Church with the Party, and the form and purpose of the journey remained similar.
>
> [Ch. 2, p. 66]

As Roy's narrator warns us, the drawback with this theory is that it ignores the actual political priorities of most business-owning 'feudal' Syrian Christians, who traditionally voted for the Congress Party. A more complex and more plausible argument might make the broader claim that in the rural restructuring attempted by the party in the 1940s, communism filled a gap created by the decline of Hindu *and* Christian social and religious structures and 'provided the answers that gods and ceremonies did not'.[106]

But the 'replacement' theory of communism, as just another faith, obscures some of the ways in which communists in Kerala accepted and reinforced existing religious and cultural structures. Although personal privilege doesn't necessarily compromise radical politics, the family background of Kerala's communist leader, E. M. S. Namboodiripad (a member of the elite *adhyan namboodiri* caste of Vedic hymn-singers but a self-described 'adopted son of the working class'), encapsulates the political contradictions of his brand of 'peaceful' communism. The irony of the situation is not lost on Roy, who describes Namboodiripad as the 'flamboyant Brahmin high priest of Marxism in Kerala' (Ch. 2, p. 67). In *TGST*, the careful reformism of Namboodiripad's politics is satirized in Chacko's revolutionary posturing (which involves intimate trade-union meetings with attractive female factory employees) and his 'unquestioning approval' of Namboodiripad's political treatise, *The Peaceful Transition to Communism*.

Roy's textual digression into the history of communism in Kerala also relates a 'second theory' which ascribes the communist victory to the famously high levels of literacy in Kerala, even though, as her narrator points out, these literacy levels were achieved largely because of the communist administration. According to the narrator of *TGST*, the most plausible reason for the communist success in Kerala – one that *TGST*'s betrayal plot reinforces – is that the Communist Party worked within the existing power structure:

> The real secret was that communism crept into Kerala insidiously. As a reformist movement that never overtly questioned the traditional values of a caste-ridden, extremely traditional community. The Marxists worked from *within* the communal divides, never challenging them, never appearing not to. They offered a cocktail revolution. A heady mix of Eastern Marxism and orthodox Hinduism, spiked with a shot of democracy.
>
> [Ch. 2, pp. 66–7]

Dilip Menon concurs with Roy when he states that Namboodiripad and other party leaders had a vested interest in seeing Kerala's history as a linear progression from a barbaric past to an enlightened Marxist present. In the process, the caste system and its *brahmin* elite could be explained as a necessary stage in the organization of production and the development of regional culture. In Menon's view: 'Ultimately, it was this neutering of the past which vitiated much Marxist history and E. M. S. [Namboodiripad]'s own *Marxisante* foray. For in not looking back in anger, E. M. S., Damodaran and others denied the long shadow of the past [and the persistence of caste] in the present.'[107]

But does this political accommodation of the existing caste structure add up to a historical betrayal of lower-caste groups by the CPI(M) in Kerala? In his historical survey of the communist party in Kerala, Menon suggests that their political strategy was not to identify completely with any group: 'The career of the party [. . .] has been characterized by political pragmatism rather than permanent affiliations of any kind. There have been conjunctural and tactical partnerships with parties and groups of all hues, justified by theoretical legerdemain.'[108] The strategic, enterprising aspects of the CPI(M), and its growing complacency, are registered in Roy's novel in the sinister figure of Comrade K. N. M. Pillai, a cynical demagogue whose house, once a hotbed of study meetings and revolutionary fervour, is now decorated with a limp, faded party flag from which, ironically, the 'red had bled away' (Ch. 1, p. 13).

Even so, while she satirizes local party organizers and caricatures specific leaders such as E. M. S. Namboodiripad, turning his ancestral home into a 'local heritage' tourist attraction in *TGST*, Roy's critique of the CPI(M) is not developed from a right-wing position, even though her Marxist detractors argue that her novel endorses liberal-bourgeois values. Instead, the communist project in Kerala is lampooned because of its failure to live up to its own liberatory ideals, a flaw that, in Roy's opinion, it shares with other corrupt 'systems' such as *laissez-faire* or 'unrestrained' capitalism (in which giant transnational corporations now

---

107 Dilip M. Menon, 'Being a Brahmin the Marxist Way: E. M. S. Nambudirpad and the Pasts of Kerala', in Daud Ali (ed.), *Invoking the Past: The Uses of History*, Oxford: Oxford University Press, 1999, pp. 55–87, at p. 87.
108 Menon, *Caste, Nationalism and Communism in South India*, p. 193.

control so much of the supposedly 'free' market). For Roy: 'Soviet-style Communism failed, not because it was intrinsically evil, but because it was flawed. It
allowed too few people to usurp too much power. Twenty-first-century market
capitalism, American-style, will fail for the same reasons. Both are edifices
constructed by human intelligence, undone by human nature.'[109]

If it were not for her scepticism about the inevitable misuse of power on a
national level, we might be forgiven for seeing in Roy's novel a covert defence of
the non-aligned, market-controlling socialism of the Nehru period.[110] However, in
her repeated statement of the need for political representation to take place on a
small, accountable scale, her politics are actually more reminiscent of Gandhi's
vision of society as a constellation of self-sufficient villages.[111] As she states in
interview, the future for India has to be local: 'Decentralized economics, decentralized control; handing some measure of power back to the people.'[112] At the same
time, Roy is deeply suspicious of the parochialism of village life and warns that
she is not 'a proselytiser for the eternal upholding of custom and tradition'.[113]
This is perhaps why her most positive political representation in *TGST* is reserved
not for Gandhi's ideas or his political successors like Vinoba Bhave, but for a left-
wing revolutionary group that espoused more violent, uncompromising methods:
the Naxalites.

## 'A keg of ancient anger': the Naxalites and environmental protest movements

The Naxalites were revolutionaries who staged an armed uprising in the north-
west Bengal village of Naxalbari in March 1967. Mostly peasants, untouchables
and people of the local Santal tribe angered by years of empty government promises,[114] the Naxalites, who advocated a brand of communism derived from the
teachings of the Chinese leader Mao Tse-tung – attacked Hindu landlords and
temporarily gained control of the district. The movement was supported by China
and, although many of the Naxalbari revolutionaries were killed in the brutal
government suppression of the rebellion, the uprising quickly spread to other states
such as Andhra Pradesh, Bihar, Kerala and Uttar Pradesh.[115] By June the Naxalites
had been condemned by the Indian Communist Party as 'an anti-party group
advocating an adventurist line',[116] and in Kerala, E. M. S. Namboodiripad dismissed them as 'a group completely bankrupt politically and organisationally'.[117]

109  Roy, *The Ordinary Person's Guide to Empire*, p. 40.
110  Mullaney, *Arundhati Roy's The God of Small Things*, p. 40.
111  See Roy's interview with David Barsamian: 'Whatever critique one may or may not have of him,
     Gandhi's understanding of politics and public imagination is unsurpassed.' (*The Chequebook and
     the Cruise Missile*, p. 135.)
112  Arundhati Roy, 'The Ecologist: Interview with Arundhati Roy', *The Ecologist*, 30(6), 2000.
     Available <http://www.paulkingsnorth.net/guts.html>. (Accessed 16 June 2006.)
113  Roy, 'The Ecologist'.
114  See H. Rai and K. M. Prasad, 'Naxalism: A Challenge to the Peaceful Transition to Socialism',
     *Indian Journal of Political Science*, 33, 1973, pp. 458–78.
115  T. J. Nossiter, *Marxist State Governments in India: Politics Economics and Society*, London:
     Pinter, 1988, p. 23.
116  Nossiter, *Marxist State Governments in India*, p. 23.
117  E. M. S. Namboodiripad, *The Communist Party in Kerala: Six Decades of Struggle and Advance*,
     New Delhi: National Book Centre, 1994, p. 235.

But where the CPI(M) seemed to work within existing (and still very unequal) social structures, the Naxalites, who became the Communist Party of India (Marxist-Leninist) in May 1969, offered many the hope of more immediate social transformation. Like contemporary Maoist movements in Europe, they enjoyed support amongst students and urban political radicals and were particularly influential in Calcutta University. In 1972 the Naxalite leader, Charu Majumdar, died in suspicious circumstances in police custody, and the movement fragmented and became involved in internal struggles and disputes with other communist groups.

In *TGST*, Velutha is rumoured to have joined the Naxalites in his four-year absence from Ayemenem (Ch. 2, p. 77), and although his murder by the police is not a response to revolutionary insurrection, it still parallels, in its 'sober, steady brutality' (Ch. 18, p. 308), the now notorious violence meted out to the Naxalite revolutionaries, who were tortured, raped and executed by police in the pay of coalitional communist state governments.[118] Because of the impressionistic quality of her presentation of Naxalite politics as a series of emotional states such as anger and a fear of dispossession, it is difficult to judge exactly how far we should read Roy's comments about the Naxalite fighters as an endorsement of their revolutionary aims. Roy has subsequently said in interview that while the 'pros and cons of violent and nonviolent resistance can be debated', there is no doubt that 'violent resistance harms women physically and psychologically in deep and complex ways'.[119] If we take her later essays into account, then Naxalbari may be more important in *TGST* as a pure sign of radical dissent – as such, the uprising works in Roy's novel as the symbolic counterpart to the revolutionary taboo-breaking transgression represented by Ammu and Velutha's affair, an act which can also be interpreted as a physical, fatal protest against 'ancient' oppressions.

There may, however, be other reasons why Naxalbari has such symbolic importance in *TGST*. On one level, Roy's references to the Naxalites cannot be disassociated from the kind of retro-revolutionary nostalgia that, in the West, has effectively repackaged Che Guevara (the photogenic Argentinian revolutionary who took part in Fidel Castro's communist coup in 1950s Cuba) as a fashion icon. The difference, as the cultural critic John Hutnyk argues, is that for writers, artists and musicians in India and in the Indian diaspora, Naxalbari may offer an alternative to the bland Bollywood culture that represents them globally.[120] Rather more importantly, Naxalbari, although a communist revolution, was sparked by some of the same environmental issues that form the basis of Roy's opposition to globalization and industrial development.

The low-caste peasants and tribal peoples of the Darjeeling foothills started their rebellion because they found themselves excluded from Indira Gandhi's (misleadingly named) 'Green Revolution', a state agricultural plan that promoted fertilizers and high-yield grain to India's farmers in the 1960s. Pushed off their land, the peasants of Naxalbari lost out on this agricultural modernization and faced greater impoverishment as a result. But while increased crop production

---

118 John Hutnyk, 'Music for Euro-Maoists: On the Correct Handling of Contradictions among Pop Stars', *Theory, Culture and Society*, 17(3), 2000, pp. 136–58, at p. 146.
119 Roy, *The Chequebook and the Cruise Missile*, p. 125.
120 Hutnyk, 'Music for Euro-Maoists', p. 151.

allowed India to escape from the threat of widespread famine, the Green Revolution was never a total success. Farmers and environmentalists soon realized that introducing costly high-yield crops and industrial agricultural practices to India locked small producers into a dependency on fertilizers and pesticides in place of the more resilient native strains of rice and wheat they had grown before. The changes in agriculture also affected local ecosystems and led to a decrease in the biodiversity of the Indian countryside – something that many poorer rural communities relied upon to augment their farming. At the same time, peasant communities (and particularly rural women) in North India started to protest against similarly damaging agricultural policies such as deforestation, most notably in the 'Chipko' movement of the early 1970s,[121] and the NBA is the present-day successor to these early environmental lobby groups.

Although they trace their origins back to events such as the Khejarli massacre in 1730 (in which villagers from the Bishnoi community were killed because they opposed tree-fellings by the Maharaja of Jodhpur), Indian environmentalist and 'ecofeminist' movements have largely taken their cue from these political challenges to the Green Revolution, and activists and thinkers such as Vandana Shiva, Medha Patkar and Ramachandra Guha have all emphasized the human costs of environmental damage and reasserted the fact that issues of social justice and human rights are intimately linked to the environment.[122] Recently, these issues have become more urgent with the promotion of genetically patented sterile crop strains that force farmers to purchase new seed grain and specific fertilizer brands yearly (and make them liable for prosecution if they do not follow their contractual obligations). In many cases, the specialist knowledge that enables multinational chemical companies to patent these new crops comes from local producers themselves, a process of intellectual theft that Vandana Shiva terms 'biopiracy'.[123]

For Roy, agricultural modernization and hydroelectric schemes such as the Narmada dam projects have dispossessed India's most vulnerable rural communities in the name of 'development'. In Roy's view, the Western notion of development, when applied to India, reveals a profound 'lack of imagination',[124] and by blindly following a 'developmental' path, the Indian state, which courted outside investment as part of its economic liberalization in the early 1990s, has impoverished its own citizens and become embroiled in corrupt deals with global multinationals such as the energy giant Enron. The impact of foreign investment and India's increased economic growth rate is apparent in *TGST* in the way the small town of Ayemenem changes and becomes 'globalized' between the two time schemes of the novel; its inhabitants find themselves able to make money working 'unhappily' in the gulf states, but their new wealth coexists with increased poverty and questionable imports such as tourism and satellite television.

121 For an account of the Chipko protests, see Ramachandra Guha, *The Unquiet Woods: Ecological Change and Peasant Resistance in the Himalaya*, Berkeley, Calif.: University of California Press, 1989.
122 See Graham Huggan, 'Greening Postcolonialism: Ecocritical Perspectives', *Modern Fiction Studies*, 50(3), 2004, pp. 701–33, at p. 704.
123 See Vandana Shiva, *Biopiracy: The Plunder of Nature and Knowledge*, Boston, Mass.: South End Press, 1997.
124 Roy, *The Chequebook and the Cruise Missile*, p. 17.

Without specific policies to target poverty, argues the historian Sunil Khilnani, economic liberalization is likely to increase social inequalities in India in several ways: widening disparities in social opportunities, sharpening the divide between rural and urban India and increasing differences in wealth between regions.[125] Much of Roy's writing since *TGST* has questioned the dominance of the narrative of neo-liberal capitalism, and her support for groups like the NBA can be seen as an attempt to protect its alternatives – political stories 'that are different from the ones we're being brainwashed to believe'.[126] For Roy, India's political alternatives are local: 'Decentralized economics, decentralized control; handing some measure of power back to the people.'[127] And in the end, her political hopes are founded on India's inherent resistance to a 'single idea'. Like her vision of the novel as a story that cannot be told in one way, India's future depends, in her work, on its plurality:

> India's redemption lies in the inherent anarchy and fractiousness of its people and its political formations [. . .] Corporatizing India is like trying to impose an iron grid on a heaving ocean, forcing it to behave. My guess is that India will not behave. It cannot. It's too diverse, too grand, too feral, and – eventually, I hope – too democratic to be lobotomized into believing in one single idea, which is, eventually, what corporate globalization really is: Life is Profit.[128]

## Ammu's 'unsafe edge': gender politics and sexuality

The last political context which we will deal with here – women's rights, and the politics of gender and sexuality – is the most important in terms of the plot and thematic focus of *TGST*. It is also the most difficult to summarize because of the varying perceptions of gender differences held by India's diverse cultural and religious communities and the close historical association between women's-rights groups and other political movements, such as the nationalist struggle and later environmental and land-rights campaigns. Nevertheless, in *TGST*, Roy's narrative is unrelenting in its need to bear witness to the routine cruelties of patriarchy (male authority), and women characters are consistently bullied, harassed and made to defer to the needs of male relatives and family members. If we describe the structure of Roy's novel in musical terms (as critics such as Baneth-Nouailhetas have done, see Critical readings, **p. 145**), then the oppression of women forms a central refrain that recurs, in various elaborations, throughout the text. At one point, Roy emphasizes the critical nature of Ammu's predicament, and, by extension, the desperation of all women marginalized and 'gendered' in traditional Indian communities, in a remarkable 'terrorist' metaphor: 'What was it that gave Ammu this Unsafe Edge? [. . .] It was what she had battling inside her. An unmixable mix. The infinite tenderness of motherhood and the reckless rage of a suicide bomber' (Ch. 2, p. 44). Here

125 Sunil Khilnani, *The Idea of India*, Harmondsworth: Penguin, 1997, pp. 100–1.
126 Roy, *The Ordinary Person's Guide to Empire*, p. 77.
127 Roy, 'The Ecologist'.
128 Roy, *The Algebra of Infinite Justice*, p. 190.

the conflicting, potentially taboo-breaking force of Ammu's frustration is described in the most self-destructive terms, and we will return to it after we have reviewed the history of the struggle for women's political self-representation in the subcontinent.

The women's movement in India originated in religious reform associations in the early nineteenth century, and by 1917 women had started to set up their own pressure groups (such as the Women's Indian Association [WIA] founded by Annie Besant, Dorothy Jinarajadasa and Margaret Cousins), which lobbied for women's greater participation in education and politics. Indian women played a critical role in the anti-colonial nationalist struggle of the 1930s and 1940s and took part in numerous political and land-rights struggles after independence, such as the 1948 Telangana peasant uprising.[129] As Radha Kumar notes, in these early social-reform and nationalist movements, women were mobilized primarily in their symbolic capacity as mothers: 'The first half of the twentieth century saw a symbolic use of the mother as a rallying device, from feminist assertions of women's power as mothers of the nation, to terrorist invocations of the protective and ravening mother goddess to the Gandhian lauding of the spirit of [maternal] endurance.'[130] In the post-independence period, however, more empowering feminist images of women as daughters and workers replaced an older cult of the mother, as women's groups drew attention to the social mistreatment of women and their right to political recognition and economic autonomy. Early on in the women's movement, calls for reform were made primarily by middle-class women, sometimes (as was the case with the WIA) in unison with European radicals and suffragettes. In contrast, during the nationalist struggle, and in the years that followed, poorer, lower-caste woman became increasingly politicized, protesting on a range of issues themselves, from rape, dowry murders and *sati* (ritual self-immolation after the death of a husband), to food-price rises and the sale of illegal alcohol. The movement for women's rights witnessed a resurgence after the publication of the *Towards Equality* report (discussed below) in 1974, and Indian feminist thinkers also started to critique aspects of Western feminism and question the ethnocentrism or cultural biases of work by 'First World' feminists in the following decade (see Critical history, **pp. 88–92**). At the same time, *dalit* and tribal women began to form their own lobby groups, and it is more accurate to speak of the present 'women's movement' in India as a broad spectrum of different political struggles, carried out by women from diverse backgrounds, rather than a cohesive nationwide campaign.

Given the involved history of the Indian women's movement, we should be wary of generalizing Roy's concerns as feminist without also thinking about their local articulation. It is useful to remember at this point that 'gender' is a term which describes the cultural and social construction of femininity or masculinity and, therefore, cannot be separated from the culture that produces it. In contrast to Western or 'First World' feminism, the struggle for women's rights in the so-called 'Third World' must be seen in the context of a colonial past, as well as

129  See Kumkum Sangari and Sudesh Vaid (eds), *Recasting Woman: Essays in Indian Colonial History*, New Brunswick, NJ: Rutgers University Press, 1990.
130  Radha Kumar, *The History of Doing: An Illustrated Account of Movements for Women's Rights and Feminism in India, 1880–1990*, New Delhi: Kali for Women, 1993, p. 2.

the gender politics of particular religious and regional communities. Thinking about exactly this issue, some critics have envisaged women's experiences in the Caribbean, Africa and India in terms of a process of 'double colonization'. First conceptualized by Kirsten Holst Petersen and Anna Rutherford, this term refers to the dual oppression of women by colonialism *and* by indigenous patriarchal structures.[131] It is this fact of 'double colonization' that informs the historical background of Roy's novel and underlies her subsequent non-fiction statements on women's rights.

A striking example of this nexus of oppressions occurs in *TGST* in Ammu's early married life, when Mr Hollick, the English tea-estate manager who employs her husband, proposes that he 'look after' Ammu in return for her partner's continued employment. Ammu divorces her husband after he beats her for not agreeing to the offer, and returns to Ayemenem where, as a divorcee, she faces the disapproval of local society. Ammu's predicament then, is one in which her body becomes a gendered sign of both desire and disgrace, and the terrible price of her refusal to prostitute herself in the archetypally colonial setting of the tea plantation is her transformation into a 'shameful' figure in the patriarchal Syrian-Christian community. (When Ammu tries to claim recognition under the law by making a statement at the police station after Velutha's arrest, the police inspector refuses the statement, assaults her and calls her a *veshya* or prostitute.) Nowadays, the 'double colonization' that imprisons women in post-independence Kerala is less likely to take the form of a negotiation between oppressive traditional values and colonialism than between tradition and 'neo-colonial' aspects of globalization (such as the objectification of women in the global media). As Roy points out in one of her interviews:

> A lot of the women who are involved in resistance movements [. . .] are also redefining what 'modern' means. They are really at war against their community's traditions, on the one hand, and against the kind of modernity that is being imposed by the global economy, on the other. They decide what they want from their own tradition and what they will take from modernity. It's a high-wire act.[132]

A milestone in the Indian women's movement came in 1974, when a report into the social, political and economic condition of women commissioned by the United Nations and entitled *Towards Equality* revealed that, even though women's rights were written into the Indian constitution, there was a gap between these principles and women's actual experiences. As the report committee made clear, a lack of understanding of their legal rights and an inability to claim them meant that Indian women were, in some cases, in a worse situation than they had been at independence in 1947.[133] The report revealed the lack of attention that the

---

131 Kirsten Holst Petersen and Anna Rutherford, *A Double Colonisation: Colonial and Postcolonial Women's Writing*, Mundelstrop: Dangaroo Press, 1986. Compare with Gayatri Spivak's concept of 'double-effacement', p. 83.

132 Roy, *The Chequebook and the Cruise Missile*, pp. 125–6.

133 See Indian Government, Committee on the Status of Women in India, *Towards Equality: Report of the Committee on the Status of Woman in India*, New Delhi: Government of India, Ministry of Education and Social Welfare, 1974, p. 359.

government had paid to feminist issues and acted as a catalyst for pressure groups to educate women about their civil rights. However, in certain cases, the rights which could be claimed by the majority of women in India were suspended by older laws which concerned particular minority communities. Important instances of this were the Travancore Christian Succession Act of 1916 and the Cochin Christian Succession Act of 1921, laws which applied only to the Syrian-Christian community and severely limited the inheritance rights of Syrian-Christian women. As a divorcee and daughter of a Syrian-Christian landowner, Arundhati Roy's mother, Mary Roy, would successfully appeal against these acts in the Indian Supreme Court in 1986 (arguing in a landmark case that they violated her constitutional rights; see Text and contexts, **p. 13**). In *TGST* we find that the intersecting forms of subjugation that Ammu faces are further reinforced by her poor legal status or *locus standi* or, as her children misinterpret it, her lack of 'Locusts Stand I', as a Syrian-Christian woman (Ch. 2, p. 57). By including references to the legal inequality between Ammu and her brother Chacko – who recognizes his own power of inheritance by telling her 'what's yours is mine and what's mine is also mine' (Ch. 2, p. 57) – Roy draws attention, obliquely, to a history of dispossession and a struggle for women's rights in which her own mother was deeply involved.

The legal and social forces that conspire against Ammu in *TGST* and create a situation where 'there would be no more chances' (Ch. 2, p. 43) are especially disturbing when we recall that, by the late 1960s, Kerala was starting to gain a reputation as a social and economic success story. (The region still has some of the best life-expectancy and literacy levels, and the lowest infant-mortality rates, in India.) As Robin Jeffrey points out, women's literacy and ability to find salaried work and a willingness amongst families to educate their daughters and allow them to marry later than usual have been crucial factors in the state's development. Jeffrey goes on to warn, however, that even given these breakthroughs, 'women still do not play a major role in public politics'.[134]

In contrast to the traditional lack of women's property rights in the Syrian-Christian community, the pre-colonial social structure of certain Hindu castes such as the *nayars* (discussed earlier in Text and contexts, **p. 28**) may have actually laid the foundations for Kerala's present, comparatively progressive, record on women's rights. Unlike the great majority of Hindu family structures, the *nayars* operated a matrilineal family system in which women had inheritance rights on land and property. Not to be confused with matriarchy (*nayar* women did not rule households or establish government), the matrilineal system developed across Kerala from the fourteenth century, and its origins have been variously attributed to the need for young *nayar* men to be free to participate in military duties and to a custom of selective but unacknowledged liaisons between high-caste *namboodiri* men and *nayar* women.

Whatever its origins, the matrilineal system meant that *nayar* women in pre-nineteenth-century Kerala had some sexual independence and certainly more personal freedom than many women in Europe and America at the time. Both *nayar*

---

134 Robin Jeffrey, *Politics, Women and Well-Being: How Kerala Became 'a Model'*, Basingstoke: Macmillan, 1992, p. 11.

women and men might have several partners during their lifetimes, and any children from these relationships would be brought up in the mother's home where her brothers acted as male guardians. With the British incursions into the region in the early nineteenth century came new colonial law systems and forms of trade, and because of these legal and commercial changes, the matrilineal family structure declined and all but disappeared by the 1930s.[135] As Jeffrey suggests, the decline of matriliny in Kerala meant that 'by the 1980s, some groups of Kerala women probably enjoyed less autonomy, particularly over their sexual lives, than their grandmothers had done. Kerala women nevertheless had more influence over their own lives and those of their families than most women elsewhere in India'.[136] With the arrival of British colonialism in Kerala, Syrian-Christian women experienced similar contradictory changes in their status: even though they were legally discriminated against and had to conform to inflexible codes of sexual behaviour and endogamy (marriage within one's own community), they were, in the first half of the twentieth century, often better educated than other Indian women due to their attendance at vocational and educational institutions set up by missionaries.[137]

In *TGST*, Ammu's 'unsafe edge' is a threat to the established order not only because it carries the promise of her 'reckless' challenging of sexual prohibitions – it also brings into play supposedly 'unmixable' aspects of her sexuality (motherhood and eroticism) that society and especially caste laws would normally keep separate. In some striking ways, the taboo-breaking force of Ammu's sexuality is reminiscent of powerful Hindu goddesses, such as the destroyer goddess Kali, incarnation of divine energy or *shakti*, who were mobilized as political symbols in the early nationalist movement and who have since been reappropriated by Hindu feminists. As Radha Kumar reminds us, one of the most important developments in Indian women's demands for equality has been a shift away from the 'concern for women's bodies as sites of racial and national regeneration' (represented, as we have seen, as forms of motherhood), towards more rights-based assertions that women's bodies must not be treated as the 'subjects of social control'.[138] It is the fact of her (divorced) maternal status that makes Ammu such an easy subject of social control, and her response to her children, whom she loves intensely but describes in a moment of rage as the 'millstones around my neck' (Ch. 13, p. 253), accentuates this tension.

While traditional gender roles make Ammu's position as a divorced mother intolerable, Roy's novel also continually traces the limitations of masculine gender norms in tyrannical or sexually predatory male characters such as Pappachi, Kari Saipu and the Orangedrink Lemondrink man. Indeed, if we see Ammu and Velutha's affair as an idealized 're-envisioning' of the actual families in *TGST* – argues Anuradha Dingwaney Needham – 'it is the roles of the father and husband/partner [the novel . . .] suggests, that need to be recast'.[139] On these terms we can

135 See G. Arunima, *There Comes Papa: Colonialism and the Transformation of Matriliny in Kerala, Malabar, c. 1850–1940*, New Delhi: Orient Longman, 2003.
136 Jeffrey, *Politics, Women and Well-Being*, p. 9.
137 See Committee on the Status of Women in India, *Towards Equality*, p. 46.
138 Kumar, *The History of Doing*, p. 2.
139 Anuradha Dingwaney Needham, ' "The Small Voice of History" in Arundhati Roy's *The God of Small Things*', *Interventions* 7(3), 2005, pp. 369–91, at p. 385.

read Ammu and Velutha's affair not so much as a *transgression* of gender politics but as a utopian moment that envisages their transformation and imagines the possibility of a family unit in which women and children are freed from long-established patterns of subordination.

## *Kathakali* dance-drama in performance

In *Pather Panchali*, a famous Bengali novel of village childhood adapted for cinema in 1955 by Satyajit Ray (and discussed in Text and contexts, **pp. 58–9**), one of the child protagonists, Opu, is spellbound by a travelling *jatra* theatre troupe. The all-night *jatra* performance provides an entrancing play-within-the-novel, and Roy exploits a similar formal technique when she includes a complete night-long *kathakali* dance-drama, watched by Estha and Rahel, in Chapter 12 of *TGST*. The drama echoes some of the traumatic events of the twins' earlier life – amongst them Estha's abandonment and Velutha's violent death – and also provides Roy with a way of reflecting on some of the cultural predicaments faced by Indian performers and writers. In order to appreciate these correspondences and internal echoes in *TGST*, it is important to understand the dramatic shape and cultural origins of this regional performance tradition.

*Kathakali* is one of the most elaborate and distinctive of the South-Asian classical dance forms, differing significantly from other styles (such as *bharatnatyam* and *kathak*) in its use of ornate make-up and costumes, its characteristic dramatic stance in which actors balance on the outer edges of their feet and its tradition of male performers taking on both male and female roles. Narrated in a mixture of Malayalam and Sanskrit, it has roots in the oldest continuous dramatic form in the world, the ancient South Indian Sanskrit theatre tradition, *kudiyattam*, which is performed to high-caste audiences at temples and can be traced back to the fourth century CE. As we shall see, a later cycle of devotional temple dramas, *Krishnattam*, dedicated to the Hindu god Krishna and devised by the Zamorin King of Calicut around 1650, and another contemporary drama form, *Ramanattam*, invented by a prince of the *nayar* Kottarakkara family, are also integral to the development of *kathakali*. Decorations such as the white ruff or face frame and the frilled head dresses that certain characters wear have made the *kathakali* actor Kerala's unofficial cultural representative and, as Roy emphasizes in *TGST*, although still staged at numerous temples and villages, *kathakali* performances now form part of the cultural itinerary of Kerala's tourist trade.

The actor-dancers of the *kathakali* (literally a 'story play') are accompanied by musicians who control the rhythm of the drama and vocalists who sing the verses of the dramatic text. The actors themselves have no vocal role and augment the narrative through a sophisticated figurative language of hand gestures (*mudras*). Rhythmic accompaniment is provided by side-stage drummers who play an upright *chenda* (alternating with a melodic hourglass-shaped *ettaka* to signify female characters) and a wide horizontal drum called a *madalam*. According to the ancient Sanskrit treatise on drama, the *Natyashastra*, the choreographic and musical aspects of the performance are categorized as *angika abhinaya*, or physical gesture, and *vachika abhinaya*, vocal or musical elements of the play. Two more key components of classical dramatic performance described in the *Natyashastra* – *satvika abhinaya*, the evocation of specific moods and emotions, such as love, anger, fear and astonishment (conveyed through stylized facial expressions), and *ahraya abhinaya*, the use of dramatic make-up and costume – are also integral to the drama.

In *kathakali*, the arts of *ahraya abhinaya* are particularly noticeable, and the ornate make-up and dress of the actor-dancers follow a colour code that denotes motivating character traits. Noble, heroic characters such as Krishna or Arjuna are termed *pacca* (green), because of their green face paint, which symbolizes purity. More popular are *katti* (knife) characters, such as the demon Ravana or villainous Duryodhana, who are noble and have some green colouring, but who are governed by base instincts such as greed, jealousy and arrogance. Another important category is *tadi* (bearded) characters. Demonic or villainous *chuvanna tadi* (red beard) figures such as Dushasana have black faces and red hair and are driven by hubris and a lust for power,[140] the faithful Hindu monkey god, Hanuman, who helps Rama in the *Ramayana*, always appears in a furry coat and with a grey/white beard and is thus known as *velupputadi* (white beard), and hunters or forest people are *karupputadi* (black beards) and have black faces with white decorative flowers on their noses. The symbolic colour of monsters and witches is *kari* (black), and these characters have faces marked with black-and-white patterns. Women, holy men, messengers and *brahmins* – who generally symbolize gentleness and spiritual virtue – are termed *minnukku* ('shining' or 'softly coloured'), and the presiding colours here are orange and yellow. Finally, some minor figures and animals, known as *teppu* characters, are not placed in any specific category and have their own make-up. These include the snake Karkotaka, the mythical birds Garuda and Jatayu and the man-lion Narasimha.[141]

Roy's partial use of a similar colour symbolism makes it tempting to compare the schematic rules of characterization in *kathakali* with the depiction of the protagonists in *TGST*. For instance, we might interpret Velutha as an updated *velupputadi* 'helper' figure or explore figurative connections between the evil *kari* characters in *kathakali* and the cigar-loving colonial ghost 'Kari Saipu'. In his critical essay on *TGST*, Pier Paolo Piciucco discusses Roy's use of colour, especially green, although this is a technique he associates with the novel's child perspectives rather than colour codes in *kathakali*.[142] In fact, Roy's use of myth and performance in *TGST* is more complex than a straightforward set of correlative figures, and her references to some of the conventions of *kathakali* are loosely evocative rather than schematic. As I argue below (see Critical readings, **pp. 155–6**), Roy's inclusion of a complete *kathakali* performance in *TGST* poses searching questions about the political potential of the novel form and the role of the postcolonial author.

The conventions governing the staging of *kathakali* dance-drama have changed little since its formalization in the mid-seventeenth century. Performed annually from January through to April/May, the plays were paid for by a wealthy patron

---

140  David Bolland, *A Guide to Kathakali*, Delhi: National Book Trust, 1980, p. 4.
141  Bolland, *A Guide to Kathakali*, p. 5.
142  Pier Paolo Piciucco, 'The Goddess of Small Things: Some Observations on the Fictional Technique of Arundhati Roy's First Novel', in R. K. Dhawan (ed.), *Arundhati Roy: The Novelist Extraordinary*, New Delhi: Sangam, 1999, pp. 319–327, at p. 324.

and, as a form of auspicious ritual, were always free to the audience. In theory, this meant that anyone could watch the play – although rules governing caste interaction and the exclusion of untouchables would still have applied.[143] In rural areas, performances often occurred in the courtyard of the patron's house, although a more traditional setting, and one reproduced in *TGST*, is the temple courtyard. In common with other forms of Hindu religious ritual, *kathakali* could not be performed completely in the open, and a temporary thatched canopy usually provided covering. Like the *kathakali* performance watched by the twins in *TGST*, the dramas performed today still take place at night, starting at nine or ten o'clock and lasting until dawn. The performers are illuminated by a single oil lamp and are preceded by ritual drumming and dance and the *vandanaslokam* or prayer song as well as a short introduction to the main characters (the *purappad*) and a musical interlude where the vocalists and drummers showcase their talents (the *melappadam*). At the conclusion of the main dramatic narrative, usually at dawn, there is a final dance piece, the *dhanasi*, that marks the end of the whole performance.[144]

## A theatre of war: the history of *kathakali*

The rigidly structured caste hierarchies of Kerala, outlined earlier, have been instrumental in preserving and perpetuating Sanskrit *kudiyattam* temple drama and later forms such as *kathakali*. Throughout Kerala's history, *kathakali* has been associated with the landowning *nayar* caste. A *nayar* author, Tuncattu Ramanujan Ezhuttacchan, translated the great Sanskrit epics of the *Mahabharata* and the *Ramayana* into Malayalam in the late sixteenth and early seventeenth centuries, giving lower-caste groups, who were barred from the temple performances of the *kutiyattam* (and were not educated in the elite Sanskrit traditions anyway), a chance to read and recite the epics themselves. Another significant development was the composition of eight plays in Malayalam, known as the *Ramanattam*, in the latter part of the sixteenth century. Based on the *Ramayana* and written by a prince of the *nayar* Kottarakkara family, these plays are seen by some historians as a direct response to the rival, more elitist, *Krishnattam* form. However, the *Ramanattam* borrowed recognizable aspects of staging, such as the use of a hand-held curtain as a backdrop, details of decoration and a single oil lamp to light the players, from the older Sanskrit *kudiyattam* tradition. Unlike *kudiyattam* and anticipating *kathakali*, the *Ramanattam* actors sang their lines rather than chanting them.

The drama-dance form now known as *kathakali* was conceived between 1665 and 1681, by another prince from the northern Kottayam principality, who composed four plays in a verse combination of Sanskrit and Malayalam based on stories from the *Mahabharata*. The major technical breakthrough of the Kottayam prince was the realization of a wider range of *bhava* or emotional moods in the drama and, hence, a greater level of complexity than the more idealized

143 Zarrilli, *Kathakali Dance-Drama*, p. 6.
144 M. P. Sankaran Namboodiri, 'Kathakali: Dance-Drama of Kerala', 1996. Online. Accessible HTTP: <http://www.vvm.com/~pnair/htm/k_kali.htm>. (Accessed 30 May 2005.)

*Ramanattam* plays: 'In the Kottayam [*kathakali*] the heroes show many facets of their characters. Bhima sometimes blusters; he is headstrong; at other times he is awkwardly embarrassed. Dharmaputra becomes tired and discouraged.'[145] Innovations in staging, musical accompaniment and costume have also been attributed to the Kottayam prince, and under his direction the ornate conical crowns of Krishna, Rama and Lakshmana were introduced and the headgear of demonic characters developed into their present, elaborate shapes. A number of subsequent developments were made to the drama by a member of the elite *namboodiri* caste, Kaplingattu Namboodiri, who was interested in theatre and set up his own *kathakali* troupe in 1765. Kaplingattu's great innovation was to increase and systematize the vocabulary of *mudras* or formal hand gestures used by the actors and to develop the role of the ambivalent *Katti* characters as the most important figures in the drama. These roles – which include the demon Ravana who abducts Sita in the *Ramayana* – offer the audience (and actors) the same flawed complexity as the great tragic heroes of the Western tradition, and new plays such as the *Ravanotbhavam* (*The Origin and Rise of Ravana*, 1777) by Raghava Pisarati were written to cater for them. Kaplingattu's legacy was carried on, with some developments, by other teacher-performers, but the basic form of *kathakali* remained the same from this point.

In *TGST*, the *kathakali* performance concludes in a violent, highly stylized confrontation between Bhima and Dushasana dramatized from the *Mahabharata*: 'Bhima cornered Dushasana in a battlefield already strewn with corpses. For an hour they fenced with each other [. . .] Their breathless battle spilled out of the kuthamabalam and spun around the temple. They chased each other across the compound, twirling their papier-mâché maces' (Ch. 12, pp. 234–5). In Roy's novel the fight harks back to the violent reassertion of order carried out by the touchable policemen against Velutha, but the acrobatic 'fencing' of the *kathakali* men also has a martial historical origin in the dual role of earlier *kathakali* actors. At the end of the seventeenth century, *kathakali* performers acted as officers in local armies, and the arduous physical training they undergo has its beginnings in the military traditions of the *kalari* or gymnasium.[146] Today, *kathakali*'s military origins are still recalled in the presiding goddess of the drama, Bhagavati, who protects the dressing room and stage and is honoured by the actors in her incarnation as the goddess of war.

In the seventeenth and eighteenth centuries, the feudal structure of South Indian society, with its network of minor fiefdoms and kingdoms, was thus a fertile ground for the patronage, growth and development of *kathakali*. Most local rulers maintained small military forces attached to a *kalari* which could always form the training centre for a *kaliyogam* or *kathakali* troupe. Setting up a *kaliyogam* conferred considerable prestige on its founder, and the warlike content of the stories, often with a culminating battle between good and evil, supported the military ethos and heroic codes of local rulers who were often involved in battles over territory. As we have already seen, the links between *kathakali*

---

145 Betty T. Jones, 'Kathakali Dance-Drama: An Historical Perspective', in B. C. Wade (ed.), *Performing Arts in India: Essays on Music, Dance and Drama*, Berkeley, Calif.: Centre for South and Southeast Asian Studies, 1983, pp. 14–44, at p. 22.
146 Jones, 'Kathakali Dance-Drama', p. 20.

and military combat were very close, and the traditional award of a gold bracelet, presented by a royal patron for an outstanding *kathakali* performance, was also the prize for heroism in battle. Some of the most popular *kathakali* are plays with 'killing' (*vadham*) in their titles, such as the *Duryodhana Vadham* (which the twins watch in *TGST*), and even dramas which do not feature military conflict often conclude with a symbolic death. As a 'dominant metaphor for conceptualizing relations of spiritual and socio-political power',[147] combat is celebrated as a heroic ideal in *kathakali* and the killing of an anti-hero or demon king re-establishes the cosmic order through the process of sacrifice.[148] By the late eighteenth century, feudal society in Kerala had started to break down following invasions by Haidar Ali and Tipu Sultan and the subsequent colonial control of the region by the British. As a consequence, *kathakali* lost much of its established patronage and declined throughout the nineteenth century.

In the 1920s, a celebrated poet, Mahakavi Vallattol, who was dismayed by the state of Kerala's traditional drama, campaigned for a regional *kathakali* training school and, with the help of a local raja, opened the new institution, the Kerala Kalamandalam, in 1930. Vallattol soon realized that, without traditional structures of patronage and support, *kathakali* would have to become a more widely recognized cultural form in order to survive and organized national and international *kathakali* tours in the late 1930s and 1940s. When the communists came to power in 1957, management of the Kalamandalam was given to the Kerala state government and, funded by subsidies and the profits from performances, it has since expanded and now also trains students in dramatic dance forms such as *bharatnatyam* and *mohiniyattam*. With increased government involvement, the Kalamandalam has both preserved *kathakali* and changed the structure of its tuition, transforming the older *kaliyogam* system (where students learned under one or two acknowledged masters) into a broader-based institutional curriculum.

### *Kathakali* intertexts: *Karna's Oath* and *The Killing of Duryodhana*

Roy's memorable description of the *kathakali* performance in *TGST* as a dramatization of culturally familiar 'Great Stories' which encapsulate epic or heroic archetypes tends to divert our attention from the fact that some *kathakali* plays, although based on ancient Hindu epics, are actually quite recent. The first play the adult twins watch, *Karna Shabadam* or *Karna's Oath*, is a case in point, as it was adapted from episodes in the *Mahabharata* by V. Madhavan Nayar ('mali') in 1966. *Karna's Oath* thus has an interesting chronological resonance with *TGST*, because its first performances – and presumably its reception by audiences in Kerala – coincide with the late-1960s strand of Roy's narrative. In recent years, *Karna's Oath* has become, along with *King Nala's Law*, one of the most frequently performed and best-loved *kathakali* dramas. As Roy tells us, the play follows the birth and abandonment of Karna, the son of Kunti and the Sun god Surya, and his subsequent search for his true parentage. After birth, Karna is put in a basket and cast adrift in a river because of the stigma Kunti fears as an

---

147 See Zarrilli, *Kathakali Dance-Drama*, p. 6.
148 See Zarrilli, *Kathakali Dance-Drama*, pp. 5–6.

unmarried mother. Adopted by a charioteer of the Kaurava family and transgress-
ing caste laws to study under the great sage Parshuram, Karna is subsequently
given a kingdom by the eldest of the Kaurava brothers and is finally reunited with
his mother on the eve of battle between the Kauravas and their enemies the
Pandavas. Tragically, Karna finds that Kunti is also mother to the Pandavas and
realizes that he is about to fight his half-brothers. He therefore makes an oath to
harm none of them except Arjuna, who has insulted him. After giving his special
powers of invincibility away to the God Indra, Karna is finally defeated by
Arjuna.

As Phillip Zarrilli points out, *Karna's Oath* is distinctive because of the 'close
focus on the title character's emotions, and his quest to discover his parentage',
and he goes on to note that 'because the role of Karna depends almost exclusively
on the histrionic virtuosity of the actor playing the title role, and not so much on
the choreographic structure of the play-in-performance as a whole', the play has
generated 'considerable controversy' among actors and *kathakali* purists.[149]
Given the high emotional pitch of her novel, it is revealing that Roy selects a
contemporary play that involves such 'histrionic' complexity for the *kathakali*
sub-performance in *TGST*. Karna's abandonment mirrors the Ipe children's
parental loss and his fate, as 'a prince raised in poverty. Born to die unfairly'
(Ch. 12, p. 232), is also Velutha's. Roy reinforces the connection in the contained
boundary-crossings and transgressions that are a routine feature of the drama.
In the *kathakali*, Karna's mother is played by a man, 'but a man grown soft and
womanly [. . .] from doing female parts for years' (Ch. 12, p. 232), and the last
time the children see Velutha, similar impromptu gender-blurrings occur. Dressed
in saris, and posing as 'Mrs Pillai, Mrs Eapen, Mrs Rajagopalan', the children
visit Velutha, who preserves the 'porcelain' conspiracy of their act by allowing
them to varnish his nails with Ammu's discarded red Cutex. As well as being an
omen of his violent death and a 'scarlet letter' connecting him to Ammu, Velutha's
painted nails become a confirmation, for his killers, of (bisexual *and* caste-
breaking) deviancy: 'The posse of Touchable Policemen had looked at [his nails]
and laughed. "What's this?" one had said. "AC-DC?" ' (Ch. 9, p. 190).

The second play that the twins watch is the more conventional *Duryodhana
Vadham* (the killing of Duryodhana). Rather older than *Karna's Oath*, this play
was written by Vayaskara Aryan Narayanan Moosad in the latter part of the
nineteenth century and recounts some of the most important episodes of the
*Mahabharata*, including the defeat of the Pandava brothers by the Kaurava family
in a game of dice. Having lost everything, the eldest Pandava brother, Yudhisthira
– sometimes known as Dharmaputra – stakes his wife Draupadi, who is also
married to the other Pandava brothers, and loses her too. The eldest Kaurava,
Duryodhana, orders his younger brother Dushasana to disrobe Draupadi,[150] but,
protected by the god Krishna, her sari becomes endless and cannot be unravelled.
Draupadi curses the Kauravas for the insult to her honour and, persuaded to play
a final dice game, the Pandavas lose and are banished to the forest for twelve
years. When the Pandavas finally return from exile, the Kauravas refuse to restore

149 Zarrilli, *Kathakali Dance-Drama*, p. 180.
150 See Bolland, *A Guide to Kathakali*, p. 42.

their kingdom, precipitating the eighteen-day battle at Kurukshetra (a conflict that forms the basis for one of the most revered Hindu texts, the *Baghavad Gita*). In the course of the fight, Bhima, the second eldest Pandava brother, is transformed into a terrifying form (*Roudra Bhima*) by the god Krishna, and hunts down Dushasana on the battlefield, killing him and drinking his blood. By doing so he avenges Draupadi, and in a scene which is not usually performed, Bhima finds and kills Duryodhana to complete his vengeance. As we noted above, there are structural parallels between the 'concluding' sacrifice of *kathakali* such as *Duryodhana Vadham* and Velutha's death, although the connection is a deeply problematic one in *TGST*, because it brings into question the whole concept of a mythical restoration of 'order' in the original dramatic narrative.

## Literary and cinematic contexts

### The God of Small Things and contemporary Indian fiction

The literary influences that shape *TGST* are extensive and culturally varied. This is due, in part, to Roy's cultural background, which encompasses traditions of Indian literature in English and Malayalam that stretch back to the nineteenth century but also takes in canonical English and American fiction. Like many contemporary Indian authors, Roy draws freely on Indian mythic and epic narrative traditions as well (see Critical readings, **pp. 155–66**). The simple fact of *TGST*'s international success has led many critics to make immediate and, in Roy's view, somewhat simplistic comparisons between her fiction and Salman Rushdie's ground-breaking novel *Midnight's Children* (1981). The critic Jon Mee underlines the influence of *Midnight's Children* when he argues that 'the appearance of a certain postmodern playfulness, the turn to history, a new exuberance of language, the reinvention of allegory, a sexual frankness, even the prominent references to Bollywood' in contemporary Indian-English writing 'all seem to owe something to Rushdie's novel'.[151] As Mee warns, however, the reinvigoration of Indian-English fiction in the 1980s and 1990s should not be attributed to Rushdie's work alone. Other factors, such as changes in India's political identity after independence, especially the threat to democratic freedoms in the 'Emergency' of 1975–7 (during which the Prime Minister, Indira Gandhi, curbed free speech and jailed many of her political opponents) and the growth of dynamic and influential Indian 'diaspora' communities in the West, have been just as important in shaping the political and cultural concerns of the contemporary Indian-English novel.

In India, Rushdie's role as an ambassador for Indian-English fiction has always been a controversial one, and fellow novelists such as Amit Chaudhuri have suggested that the very fact of Rushdie's fame has made *Midnight's Children* into an unrepresentative literary-historical landmark: a 'gigantic edifice that all but obstructs the view of what lies behind it'.[152] As a fellow Booker prize-winner

151 Jon Mee, 'After Midnight: The Indian Novel in English of the 80s and 90s', *Postcolonial Studies* 1(1), 1998, pp. 127–41, at p. 127.
152 Amit Chaudhuri (ed.), *The Picador Book of Modern Indian Literature*, London: Macmillan, 2001, p. xxiii.

(Rushdie received the award for *Midnight's Children* in 1981, and also won the 'Booker of Bookers' for the same novel in 1993), critical comparisons between Roy and Rushdie were perhaps inevitable.[153] But while not denying these influences, Roy has preferred to emphasize Rushdie's pioneering role in establishing Indian-English fiction as an international genre, thus allowing newer writers, like herself, to 'tell their stories'.[154] Inevitably, *TGST* does owe some of its formal and linguistic complexity to Rushdie's fiction, and this is clearest in the centrality of child protagonists, an attention to linguistic idioms and the manipulation of realist techniques in both novels. The plot of Rushdie's novel involves 1,001 children whose births all coincide, magically, with the moment of India's independence at midnight on 14 August 1947, and, while Rushdie's narrator Saleem Sinai 'tunes in' telepathically to the voices of the nation, becoming an All-India radio for the other 'children of midnight', Roy's twins share a more private psychic bond – a 'single Siamese soul' (Ch. 2, p. 41) that allows Rahel to open doors for her brother without hearing him knock and understand, intuitively, 'what the Orangedrink Lemondrink Man did to Estha [and] the taste of the tomato sandwiches – *Estha's* sandwiches, that *Estha* ate – on the Madras Mail to Madras' (Ch. 1, pp. 2–3).

Roy acknowledges her debt to Rushdie in the pickle/chutney theme in *TGST*, when Mammachi writes to the manager of 'Padma Pickles' (a reference to the Bombay factory run by Rushdie's Saleem in *Midnight's Children*) for advice on pickling techniques (Ch. 8, p. 167). In Rushdie's novel, pickles and preserves symbolize the fictional 'chutnification of history',[155] which involves both a highly political 'grand hope' of distilling the history of the Indian state but also a migrant desire to recapture lost time and memories of home. Roy's pickle theme, it could be argued, plays on Rushdie's figurative engagement with history, and the collapse of Mammachi's pickle business evokes the failure of the post-independence generation to 'preserve' the economic vision of a self-sufficient India cherished by the leaders of the anti-colonial Indian nationalist movement, M. K. Gandhi and Jawaharlal Nehru.[156] However, in *TGST* the pickle motif is not solely historical, and Mammachi's problems with classification (according to local government regulations, her banana jam is 'an ambiguous, unclassifiable consistency [. . .] too thin for jelly and too thick for jam' [Ch. 1, p. 30]) and containment (her pickle jars always leak [Ch. 8, p. 167]) also point to more psychological themes of transgression and the 'seeping' return of guilty, repressed memory.

Like Rushdie in *Midnight's Children*, Roy is deeply interested in the relationship between personal lives and national events in the subcontinent, and her references to the 'Big God' of 'the vast, violent, circling, driving, ridiculous, insane, unfeasible, public turmoil of a nation' (Ch. 1, p. 19) recall the allegorical connections that 'handcuff' Rushdie's narrator, Saleem to India's national history. Needless to say, for both authors, these 'national allegories' are highly unstable and are rarely presented as a straightforward connection between the public story

153 Arundhati Roy in 'Winds, Rivers and Rain'.
154 Arundhati Roy, quoted in Vir Sanghvi, 'The Rediff Special Interview'. Online. Available HTTP <http://www.rediff.com/news/apr/05roy2.htm>. (Accessed 6 October 2005.)
155 Salman Rushdie, *Midnight's Children*, London: Pan Macmillan, 1982, p. 459.
156 Mullaney, *Arundhati Roy's The God of Small Things*, p. 40.

of the nation and personal narrative.[157] In *Midnight's Children*, Rushdie's everyman narrator is a grotesque, cracked mirror of independent India, and his story constantly struggles to accommodate the subcontinent's epic variety and breadth. On the other hand, in *TGST*, Roy reshapes the epic mode in favour of a sense of the integrity and vulnerability of *petits récits*: small narratives[158] or expressions of 'personal despair', which are continually dwarfed by, but reflect, 'Worse Things' that happen on a national level (Ch. 1, p. 19). Roy also uses impressionism and tonal effects where Rushdie tends to employ irony and caricature, and her contextualized use of myth and the lyrical representations of the natural world in *TGST* complicate any broad comparisons with Rushdie's writing.

While we compare Roy's novel with fairly recent works like *Midnight's Children*, we should remember to look behind the 'edifice' of that novel and take account of the fact that traditions of Indian writing in English stretch back to the colonial nineteenth century. It is Roy's awareness of social injustice in *TGST* that gives us the strongest sense of these precursors – the lack of freedom for women in orthodox religious communities, epitomized in the entrenched sexism that faces Ammu as a divorcee in *TGST*, was an issue that troubled some of the first Indian women writers, such as the nineteenth-century Christian convert Krupabai Satthianadhan. In her two novels, *Kamala* (1893) and *Saguna* (1895), Krupabai drew attention to the need for women's education and condemned the abuses of Hindu child marriage, and her writing can be seen as part of the late nineteenth- and early twentieth-century process of religious and social reform that produced other pioneering women writers and activists such as the Muslim author Rokeya Sakhawat Hossain and the Parsi barrister Cornelia Sorabji. Similarly, one of the very first novels by a male author in Malayalam, O. Chandumenon's *Indulekha* (1889), voices reformist concerns about the oppression of women in Kerala's feudal upper castes in its story of a progressive woman who resists an arranged marriage to a decadent, lecherous *brahmin*, Sri Namboodiri.

Roy's concentration on caste in *TGST* and her proverbial descriptions of inequality ('Big Man the Laltain, Small Man the Mombatti') are foreshadowed in the social concerns of Indian fiction during the nationalist period of the 1920s and 1930s. In terms of the debate over caste, the most important of these works is Mulk Raj Anand's social-realist novel *Untouchable* (1935), which attacked caste injustice and was inspired by M. K. Gandhi's campaign against untouchability. Gandhi believed that the emancipation of India's untouchables, alongside Hindu–Muslim unity, was an essential part of the national struggle for Indian self-rule, but his spiritual vision also meant that he tended to see a nobility in the suffering of marginalized sectors of society – especially women and untouchables – and this view made his political representation of these groups controversial (see Text and contexts, **p. 26**). Recounting a day in the life of Bakha, a low-caste sweeper, and recording the numerous slights and insults he experiences, Anand's novel forms an urgent humanist protest against caste prejudice and presents a concealed critique of Gandhi's politics (see Further reading, **p. 174**).

---

157 Mee, 'After Midnight', p. 139
158 See Boehmer, 'East is East and South is South', p. 70.

Anand was a founding member of the left-wing Indian Progressive Writer's Association, and his Marxist politics inform the sharpest satires in *Untouchable*, which features slow-witted colonial missionaries and corrupt Hindu priests. Shocked by the conservatism and hypocrisy of religious orthodoxies, he would state that 'Hinduism has tended for a long time to be more the social organism of caste and less and less a unified religion'.[159] During the 1930s and 1940s, writers in India's state languages shared Anand's sense of social commitment, and in Kerala, the famous Malayalam author T. S. Pillai (whose 1956 novel *Chemmeen* (or *The Prawn*) was later adapted into the film cited in *TGST*) launched a scathing attack on untouchability in his novel *Thottiyude Makan* (*Scavenger's Son*) (1947), which charts the struggles of three generations of latrine cleaners, or *thottis*, and concludes with the triumphant victory of the central protagonist, Mohanan, over oppression and caste prejudice.[160]

While it is possible to trace Indian women's fiction and the social-protest novel back to the late nineteenth century, the post-independence decades of the 1960s and 1970s saw the emergence of a new generation of women novelists which included Anita Desai, Ruth Prawer Jhabvala, Shashi Deshpande and Nayantara Sahgal. While these writers do not exert a strong stylistic influence on Roy, they do elaborate common feminist concerns, and their work often features women who are forced to negotiate sometimes conflicting discourses of sexuality, religious faith, gender, caste and citizenship.[161] For instance, Desai's and Deshpande's fictional explorations of the frustrations of upper-class, urban Indian women, ensnared in unfulfilling home lives, anticipate Ammu's social entrapment and her fateful sexual rebellion against the 'love laws'. Commenting on Desai's *Where Shall We Go this Summer?* (1975), Deshpande's *That Long Silence* (1988) and Sahgal's *The Day in Shadow* (1971) in her discussion of alternative, reconfigured visions of home in Indian women's fiction, the critic Rosemary George argues that these novels all repeat a common plot in which a 'young or middle-aged female protagonist' experiences a domestic crisis such as 'a divorce, an extramarital affair, an unpleasant encounter with suffering, [or] a cross-class confrontation'. George goes on to state:

> Whatever its scale the event develops into the central event or crisis of the narrative, whose reverberations force the protagonist to confront the parameters of herself, her life and her worth. This period of self-examination is followed by a return (often with relief) to her life of domestic boredom [. . .] *or* by a rejection of the entire enterprise of domesticity.[162]

A cursory glance at these plot variants is telling because Roy uses all of them (in combination, and in a particularly tragic form) in her representation of

---

159 Quoted in Margaret Berry, *Mulk Raj Anand: The Man and the Novelist*, Amsterdam: Oriental Press, 1971, p. 12.
160 N. Natarajan (ed.), *Handbook of Twentieth-Century Literatures of India*, Westport, Conn.: Greenwood Press, 1996, p. 192.
161 Mullaney, *Arundhati Roy's The God of Small Things*, p. 25.
162 Rosemary M. George, *The Politics of Home: Postcolonial Relocations and Twentieth-Century Fiction*, Berkeley, Calif.: University of California Press, 1996, p. 132.

Ammu. Similarly, the building sense of frustration that initiates each of these narratives is echoed in Ammu's dismay at her own limited opportunities: 'She was twenty-seven that year, and in the pit of her stomach she carried the cold knowledge that for her, life had been lived. She had had one chance. She made a mistake' (Ch. 2, p. 38).

An awareness of how middle-class lives are built on the exploitation and labour of the poor is another relevant feature of George's analysis. In the novels she discusses, any feminist protest against patriarchal oppression has to acknowledge the very obvious *comparative* privileges of urban middle-class women in India. A keen sensitivity to privilege is a noticeable feature of *TGST* too, and Roy's description of the exasperating insignificance of personal tragedy, compared with public disaster, adds the 'small god' of middle-class guilt to her layered title motif (Ch. 1, p. 19). Not only do her middle-class characters confront poverty as a daily fact, Roy, unlike many earlier Indian novelists, is unflinching in her exploration of the way their guilty sense of privilege is exploited in cross-class confrontation. Thus, during Chacko's visit to Pillai's house, the communist leader holds his straitened circumstances 'like a gun to Chacko's head' (Ch. 14, p. 275), and after he sexually abuses Estha, the Orangedrink Lemondrink Man quells his potential protests by telling him he is a 'lucky rich boy, with porketmunny and a grandmother's factory to inherit' (Ch. 4, p. 105).

The feminist preoccupations and uncompromising emotional clarity of Roy's work connect her to another author from Kerala, the short-story writer and poet Kamala Das, who is well known for poetry collections in English, such as *Summer in Calcutta* (1965) and *The Old Playhouse and Other Poems* (1973), and also writes in Malayalam under the pen name Madhavikutty. She was one of the first Hindu women writers to discuss women's sexuality openly, and many of her most famous poems deal with the attenuated lives and emotional frustrations of Indian women caught in stifling domestic situations. Considered alongside the work of poets such as Das, and given its distinctive setting, *TGST* might be described more accurately as a *South* Indian novel in English and can be usefully compared with writing by other authors who share Roy's regional affiliation. The author Githa Hariharan spent her childhood in South India, and she anticipates Roy's interest in the restricted, idealizing roles available to women in 'traditional' Hindu narratives in *A Thousand Faces of Night* (1992); she also shares Roy's fascination with children's stories and fables such as the *panchatantra* in *The Ghosts of Vasu Master* (1994). Further intriguing comparisons can be made between *TGST* and Aubrey Menen's largely forgotten collection of prose essays, *Dead Man in the Silver Market* (1954), one of which deals with the socially fraught visit of Menen's Irish mother to his father's orthodox Hindu family in Malabar. Returning to Rushdie's work, *The Moor's Last Sigh* (1995) shares the South Indian setting and fractured family dynamic of *TGST*, although Rushdie is clearly more excited by the buzz and clamour of urban India than the brooding silence of the Kerala backwaters.

Finally, Roy's use of Ayemenem as a stage for her complex contemporary fable of power and caste transgression can be contrasted with another famous fictional South Indian setting, the small riverside town of Malgudi, which provides the sleepy locale for many of R. K. Narayan's novels. A pioneer of Indian-English fiction who started writing in the 1930s, Narayan perfected a form of

'mythic-realism'[163] in which his protagonists solve some form of personal predicament and achieve (often life-changing) self-knowledge through the transcendent truths of Hindu myth and philosophy. The striking contrast between the two
authors is that, while Roy reminds us of the social power relations supported by
Hindu myth and epic in stories such as Draupadi's disrobing (see Text and contexts, pp. 45–6), Narayan endorses their often conservative injunctions as ways
of resolving conflict. This difference is clearest in novels such as *The Dark Room*
(1938), in which Narayan tackles the theme of the oppressed middle-class wife
but does so in a way that offers little consolation to his downtrodden protagonist, Savitri, and seems to support the 'feminine' qualities of endurance and
self-sacrifice celebrated in the sacred Hindu religious text, the *Dharma Shastra*.[164]

## Colonial literary contexts

In common with many other postcolonial authors, Roy gestures 'intertextually'
towards a number of well-known English literary works in her novel, and in order
to understand the implications of these borrowings and contexts we must pause
for a moment to consider the history of English in the Indian subcontinent.
Ever since the pioneering work of critics such as Edward Said[165] and Gauri
Viswanathan,[166] postcolonial critics have argued that the teaching of English literature in colonial India was never a politically neutral process. As early as 1835,
the ideological potential of English literature as a means of inculcating the values
of the colonizer in a 'translator class' of Indians had been recognized by the
historian and policy-maker T. B. Macaulay in his famous 'Minute on Indian Education', in which he claimed that 'a single shelf of a good European library was
worth the whole native literature of India'.[167] Shortly afterwards, these convictions were converted into colonial law in the English Education Act of 1835. As
the politics of colonial rule became more complex, and missionary activity more
closely regulated, English literature was increasingly used to teach Protestant
Christian morality 'indirectly' to Indians. Teaching English literature in this way
masked the economic exploitation of empire and 'implied that moral behaviour
and English behaviour were synonymous', so that the English literary text
'function[ed] as a surrogate Englishman in his highest and most perfect state'.[168]
In Roy's novel, the consequences of this kind of dislocating colonial education are underlined in Chacko's 'Anglophilia' speech, in which he laments the
cultural mimicry of the Ipe family, who are all 'pointed in the wrong direction,
trapped outside their own history, and unable to retrace their steps because their
footprints had been swept away' (Ch. 2, p. 52).

---

163 Fawzia Afzal-Khan, *Cultural Imperialism and the Indo-English Novel: Genre and Ideology
   in R. K. Narayan, Anita Desai, Kamala Markandaya, and Salman Rushdie*, Pennsylvania, Pa.:
   Pennsylvania State University Press, 1993, p. 27.
164 Satyanarain Singh, 'A Note on the World-View of R. K. Narayan', *Indian Literature*, 24, January–
   February 1981, p. 106.
165 Edward Said, *Orientalism*, London: Pantheon, 1978.
166 Gauri Viswanathan, *Masks of Conquest: Literary Study and British Rule in India*, London: Faber
   and Faber, 1990.
167 T. B. Macaulay, 'Minute on Indian Education' in John Clive and Thomas Pinney (ed.), *Selected
   Writings: Thomas Babington Macaulay*, Chicago, Ill.: University of Chicago Press, 1972, p. 241.
168 Viswanathan, *Masks of Conquest*, p. 20.

The role of English literature as a culturally incongruous marker of 'education' is apparent in the atmosphere of formal quotation and recital which pervades Roy's novel. Canonical English literature is often reduced to a status symbol in *TGST*, and its recitation is frequently a show put on by children to impress adults. Key amongst these is the comical rendition of 'Lochinvar' (a ballad in Walter Scott's *Marmion* in which 'fair Ellen' elopes with Lochinvar at her bridal feast) by Pillai's niece, and a parroted version of Mark Antony's 'Friends, Romans, Countrymen' speech shouted at high speed by his son, Lenin. At Cochin airport, where the Ipe family welcome Margaret Kochamma and Sophie Mol, Baby Kochamma lives up to her name by taking on this childish recital role herself, quoting Ariel's speech from *The Tempest* in order 'to announce her credentials to Margaret Kochamma [and] set herself apart from the Sweeper Class' (Ch. 6, p. 144). A similar scene occurs at the sailing club, where a neo-colonial Indian elite of 'Cardamom Kings, Coffee Counts and Rubber Barons' misquote *Romeo and Juliet* in order to distance themselves from, and ridicule the demands of, militant low-caste unions: 'They raised their glasses. "*A rose by any other name . . .*" they said, and sniggered to hide their rising panic' (Ch. 2, p. 69).

Of course, all these quotations have a deeper narrative resonance and, like fragments of a mirror scattered through the novel, they reflect aspects of Roy's plot and characterization. Amongst these, Baby Kochamma's quotation of *The Tempest* deserves a little more consideration, as it reminds us of the play's colonial theme: the conquest of Sycorax's island by the exiled Prospero, and Caliban's bitter speech to his captors: 'You taught me language; and my profit on't / Is, I know how to curse',[169] a speech that evokes the Ipes' postcolonial predicament of 'adoring' their conquerors and 'despising' themselves (Ch. 2, p. 53). Even so, it is not Caliban's speech that Baby Kochamma quotes, or the (equally apt) description of the supposedly drowned King of Naples, but Ariel's lyrical account of his dance with nature: 'In a cowslip's bell I lie; there I couch when owls do cry',[170] a song which seems to gesture towards the enchanted natural world of *TGST* and reminds us that Ariel, like the Ipe twins, is passed between surrogate 'parents', Sycorax and Prospero. Elsewhere, Estha recites Caesar's accusatory dying speech, 'Et tu Brute!', from *Julius Caesar*, to the uncomprehending cook, Kochu Maria, the words becoming an omen of his own innocent complicity in Velutha's death, and the passing reference to *Romeo and Juliet* recalls the forbidden, and ultimately fatal cross-caste romance at the centre of *TGST*.

The allusions to English literature in *TGST* become more complicated when Roy cites novels *about* empire. By the late nineteenth century, the ideological role of English literature was not confined to promoting the moral superiority of 'Englishness' through exemplary fiction, poetry and drama. New, aggressively imperialist values such as 'keeping the peace', masculine duty and the colonial work ethic were being inculcated in Raj fictions by writers such as Rudyard Kipling. At the same time, however, the moral basis of imperial rule was coming under increasingly critical scrutiny in the work of authors such as R. L. Stevenson and Joseph Conrad. Roy makes use of both these strands of late colonial fiction in

---

169 *The Tempest*, Act I, Scene 2, line 363.
170 *The Tempest*, Act V, Scene 1, line 88.

the course of *TGST*, referring ironically to Kipling's children's fable *The Jungle Book* (1894), but also exploiting the more sinister tone of Conrad's famous novella of the Belgian Congo, *Heart of Darkness* (1899), when she uses it in her naming of the tourist hotel built on the site of the abandoned plantation house. Here, colonial culture and its fictional signifiers literally return to 'haunt' Roy's writing in the spectre of Kari Saipu – 'Ayemenem's own Kurtz' – who figures as a partly threatening, partly comical ghostly presence on the edges of the novel.[171]

Contemporary Indian literature in English is often read as a creative postcolonial negotiation with the language, forms and literary traditions used to legitimize colonial culture. Indeed, if we pursue this line of inquiry we might see the misquotation and re-contextualizing of English literature in *TGST* as part of a postcolonial strategy that appropriates and rewrites the 'master texts' of colonialism. At the same time, we also risk missing some of the subtler points of Roy's writing (and underestimate the way English texts like Shakespeare's plays have been absorbed into Indian culture) if we see references to English literature simply as a statement about the dislocating cultural force of colonialism. In her study of postcolonial intertextuality, the critic Judie Newman reminds us that, while postcolonial societies were shaped and culturally marginalized by colonial literature, places like Roy's Kerala also 'have their own internal centres and peripheries'.[172] As such, Roy's awareness of canonical works such as *The Tempest* and *Julius Caesar* are as much about the colonial cultural pretensions of the Indian middle classes, contrasted with the twins' 'real [and therefore supposedly more sincere] affection for the English language' (Ch. 2, p. 51), as about the actual pain of cultural disinheritance and 'Anglophilia'.

The fact that this kind of rewriting has become such a convention of postcolonial fiction has irritated some of Roy's reviewers, who feel that her symbolism and habit of textual citation is overemphatic and object to her artificial or pretentiously naïve style.[173] Certainly, for undergraduate students, Roy's novel sometimes seems to offer a misleadingly simple checklist of literary reference points that can be ticked off, in coursework essays, as evidence of her 'postcolonialism'. In Roy's defence, when we examine these embedded colonial fictions carefully, we often find that they are presented in surprising or unusual ways. Kipling's *The Jungle Book* may encode imperialist values and oblique references to the 'law' of the jungle, but it still exerts a narrative magic on the twins: 'At night Ammu read to them from Kipling's *Jungle Book*. "*Now Chil the Kite brings home the night / That Mang the Bat sets free –.*" The down on their arms would stand on end, golden in the light of the bedside lamp' (Ch. 2, p. 59). Moreover, with its fabular presentation of the animal world, and its orphaned 'man-cub' protagonist, Mowgli, *The Jungle Book* has a thematic resonance in *TGST* that escapes irony and could be interpreted as a metaphor for the 'mixed-blood' hybridity of the Ipe twins and the 'sacredness of friendship and loyalty' in both works.[174]

---

171 See David Punter, *Postcolonial Imaginings: Fictions of a New World Order*, Edinburgh: Edinburgh University Press, 2000, p. 67.
172 Judie Newman, *The Ballistic Bard: Postcolonial Fictions*, London: Arnold, 1995, p. 3.
173 For a summary of these reviews, see Mullaney, *Arundhati Roy's The God of Small Things*, p. 72.
174 Baneth-Nouailhetas, *The God of Small Things: Arundhati Roy*, p. 134.

Similarly, allusions to Conrad's modernist classic *Heart of Darkness*, criticized by some as a clumsy, incongruous endorsement of Roy's cultural politics, can, alternatively, be read as a form of textual layering, enabling associations to be made between Kerala's past and present and revealing the often invisible historical continuities that link exploitative colonial plantation economies with latter-day 'neo-colonial' incursions into the 'Third World'. Roy herself argues that the metaphor of the 'Heart of Darkness' is a deliberately ironic, 'laughing', reversal of the ideological direction of Conrad's novella and also, perhaps, its most famous adaptation, Francis Ford Coppola's film *Apocalypse Now* (1976), which transplants Conrad's African setting to South-East Asia in one of the bleakest cinematic representations of America's war in Vietnam. When questioned about these references, Roy has stated:

> It's saying that we, the characters in the book, are not the White Men, the people who are scared of the Heart of Darkness. We are the people who live in it; we are the people without stories. I keep referring to the war in Vietnam, saying we are the nameless geeks and gooks who populate the Heart of Darkness.[175]

The influence of nineteenth-century fiction and later, more imperialist genres of English literature is also clearly apparent in the fateful romance plot (reminiscent of both Gustave Flaubert's realist novel *Madame Bovary* (1857) and, as we have seen already, *Romeo and Juliet*) which forms the centrepiece of Roy's novel. The romance genre has traditionally provided a very fertile literary ground for Indian writing in English, not least because exotic 'Eastern' locations were already favoured settings for popular nineteenth-century romances by middlebrow colonial authors such as Flora Annie Steel and Maud Diver and were understood as such by contemporary European readers. Many of Kipling's early short stories in *Plain Tales from the Hills* (1888) deal satirically with Anglo-Indian romances and clandestine adulteries and, in the early twentieth century, Indian authors such as S. K. Ghosh and S. M. Mitra exploited the political potential of the genre in *The Prince of Destiny* (1909) and *Hindupore* (1909) respectively, both of which feature highly symbolic cross-cultural love affairs. Hinting at a line of literary influences which we have traced in this section, Blake Morrison, in his review of *TGST*, suggests that Roy's novel 'might begin among the spices and pickles of *Midnight's Children*', but it 'ends in the tradition of the romantic popular classic'.[176]

## Wider literary influences

Moving beyond the English and Indian-English literary precursors discussed above, *TGST* can also be compared to some well-known works of American

---

175 Roy, 'When You Have Written a Book You Lay Your Weapons Down'. See also Roy, *The Ordinary Person's Guide to Empire*, p. 62.
176 Blake Morrison, 'The Country Where Worse Things Happen', *Independent on Sunday*, 1 June 1997.

fiction. This connection is most obvious when we think of the rich sense of place and the threatening racial politics that overshadow novels from the American Deep South, such as Harper Lee's *To Kill a Mockingbird* (1960). Set in rural Alabama, Lee's famous 'rites of passage' story is narrated from the perspective of Jem and Scout, the children of Atticus Finch, a local lawyer, and takes a similarly extended view of narrative beginnings as *TGST*: 'It really began with [General] Jackson.'[177] One of Lee's primary concerns in the novel is the way small communities exact a particularly punishing form of vengeance on individuals who are marginalized or flout social convention, and the latter part of the novel follows the trial of an African American man, Tom Robinson, who is falsely accused of raping a white woman. Tom Robinson's case is defended convincingly by Atticus, but he is still convicted by the all-white jury and is eventually shot trying to escape from jail. Like *TGST*, *To Kill a Mockingbird* is thus marked by a traumatic loss of childhood innocence, and in both novels the entry to adulthood involves the sacrifice of a guiltless scapegoat figure. The use of subjective perspectives and layered time schemes in *TGST* has been compared with similar techniques developed in American jazz-age novels such as F. Scott Fitzgerald's *The Great Gatsby* (1925) – a novel Chacko habitually quotes – and modernist classics such as William Faulkner's *The Sound and the Fury* (1929). Commenting on these novelists, Roy admits 'there's an infusion or intrusion of landscape in their literature that might be similar to mine',[178] even though she has made it clear that she has never read Faulkner's work. There are interesting coincidental similarities between the two novels, however. In contrast to *TGST*'s fluid third-person narrative, Faulkner, in *The Sound and the Fury*, uses several different interlocking first-person narratives to relate the history of the dysfunctional Compson family (a decaying branch of the southern aristocracy), but both authors refuse to tell their story of sombre familial corruption 'as if it is the only one'. Time and the unreliable subjectivity of memory are also shared features and, in Michael Gorra's view, both authors' common focus on 'sex, sudden death and transgression' makes *TGST* potentially the 'first Indian attempt at the Southern Gothic'.[179]

Given Roy's awareness of the colonial linguistic history out of which she writes, another significant modernist precursor is Irish rather than American: James Joyce's early *künstlerroman* (literally, an 'artist novel', a type of novel in which the central protagonist is an artist or writer), *A Portrait of the Artist as a Young Man* (1914–15). Like the South Indian characters in *TGST* who are 'trapped outside their own history' (Ch. 2, p. 52), Joyce's semi-autobiographical protagonist, Stephen Dedalus, is trapped in a (colonial) history, a 'nightmare' from which he is 'trying to awake'.[180] In addition, Joyce's narrative virtuosity, and his interest in children's language use, stems from a 'semi-colonial' awareness of the political implications of English.[181] Another author with whom Roy has been

177 Harper Lee, *To Kill a Mockingbird*, Harmondsworth: Penguin, 1963, p. 9.
178 Roy in 'Winds, Rivers and Rain'.
179 Gorra, 'Living in the Aftermath'.
180 Stephen Dedalus makes this claim in his later appearance in James Joyce's *Ulysses* (New York: Vintage, p. 34).
181 See Derek Attridge and Marjorie Howes (eds), *Semicolonial Joyce*. Cambridge: Cambridge University Press, 2000.

compared is D. H. Lawrence,[182] a key novelist and poet of the modernist period and author of the notorious *Lady Chatterley's Lover* (1928). Lawrence's sexually explicit novel deals with an extramarital affair between the aristocratic Constance Chatterley and her gamekeeper Oliver Mellors and was the subject of a famous obscenity prosecution in Britain in 1960. However, comparisons of Roy and Lawrence's shared sense of the liberatory power of sex are perhaps less convincing than their common scepticism about modern civilization and their interest in the natural world, and animals in particular, as expressions of vital totemic power. Lawrence's use of biblical imagery in works such as *The Rainbow* (1915) and the transcendent force of symbol and visionary spirituality in his writing also bear comparison with Roy's interest in the power and cultural integrity of pre-modern, epic narrative forms.

While modernist experiments in narrative and perspective anticipate some of the structural complexities of *TGST*, the imagism and fragmentary *bricolage* style of poetry written during the 1920s and 1930s (a *bricolage* is an artistic work, similar to a collage, assembled from 'found' materials) pre-empts Roy's concentration on the quiddity of 'small' things, such as plastic hairbands and toy wristwatches. A comparable focus on everyday objects occurs in the poetry of American modernists such as William Carlos Williams and Gertrude Stein. Moreover, given Roy's interest in the natural world and the complexity of her natural settings, we should not discount the literary (and political) influence of American writing about the environment, which was pioneered in the nineteenth century in the work of transcendentalists such as Ralph Waldo Emerson and Henry David Thoreau. These themes were revisited in the twentieth century, in some of the counter-cultural verse of Richard Brautigan and in the meditational haiku and translations of the 'greenest' poet of the Beat generation, Gary Snyder. In relation to Roy's emphasis on 'connectedness' and her vision of a rural Indian poisoned by pesticides, a key American (non-fiction) work is Rachel Carson's bestselling *Silent Spring* (1962). Carson, a marine biologist, was the first person to draw public attention to the over-use of pesticides such as DDT, and her book, which revealed their damaging effect on the ecosystem, has been credited as one of the founding texts of Western environmentalism.

It could be argued that Roy's interest in 'depthless' stylistic effects such as *bricolage*, verbal artifice and forms of intertextual literary parody and citation make *TGST* a good example of the postmodern novel – a literary form distinguished by its rejection of the older literary values of realist representation, formal coherence and artistic authenticity. However, in *TGST*, as in Rushdie's work, these technical features often merge with, and are sometimes difficult to distinguish from, the novel's more inherently 'political' postcolonial concerns.[183] A good example of the crossover currency of certain 'post'-marked literary styles associated with Roy's work is magic realism, a fictional mode that combines

---

182  See, for example, Mini Chandy's 'The Love Laws' in Indira Bhatt and Indira Nityanandam (eds), *Arundhati Roy's The God of Small Things*, New Delhi: Creative, 1999, p. 83.

183  For a detailed discussion of continuities and differences between the postcolonial and the postmodern, see Ian Adam and Helen Tiffin (eds), *Past the Last Post: Theorising Post-Colonialism and Post-modernism*, Hemel Hempstead: Harvester Wheatsheaf, 1991. See also A. Mukherjee, 'Whose Post-colonialism and Whose Postmodernism?', *World Literatures Written in English*, 30(1), 1990, pp. 1–9.

realist representational conventions with surreal or supernatural effects. Magic realism developed in Latin America, notably in writing by Alejo Carpentier, Gabriel García Márquez and Isabel Allende, as a way of representing grotesque or fantastic political realities, but had a parallel growth in German fiction in the 1950s.[184] These strands combined in English fiction in the 1980s when both Angela Carter and Salman Rushdie employed magic-realist techniques to redefine the novel in terms of the marginalized voices and histories of women and cultural minorities. A number of critics have commented on Roy's 'magic realism',[185] but apart from the twins' subtle telepathy and Rahel's conviction that Sophie Mol is 'awake for her funeral' in the first chapter, most of the surreal or fantastic aspects of Roy's writing can all be justified in terms of the heightened, imaginative perceptions of her child characters. (If we look more closely at the description of the funeral in *TGST* we find that, having drowned in the river, Sophie Mol *does* die 'because she couldn't breathe', and that Rahel translates this into a claustrophobic living burial 'on her behalf' [Ch. 1, pp. 5–7].) Critical discussions of Roy's 'magic realism' are thus, in many ways, as misleading as reflex comparisons with Rushdie's fiction; both are attempts to force *TGST* into a badly fitting critical framework. A better alternative, as Mullaney notes, is Elleke Boehmer's definition of Roy's style as 'extravagant realism', which captures the emphasis on realism in Roy's novel while also taking into account its more embellished subjective variations.[186]

Alongside the manipulation of 'the real' and forms of pastiche and metafictional conceit, one of the defining features of postmodernism is a mixing of high- and low-cultural forms, and Roy's ironic juxtaposition of Hindu epics such as the performed stories of the *Mahabharata* with more popular-cultural references to cinema, television and advertising is reminiscent of contemporary American novels such as Don DeLillo's *White Noise* (1985). Roy's references to popular culture are rarely positive, however, and the way media such as television and film dislocate or marginalize the Ipe family is underlined in Western self-images and norms of beauty and 'purity' that literally colour Estha and Rahel's moral universe, shaping their association with their lighter-skinned cousin, 'beach-coloured' Sophie Mol (Ch. 8, p. 186). Similar issues underlie the work of some African-American authors, especially Toni Morrison's novel *The Bluest Eye* (1970), the title of which refers to Eurocentric concepts of beauty that effectively excluded African Americans until the late 1960s. Morrison's better-known *Beloved* (1987) deals with the personal legacy of slavery and the lingering, traumatic memories of violence that shape African-American history, and dislocated identities and the colonial erasure of non-European histories are also significant themes in writings by migrant Caribbean authors such as Jamaica Kincaid. Child perspectives and mother–daughter relationships feature heavily in Kincaid's

---

184 See, especially, Günter Grass's *The Tin Drum*, trans. Ralph Manheim, New York: Pantheon, [1959] 1961.
185 S. Kannamal, 'Magic Realism and Arundhati Roy: India's Response to Emerging Literary Theories' in T. S. Anand (ed.), *Indian Responses to American Literature*, New Delhi: Creative, 2003, pp. 133–8, and Alexandra Podgorniak, 'Magical Realism, Indian-Style; or, the Case of Multiple Submission: *The God of Small Things* by Arundhati Roy' in Gerhard Stilz (ed.), *Missions of Interdependence: A Literary Directory*, Amsterdam: Rodopi, 2002, pp. 255–63.
186 Boehmer quoted in Mullaney *Arundhati Roy's The God of Small Things*, p. 72.

depictions of colonial Antigua, *Annie John* (1985) and *The Autobiography of My Mother* (1996), and her anger at the multiple dispossessions of slavery and colonialism echoes the powerful tone of moral outrage in Roy's writing. The strongest linkage between the two writers can be found in Kincaid's polemical prose essay on tourism in Antigua, *A Small Place* (1988), which questions the neo-colonial impact of resort tourism even more fiercely than Roy's jibes at the 'lolling' foreigners at the Heart of Darkness hotel.

## Cinematic intertexts: *Chemmeen, The Sound of Music* and *Pather Panchali*

Roy's experience of screenwriting and independent film-making before her literary debut with *TGST* means that cinema is almost as strong an influence as literature in her novel. Roy's cosmopolitan cultural background is signalled, like her many literary influences, in the variety of films which are cited in the course of the novel, and the stylistic debt to film is another shared aspect of *TGST* and Rushdie's *Midnight's Children*. Two films stand out particularly strongly in Roy's novel: *Chemmeen*, a tragic 1965 South Indian musical romance adapted by Ramu Kariat from the Malayalam novel by T. S. Pillai, and *The Sound of Music*, a Hollywood musical released in the same year, which forms the basis of the 'Abhilash Talkies' episode. Ammu listens to songs from *Chemmeen* on her tangerine transistor radio, and the plot line of the film, which tells the story of an unhappy arranged marriage between a fisherman and his wife and the unrequited love between the fisherman's wife and her former lover anticipates the affair between Ammu and Velutha. Like *TGST*, the film ends tragically, and Chelva Kanaganyakam argues that 'with some changes, the novel is a self-conscious reworking of [*Chemmeen*] and, as with most instances of intertextuality, the differences are as important as the similarities'.[187] The differences are mainly to do with class, and the film's village setting bears little resemblance to the middle-class world of the Ipe family. *Chemmeen* does, however, reflect the central theme of fated romance in *TGST*, incorporates local folk myth (in the figure of the 'sea mother' whom the fisher community worships), and anticipates Sophie Mol's death in the drowning of Palani, one of the central protagonists.

For many readers, a more familiar cinematic link is Robert Wise's 1965 musical *The Sound of Music*, an adaptation of a 1959 stage hit by Rodgers and Hammerstein. The film is interesting because, with its sprightly costume changes, its mixture of song, choreography and drama and its mountain scenery, it is, arguably, the most 'Indian' of Hollywood musicals. Whereas *Chemmeen* mirrors adult relationships in Roy's novel, *The Sound of Music* reflects the childish aspirations and the guilt Estha and Rahel feel, as part of broken marriage (and, in Estha's case, as the victim of sexual abuse). At one point, the film's authoritarian father figure, Captain von Trapp, played by Christopher Plummer, delivers an unscripted, apologetic aside, 'overheard' by Estha, about the impossibility

---

187  Chelva Kanaganayakam, 'Religious Myth and Subversion in *The God of Small Things*', in Erik Borgman, Bart Philipsen and Lea Verstricht (eds), *Literary Canons and Religious Identity*, Aldershot: Ashgate, 2004, pp. 141–9, at p. 147.

of adopting the twins: ' "I'm sorry," Captain von Clapp-Trapp said. "It's out of the question. I cannot love them. I cannot be their Baba. Oh no" ' (Ch. 4, p. 107). Here, Estha's self-loathing contrasts with the moral purity and whiteness of the Von Trapp family, who are 'clean' and guilt-free, and is reminiscent, again, of the racial dislocations of novels such as Toni Morrison's *The Bluest Eye*, although the fact that in *TGST* the von Trapp family are caricatured as the *Clapp*-Trapps alerts us to the falsity of what they represent. More obliquely, Maria's departure from the convent at the start of the film echoes Baby Kochamma's unhappy novitiate at the Roman Catholic convent in Madras.

Another film that precedes, and bears a strong formal resemblance to, *TGST* is Satyajit Ray's *Pather Panchali* (*Song of the Road*, 1955). As Ray's first production, it was filmed on a shoestring budget in a village outside Calcutta and is now regarded as one of the great works of twentieth-century cinema. Adapted from a semi-autobiographical 1928 Bengali novel by Bibhutibhushan Banerji, *Pather Panchali* (mentioned in relation to *kathakali*, see Text and contexts, **p. 40**) tells the story of the family of an impoverished village priest, and follows his children, Opu and Durga, as they grow up amidst the fields and forests of rural Bengal. Both Ray's interest in capturing a kind of pastoral idyll and his cinematic technique, which concentrates on small significant details and meticulous scene-setting, are features *Pather Panchali* shares with *TGST*. Comparisons can also be made between the deft cinematography and composition of *Pather Panchali* and Roy's 'framing' of key scenes in her novel. Describing the children's expedition to the river as 'a small procession (a flag, a wasp and a boat-on-legs) wend[ing] its knowledgeable way down the little path' (Ch. 10, p. 205), Roy may be recalling a similar procession in which the children in *Pather Panchali* follow a passing sweet-seller. Moreover, both texts share an abiding interest in the talismanic qualities of small objects. In a poignant scene near the end of *Pather Panchali*, Opu finds a string of beads which had been stolen and hidden on a high shelf by his sister, who is now dead. A strikingly similar act of retrieval takes place in *TGST*, although here the string of beads becomes, appropriately enough, a rosary: 'Rahel groped behind the row of books and brought out hidden things [. . .] A silver crucifix on a string of beads [. . .] "Imagine [she said to Estha]. It's still here. I stole it. After you were Returned" ' (Ch. 7, pp. 155–6). *Pather Panchali* ends, like *TGST*, in the tragic uprooting of its central characters, and in its two sequels (*Aparajito* and *The World of Apu*), Ray extends some of the themes of parental loss and familial reconciliation that feature so strongly in Roy's novel.

# Chronology

Bullet points are used to denote significant events in India's political history, and asterisks to denote literary and cultural milestones.

1200–1000 BCE
* The *Rig Veda*, the earliest text of Hinduism, compiled.

1–200 CE
* *Manusmriti* (the law books of Manu) compiled.

52 CE
- The alleged date of the arrival of the apostle St. Thomas near the South Indian port of Cranganore.

345
- The supposed date of the arrival in south-west India of Christian refugees from Syria and Mesopotamia under the leadership of a merchant, Thomas of Cana.

520
- Cosmas the Alexandrian, a theologian and merchant, visits Malabar and reports the existence of Christian communities in India.

1054
- The Christian church is split in the 'East–West Schism'.

1498
- The Portuguese explorer Vasco da Gama lands north of the Malabar port of Calicut after discovering a southern passage to India around Africa.

1510
- Goa becomes the capital of Portugal's empire in the East.

1599
- The Synod of Diamper (Udiamperer) is convened. The Portuguese force the Syrian-Christian community to convert to Roman Catholicism.

1600
- The British East India Company is formed in London.

1653
- The Syrian-Christian community reaffirms its allegiance to the Eastern Church in the Coonan Cross Oath.

1665
- Mar Gregorios of Jerusalem, a bishop of the Eastern Church tradition, arrives in Malabar and is welcomed by the Syrian- Christian community.

1665–81
* The Kottayam Prince invents *kathakali* during the composition of four new plays based on the *Mahabharata*.

1757
- Robert Clive strengthens British colonial rule in Bengal after his victory at the battle of Plassey.

1799
- British forces defeat Tipu Sultan of Mysore at the battle of Seringapatam. The British consolidate their control of southern India.

1816
- The Church of England sends missionaries to Travancore and Cochin.

1835
- Thomas Babington Macaulay's 'Minute on Indian Education' proposes the use of English in the colonial education system.

1857
- Indian soldiers rebel against the British in North India in what becomes known as the 'Indian Mutiny'. The British regain control after several months of fighting.

1860
* Vayaskara Aryan Narayanan Moosad's *kathakali* play, *The Killing of Duryodhana*, becomes increasingly popular.

1889
- The Syrian Christian community divides between Orthodox Syrian and the newly founded reformist Mar Thoma church.

1889
* O. Chandu Menon publishes the first novel in Malayalam, *Indulekha*.

1893–5
* Krupabai Satthianadhan publishes *Kamala* and *Saguna*.

1894
*    Rudyard Kipling publishes his children's story *The Jungle Book*.

1899
*    Joseph Conrad's *Heart of Darkness* is published in serial form.

1914–15
*    James Joyce publishes *A Portrait of the Artist as a Young Man* in serial form.

1916–21
•    The Travancore and Cochin Christian Succession Acts are passed, limiting the amount Syrian-Christian women can inherit from their families.

1920
•    M. K. Gandhi starts the non-cooperation movement as part of the struggle for Indian independence.

1929
*    William Faulkner publishes *The Sound and the Fury*.

1930
•    M. K. Gandhi launches the civil-disobedience movement and campaigns against untouchability.

1935
*    Mulk Raj Anand publishes *Untouchable*.

1937
•    The Kerala unit of the Congress Socialist Party is formed.

1947
•    India gains independence. The subcontinent is partitioned to create India and Pakistan.

1950
•    B. R. Ambedkar helps draft the Indian constitution, and defends the rights of untouchables.

1955
*    Satyajit Ray's cinematic adaptation of Bibhutibhushan Banerji's novel *Pather Panchali* is released.

1957
•    Kerala elects a communist state government. E. M. S. Namboodiripad becomes Chief Minister.

1961
•    Arundhati Roy is born in Assam.

1964
• The Communist Part of India splits. E. M. S. Namboodiripad forms a new Communist Party of India (Marxist), CPI(M).

1965
* First screening of Ramu Kariat's film adaptation of T. S. Pillai's *Chemmeen* (*The Prawn*); Robert Wise's film adaptation of the Rodgers and Hammerstein stage hit *The Sound of Music* is released.

1967
• A peasant uprising in Naxalbari heralds the start of the Naxalite movement. The CPI(M) comes to power in a coalition victory in Kerala and E. M. S. Namboodiripad becomes Chief Minister for a second, two-year term.
* First staging of V. Madhavan Nayar's *kathakali* play *Karna's Oath*.

1969
• The Naxalites form the Communist Party of India (Marxist-Leninist), CPI(M-L).

1973
• The Chipko environmentalist movement starts protests against logging in Uttarakhand.

1974
• Publication of the *Towards Equality* report investigating women's rights in India.

1975–77
• Prime Minister Indira Gandhi establishes a State of Emergency. Democratic government is suspended.

1981
* Salman Rushdie wins the Booker Prize with his novel *Midnight's Children*.

1984
• The Bhopal industrial disaster. Fifteen thousand people die after poisonous gas leaks from the Union Carbide pesticides plant in Bhopal.

1985
• The Narmada Bachao Andolan (Save the Narmada Movement) begins protesting against dam schemes in the Narmada valley.

1986
• Arundhati Roy's mother, Mary Roy, wins her appeal against Syrian-Christian inheritance laws at the Indian Supreme Court.

**1988**

\*    Roy's screenplay *In Which Annie Gives It Those Ones* is shown on the national television channel, Doordarshan.

**1991**

•    India relaxes trade restrictions and encourages foreign investment.

**1992**

•    The demolition of the Babri Mosque in Ayodhya sparks communal rioting between Hindu and Muslim communities.

**1994**

\*    Shekhar Kapur's controversial film *Bandit Queen* is released. Roy writes several highly critical reviews.

**1997**

\*    Roy publishes *The God of Small Things* and wins the Booker Prize.

**1998**

•    The Indian government tests a thermonuclear device at Pokhran.

**1999**

•    Roy publishes her first essays on the Narmada dams and India's nuclear tests in *The Cost of Living*.

**2001**

•    Roy is charged with criminal contempt for demonstrating with the leaders of the *Narmada Bachao Andolan* outside the Indian Supreme Court.

**2002–6**

•    Roy publishes further essay collections and speaks out against globalization and the US-led 'War on Terror'.

# 2

# Critical history

# Overview

*TGST* is one of the most popular Indian novels ever written in English, and, as well as enjoying a global best-seller status (in numerous translations), it now features strongly on university literature programmes, college courses and book-group reading lists. Roy's Booker Prize win, while not an infallible indicator of merit, assured her novel a certain level of literary respectability, and *TGST* has generated a constant stream of scholarly criticism ever since. Several critical studies, most of them essay collections, have been published in India, in addition to reader's guides, monographs and edited collections from academics working in Europe and the USA, and critical articles in an international range of journals. This section provides an overview of the existing secondary material on *TGST* and maps out common themes and approaches. As part of this survey, key critical contexts and ideas will be summarized, among them the marketing of *TGST*, theoretical developments in postcolonial studies, Marxist criticism and the concept of the subaltern, feminism and gender studies, linguistics-based approaches and criticism that draws on ecology and environmentalism.

For readers and students, the two most useful single-author studies of *TGST* are Émilienne Baneth-Nouailhetas's monograph *The God of Small Things: Arundhati Roy*[1] and Julie Mullaney's *Arundhati Roy's The God of Small Things: A Reader's Guide* (both published in 2002).[2] Although aimed at different readerships, both works are insightful in their critical assessments of Roy's fiction. Baneth-Nouailhetas's monograph (which is excerpted in the Critical readings section, **pp. 142–54**), contains some of the most perceptive close readings of *TGST* so far, and the fact that the publishers, Armand Colin/VUEF-CNED, do not distribute widely outside France is a loss to students of Roy's work. Featuring topic headings such as 'Colonial Heritage, Postcolonial Fiction', 'The Structures of Memory', 'Expression and Repression' and 'Transgressions', Baneth-Nouailhetas's study is especially strong in its discussion of Roy's language use and provides meticulous

1   Baneth-Nouailhetas, *The God of Small Things: Arundhati Roy.*
2   Mullaney, *Arundhati Roy's The God of Small Things: A Reader's Guide.*

critical assessments of the narrative structure of *TGST*. In its approach, her work reflects the dominance of narratology as a critical mode in French literary studies and draws on work by well-known narratologists such as Gérard Genette.[3] Baneth-Nouailhetas's reading of Roy's fictional presentation of history and her structural use of memory is particularly acute, as is her discussion of the thematic significance of purity and pollution in the novel. She is, however, less willing to engage with postcolonial theory and avoids detailed discussions of contextual issues or extensive comparisons between Roy and other postcolonial authors.

More accessible is Julie Mullaney's 'reader's guide', *Arundhati Roy's The God of Small Things*, published as part of the pocket-sized Continuum Contemporaries series. Mullaney's guide is short and synoptic but still presents a theoretically informed introduction to the central themes of *TGST* and includes sections on the novel's reception and its commercial 'performance'. In fact, alongside her summary of the language politics of the 'Indo-Anglian' novel, Mullaney's grasp of the agreements and differences between Roy's reviewers is one of the most useful aspects of her work and provides a good map of critical opinion following the novel's meteoric publication success. Mullaney's casebook also provides more comparative range than Baneth-Nouailhetas's monograph and looks, albeit briefly, at *TGST* in relation to contemporary Indian authors in English such as Salman Rushdie, Nayantara Sahgal and Anita Desai, as well as contrasting Roy's idiosyncratic fictional 'return to the colonial historical archive' with similar techniques by Canadian authors such as Margaret Atwood and Robert Kroetsch.

Several noteworthy collections of critical essays on *TGST* have also appeared in the past few years, the majority of them from India. They include R. K. Dhawan's *Arundhati Roy: The Novelist Extraordinary*,[4] Indira Bhatt and Indira Nityanandam's *Explorations: Arundhati Roy's The God of Small Things*,[5] J. Dodiya and J. Chakravarty's, *The Critical Studies of Arundhati Roy's The God of Small Things*[6] and R. S. Pathak's *The Fictional World of Arundhati Roy*.[7] A collection entitled *Reading Arundhati Roy's The God of Small Things*, edited by Carole Durix and Jean-Pierre Durix, was also published in France in 2002[8] and another volume of essays, *Arundhati Roy: Critical Perspectives*, edited by Murari Prasad, was produced by the Delhi-based publisher Pencraft, in 2006. Of these, the most expansive is R. K. Dhawan's collection, which includes essays from an international range of critics arranged in sections on media and marketing, women's writing, 'The Big and the Small', setting, 'Architectonics', 'The Language' and Roy's prose essays. The quality of the essays in Dhawan's collection tends to be uneven, however, and some of the contributions are much too short and have minimal bibliographies. Bhatt and Nityanandam's edition suffers from similar problems of variable quality, with a number of essays simply reprising plot

3    See Gérard Genette, *Narrative Discourse*, trans. Jane Lewin, Oxford: Blackwell, 1986.
4    Dhawan (ed.), *Arundhati Roy: The Novelist Extraordinary*.
5    Bhatt and Nityanandam (eds), *Explorations: Arundhati Roy's The God of Small Things*.
6    Jaydipsinh Dodiya and Joya Chakravarty (eds), *The Critical Studies of Arundhati Roy's The God of Small Things*, New Delhi: Atlantic, 2001.
7    R. S. Pathak (ed.), *The Fictional World of Arundhati Roy*, New Delhi: Creative, 2001.
8    Carole Durix and Jean-Pierre Durix (eds), *Reading Arundhati Roy's The God of Small Things*, Dijon: Éditions Universitaires de Dijon, 2002.

details, but the collection takes some interesting angles on Roy's novel and includes articles on myth, 'the gaze' and oppositional discourses in *TGST*.

Pathak's collection, although it includes two essays from Dhawan's, has fewer high-quality contributions than the latter. In fact its most useful feature is the extensive introduction, which provides a thematic summary that covers the marketing of the novel and touches briefly on Roy's environmentalism. Like Pathak's, Dodiya and Chakravarty's volume reproduces papers from earlier collections and monographs (such as K. V. Surendran's *The God of Small Things: A Saga of Lost Dreams*),[9] without necessarily choosing the best contributions. Finally, Durix and Durix's selection features illuminating essays by French critics who examine *TGST* from psychoanalytic, post-structuralist and postmodernist perspectives. These approaches are all valid and provide the foundations for some perceptive accounts of *TGST* – especially when they are read alongside Jean-Pierre Durix's essay 'The Postcoloniality of *The God of Small Things*', but a reliance on European theoretical frameworks in some of the contributions sometimes sidelines Roy's political and cultural concerns as an *Indian* writer. Lastly, Murari Prasad's *Arundhati Roy: Critical Perspectives* brings together a number of key essays on Roy, reproducing two that appear in this guide – Aijaz Ahmad's 'Reading Arundhati Roy *Politically*', Brinda Bose's 'In Desire and in Death: Eroticism as Politics in Arundhati Roy's *The God of Small Things*' alongside my own essay *The God of Small Things*: Arundhati Roy's Postcolonial Cosmopolitanism'. Most useful for those studying *The God of Small Things* in relation to Roy's political essays, the collection also includes important theoretical commentaries on the ethics and representational politics of Roy's non-fiction, as well as reproducing a 2001 *Frontline* interview with Roy. Rather than covering each of these essay collections in turn in the following pages, I will refer to specific articles and texts where they are especially insightful or have some relevance to a key approach or theme.

## Cultural and commercial contexts

There is a memorable scene in Mira Nair's 2001 film *Monsoon Wedding* in which a middle-class Indian family, gathered for pre-wedding drinks in their New Delhi mansion, discuss the possibility of sending their daughter to America for her education. Asked what she wants to study, the daughter expresses an interest in creative writing and, instead of dissuading her, or suggesting a more conventional profession, her parents applaud the choice as a good career move, citing 'that woman who won the Booker' as a model.[10] More than any previous Indian author, Roy now figures in India's public consciousness as an example of the power of the Indian-English novel (and novelist) as an international commodity. In contrast to earlier, predominantly male Indian writers, many of whom had followed a common educational path from elite Indian schools to prestigious

9  K. V. Surendran, *The God of Small Things: A Saga of Lost Dreams*, New Delhi: Atlantic, 2000.
10  Roy herself notes, 'Ambitious middle-class parents, who, a few years ago, would only settle for a future in engineering, medicine or management for their children, now hopefully send them to creative writing schools' (*The Algebra of Infinite Justice*, London: HarperCollins, 2002, p. 173).

universities in Britain and North America,[11] Roy was entirely 'home grown' and still lives in New Delhi, a fact that endears her to Indian readers. Moreover, her rise to fame coincided with the fiftieth anniversary celebrations of Indian independence and thus took on an added symbolism, seeming, in the public consciousness, to represent India's cultural and economic dynamism – a slightly ironic connection, since *TGST* itself paints a bleak picture of India's new openness to the global economy.

Although Roy's novel was always promoted as an 'authentically' Indian-English work, the narrative that her publishers formulated to market the novel (a story of hidden, photogenic genius, fortuitous discovery and instant international fame) reproduces one of the founding celebrity myths of the global US-dominated media.[12] As two of the earliest critics of the American culture industry, Theodor Adorno and Max Horkheimer, point out, the relationship between planning and chance in the marketing of creative talent is a highly involved one, since the Hollywood studio-system myth of the unknown typist who is 'discovered' and becomes a star serves to mask the rationalized nature of the industry itself. In the culture industry, they argue, 'chance itself is planned [. . .] precisely because it is believed to play a vital part. It serves the planners as an alibi'.[13] While not detracting from the technical achievement of *TGST*, the story of Roy's 'discovery' probably tells us as much about publishing as a billion-dollar global business and about the preferences of its networked personnel of authors, agents and editors (who recognized that Roy was 'the rarest sort of commodity in publishing [. . .] an amazing elfin beauty and an incredible talent')[14] than it does about Roy's fiction itself.

Even so, since it has such an important bearing on subsequent critical discussions of Roy's novel, the 'discovery story' is worth reviewing here. Roy completed *TGST* in April/May 1996, and the novel was launched in Delhi a year later. She had shown a copy of the manuscript to Pankaj Mishra, the writer and Indian agent for HarperCollins, who read it on a night train to Dehra Dun in the Himalayan foothills. Mishra thought the work a masterpiece and got off the train at a remote station early in the morning to phone Roy and congratulate her. He subsequently sold the Indian rights to the novel for the biggest advance ever paid by an Indian publisher. He also couriered the manuscript to the British agent David Godwin, who flew to Delhi shortly afterwards, asking to represent Roy. Within a week, HarperCollins and Random House had bought the British and American rights to *TGST*, and the sale of translation rights in a further eighteen languages brought Roy's advance to over half a million pounds, possibly the largest sum ever paid for a first novel. Matching these massive advances was a sophisticated advertising campaign and an extensive worldwide promotional tour, during which Roy's publishers bought space in large bookshop chains in Europe and North America and took out advertisements in major newspapers.

---

11  See Harish Trivedi, 'The St. Stephen's Factor', *Indian Literature*, 145, 1991, pp. 183–7.
12  See Petri Pietiläinen, 'The American Dream as Authentic Experience: The Reception and Marketing of Arundhati Roy as a Post-Colonial Indian Writer', in A. Blake and J. Nyman (eds), *Text and Nation*, Joensuu: University of Joensuu, 2001, pp. 103–25.
13  T. W. Adorno and M. Horkheimer, *Dialectic of Enlightenment*, trans. John Cumming, London: Verso, 1997, p. 146.
14  Peter Popham, quoted in Pietiläinen, 'The American Dream as Authentic Experience', p. 108.

In October 1997, *TGST* won the prestigious Booker Prize – an award that virtually guarantees a higher literary profile and substantially larger sales for its recipient. *TGST* went on to sell 6 million copies worldwide and has been translated into forty languages.

It was not only Roy's astronomical advances that contributed to the marketing mythology of *TGST*. Her authorial persona was also carefully managed, and promotional images tended to stage her as the attractive incarnation of her own, intricately wrought prose. The fact that Western publishers, following the success of Vikram Seth's *A Suitable Boy* (1993), seemed primed for the next Indian best-seller only increased the scepticism of some readers and critics who were suspicious of the marketing 'frenzy' that surrounded Roy and regarded the novel's promotion as meretricious. The Booker Prize has always had a controversial role in the promotion of 'commonwealth' or postcolonial authors,[15] and in Britain Carmen Callil, a previous Booker judge, derided the novel as 'execrable' and argued that it should never have made the shortlist. Other critics, echoing Callil, viewed the judges' preference for Roy's novel as a triumph of political correctness over literary merit,[16] and a 'safe' choice in a year that featured a weak shortlist for the award.

We noted earlier that *TGST*'s publication in 1997 coincided with the fiftieth anniversary of Indian independence, an event that had already generated interest in India and Indian culture in Europe and North America at the time. The trend was noticed by Somini Sengupta, who stated wryly in *The New York Times*, that 'ever since the Beatles popularized Hinduism and Nehru jackets in the late 1960s, Indian cultural artefacts have had a vague currency in the American imagination [. . .] but lately India and its inhabitants are indisputably chic'. She went on to suggest that 'the starkest example of Indo chic can be found in the new popularity of literature out of India and its diaspora'.[17] Salman Rushdie and Elizabeth West's collection, *The Vintage Book of Indian Writing 1947–1997* (which included an excerpt from *TGST*), fed the burgeoning interest in Indian-English fiction, and literary magazines such as *Granta* and *The New Yorker* ran special editions devoted to India that year. In Britain, the culture of the South-Asian diaspora entered the mainstream in the late 1990s with the success of musicians such as Talvin Singh, Nitin Sawhney and the group Asian Dub Foundation,[18] and the popularity of television shows such as *Goodness Gracious Me*.

The growing cultural currency of India seemed to reflect, on the surface at least, an increasing awareness (and celebration) of Britain's cultural diversity and a new self-assurance amongst British-Asian communities. In marked contrast to Salman Rushdie's novel *The Satanic Verses* (1988), which had outraged Muslims worldwide and led to death threats against Rushdie, book-burnings and a racist backlash against South-Asians in Britain in the late 1980s, Roy's literary success was regarded by many as a cause for collective celebration, and

15  See Luke Strongman, *The Booker Prize and the Legacy of Empire*, Amsterdam: Rodopi, 2002.
16  See Lakshmi Gopalkrishnan, 'Booker Snooker'. Online. Available HTTP: <http://slate.msn.com/id/1837/> (Accessed 6 October 2005).
17  Somini Sengupta, 'Beyond Yoga, Curry and Nehru Jackets into Film, Publishing and Body Painting', *New York Times*, 30 August 1997, p. 13.
18  See John Hutnyk, 'Music for Euro-Maoists: On the Correct Handling of Contradictions among Pop Stars', *Theory, Culture and Society*, 17(3), 2000, pp. 136–58.

Sanjay Suri reported from the predominantly South-Asian community of Southall that her Booker win 'felt like a team-mate winning the finals of a literary kabaddi'.[19]

In India, Roy was similarly fêted and received a formal congratulation on her success from the president, K. R. Narayanan, an untouchable from Kerala. She remembers the process of her transformation into a national icon somewhat equivocally: 'Last year I was one of the items being paraded in the [Indian] media's end-of-the-year National Pride Parade. Among the others, much to my mortification, were a bomb-maker and an international beauty queen.'[20] The fact that *TGST* was also such a commercial triumph reinforced the sense of shared pride amongst 'resident' and non-resident' Indians alike and evened old scores in the same way that cricket victories against the former colonizer have always been occasions for celebration in India. As the poet and playwright Kamala Das stated at the time (using a telling combination of game-playing and commercial metaphors), Indian writers don't 'take English lightly [. . .] we had to beat the English at their own game [. . .] we are trying to sell India to the West and [Arundhati Roy] has succeeded'.[21]

## Postcolonial approaches

The cultural and financial stakes involved in the marketing of *TGST* reached such extraordinary proportions that they could hardly be ignored in critical discussions of the novel. Indeed, as we will see shortly, some critics of *TGST*, such as Padmini Mongia and Graham Huggan, have argued that Roy's novel seems to betray an awareness of its own 'exotic' retail value. However, before we review these critical assessments, it is important to step back for a moment and reflect on the postcolonial – a perspective which has been more influential than any other in critical readings of *TGST*.

The postcolonial is used here as an umbrella term to cover a range of (increasingly well-known) literary-critical and theoretical approaches that concentrate on the economic, cultural and ideological experience of European colonialism and its historical legacy, especially in writings from formerly colonized countries. Postcolonial critics and theorists are not only interested in the 'mis'-representation of non-Europeans in colonial writings, they also look at the strategies by which authors from countries such as India appropriate and revise the English language and English literary traditions to articulate their own identities *after*, and often *in opposition to* colonial rule. For a number of influential critics, the smooth processing of Roy's novel by a globally networked publishing and marketing industry seemed to be further evidence that the 'postcolonial' (in its immigrant journey into Western university courses and publishing lists) had started to reflect Western preconceptions and a commercially defined multiculturalism, instead of representing the actual political and artistic concerns of formerly

19  Quoted in Somdatta Mandal, 'From Periphery to Mainstream: The Making, Marketing and Media Response to Arundhati Roy' in R. K. Dhawan, *Arundhati Roy*, pp. 23–37 at p. 34.
20  Roy, *The Cost of Living*, p. 139.
21  Kamala Das quoted in Mandal, 'From Periphery to Mainstream', p. 32.

colonized peoples. As such, the international success of *TGST* appeared to reveal and widen a conceptual fault line that had been developing in postcolonial theory for some time.

Postcolonial theory, which revolutionized forms of literary and cultural analysis from the early 1980s, has never been a unified intellectual movement, and is divided, very broadly, between two schools of thought.[22] This split in the conceptual framework of the postcolonial goes back to the mixed heritage of the discipline itself and, recalling the broken families which we encounter in *TGST*, we could use the metaphor of parent–child relationships to think about the dual inheritance of the postcolonial in its current form. On one hand, postcolonialism is the offspring of a historically embedded, economically informed Marxist criticism, which builds on traditions of collective resistance developed in anti-colonial national liberation movements (armed struggles against colonial rule which took place across the world, in numerous countries, in the mid-twentieth century). It is also, on the other hand, indebted to the work of the radical French intellectuals and philosophers of the 1960s and is thus the heir to a less clearly historicized cultural theorizing that employs the linguistic guerrilla tactics of post-structuralism and psychoanalysis – disciplines which both ask searching questions about the connection between language, power and identity. Post-structuralism in particular has concerned itself with the instability of meaning and, through its focus on ambiguity in language, challenges concepts such as objectivity, difference and truth. Although, at first glance, it may seem as though both postcolonialism's 'parents' agree that their offspring is concerned with resistance to, and critique of, 'empire' (in both its old colonial form and its new neo-colonial economic guise), they have differed widely over the forms this resistance takes.

The potentially divisive theoretical parentage of the postcolonial was already apparent in some founding works of postcolonial studies such as Edward W. Said's *Orientalism* (1978), which drew, in a sometimes contradictory way, on the thought of the Italian Marxist intellectual Antonio Gramsci and the French philosopher and political historian Michel Foucault. Said argued in *Orientalism* that the extensive study and representation of the Orient across several centuries of Western history was actually a highly political construction of Arabic culture as the 'Other' – the negative reflection – of a more rational, civilized and developed European 'Self'. For Said, the representation/construction of the Orient thus acted as an ideological complement to colonialism. In the 1980s and 1990s, a number of theorists critiqued and built on Said's ideas, and perhaps the most influential of these was Homi Bhabha. Drawing on post-structuralist and psychoanalytic thought in order to question concepts of transcendent meaning in Western humanist philosophy, Bhabha nuanced Said's reading of colonialism by exploring its more subjective and psychological aspects.[23] In his view, colonialism was defined not so much by binary constructions of colonial Self and colonized Other, as Said suggested, but by moments of unsettling mimicry, hybridity and linguistic ambiguity between colonizer and colonized, which seemed to reveal hidden flaws and anxieties in the operation of colonial rule.

---

22 I am indebted to Elleke Boehmer's unpublished work on 'Postcolonialism, Globalization and Terror' in my summary of the bifurcated theoretical development of the postcolonial.
23 See Homi K. Bhabha, *The Location of Culture*, London: Routledge, 1994.

Because Bhabha, like Said, regards language as central to the construction of identity, the postcolonial text (especially fiction that mixes colonial forms and languages and unsettles unitary models of the self) exemplifies, in his work, the rebellious potential of the migrant, the mimic-man and the cultural hybrid. However, as the field diversified and became increasingly influenced by language-orientated approaches such as post-structuralism, some Marxist critics such as Aijaz Ahmad and Arif Dirlik reasserted their materialist claim that postcolonial-ism should not be disassociated from the collective, and often violent, national liberation struggles of the mid-twentieth century. For these critics, the institutional growth of postcolonial studies, with its emphasis on psychological and textual forms of cultural 'resistance' and hybrid or migrant identities,[24] simply masked continuing inequalities between the West and its former colonies. Moreover, in Dirlik's view, the turn to 'subjective' forms of politics in postcolonial studies (in other words, forms of politics that concentrated on details of language or the psychology of identity) represented a 'diversion of attention from contemporary problems of social, political and cultural domination'. Thus, in concentrating on issues of 'representation' and 'identity', postcolonial studies disguises its close relationship with the 'condition of its own emergence, that is, global capitalism'.[25] According to this perspective, postcolonialism, instead of opposing and 'de-centring' neo-colonial values, merely operates alongside dominant Western aes-thetic modes, such as postmodernism, providing 'suitable' instances of cultural difference.[26]

This is a very basic account of the development of postcolonial thought, and it is important to realize that not all commentators fall so neatly into the two intellectual parent strands of the discipline. In fact, some of the most interesting and provocative theorists working in the field, such as Gayatri Spivak, have repeatedly combined forms of Marxist analysis, feminism and deconstruction (the critical methodology of post-structuralism) in their work. And while Marxist critics such as Aijaz Ahmad and Benita Parry[27] have questioned her contribution to a discursive postcolonial theorizing, Spivak's interest in how writers and intel-lectuals represent socially and economically disadvantaged groups in India makes her, as we shall see below, one of the most useful theoretical reference points for the study of *TGST*. Other intra-disciplinary negotiations have also taken place between the two (broadly textual and materialist) factions, and recently the critic and theorist Robert Young has attempted a *rapprochement* (or, in our terms, a kind of marital reconciliation) between the warring parent theories of the postco-lonial, by arguing that post-structuralist thought is more deeply informed by the history of French colonialism in North Africa and anti-colonial struggle than many critics previously supposed.[28]

---

24  Aijaz Ahmad, 'The Politics of Literary Postcoloniality', *Race and Class*, 36(3), 1995, pp. 1–20.
25  Arif Dirlik, 'The Postcolonial Aura: Third World Criticism in the Age of Global Capitalism', *Critical Inquiry*, 20, 1994, p. 331.
26  See Ziauddin Sardar, *Postmodernism and the Other: The New Imperialism of Western Culture*, London: Pluto, 1998.
27  See Benita Parry, 'Problems in Current Theories of Colonial Discourse', *Oxford Literary Review*, 9(1–2), 1987, pp. 27–58, and, more recently, *Postcolonial Studies: A Materialist Critique*, London: Routledge, 2004.
28  Young, *Postcolonialism: An Historical Introduction*.

As we saw in the introduction, Roy has always been highly suspicious of the 'colonizing' knowledge claims and 'Brahminical instincts' of academic specialists,[29] and, given her views on self-serving forms of institutional power, we might expect her to be sceptical about the critical disputes outlined above. Moreover, amongst Indian critics and authors there has been a long-running debate about the limitations of the 'postcolonial', which is seen by some as a restricting or ghettoizing category.[30] And yet, when we think about the distinctive shape of *TGST*, which juxtaposes heroic images of revolutionary Naxalite protest alongside detailed accounts of Ammu's lonely personal battle against local disapproval and her children's playful subversion of 'Anglophile' texts and attitudes, the novel appears to acknowledge both the collective and subjective forms of postcolonial resistance outlined above. The critical usefulness of postcolonial theory in exploring *TGST* also becomes apparent when we remember that one of the novel's central themes is the perpetuation of old, colonial histories of domination in new 'neo-colonial' forms in South India. Roy is quick to point out that 'late' or global capitalism, which has been invited into India through economic privatization and a new investment culture, involves 'barbaric dispossession' and may be simply another 'mutant variety of colonialism, remote-controlled and digitally-operated'.[31] The fact that Roy's success was made possible, in part, by the remote-controlled information networks and multinationals which she treats with such distrust complicates an understanding of her work and brings us to a more involved critical discussion of the commercial aspects of her fiction.

## Marketing, cosmopolitanism and the exotic

In the first of the essays reproduced in the Critical readings section, 'The Making and Marketing of Arundhati Roy' (see **pp. 103–9**), Padmini Mongia examines the growth of a 'Roy phenomenon' that accompanied the publication of *TGST*. In the USA, Mongia argues, a growing economic interest in India as a place of potential investment combined very neatly with older colonial tropes of discovery in the sophisticated marketing myth of Roy's hidden and suddenly revealed literary genius. Concentrating on non-textual aspects of the novel, Mongia argues that the promotional narrative of Roy's discovery is reinforced in the book's cover images and careful use of author photos by her publishers. This marketing myth was made all the more potent by Roy's status as an author who 'partook of the cosmopolitan moment' but was (unlike her diasporic contemporaries) also reassuringly 'home grown' and 'authentically' Indian. Mongia was one of the first critics to discuss the marketing of *TGST*, and her essay is noteworthy because it signals a growing awareness, among academic commentators, of the commercial value of 'cosmopolitan' postcolonial fictions and their promotion as a type of exotic commodity.

---

29  Roy, *The Algebra of Infinite Justice*, p. 187; Roy, *The Chequebook and the Cruise Missile*, pp. 120–1.
30  See Harish Trivedi and Meenakshi Mukherjee, eds, *Interrogating Postcolonialism: Theory, Text and Context*, Simla: Indian Institute of Advanced Study, 1996.
31  Roy, *Power Politics*, p. 14.

As we saw earlier, in the early 1990s postcolonial critics had already started to notice a potential complicity between postcolonialism and global capitalism. The critic Timothy Brennan went on to explore these ideas in relation to postcolonial writing in his monograph *At Home in the World: Cosmopolitanism Now*,[32] in which he argued that a form of ironic literary 'cosmopolitanism' (epitomized in works such as Rushdie's *Midnight's Children*) had become, in the West, the recognized generic template for the successful postcolonial novel. In his book *The Postcolonial Exotic: Marketing the Margins*, Graham Huggan developed some of Brennan's ideas when he argued that 'links clearly exist between postcoloniality as a regime of value and a cosmopolitan alterity industry'[33] (the commercialization of cultural difference in a range of forms, from Caribbean holiday resorts to Indian curry sauces). One of the central ways that this global 'alterity industry' processes cultural difference is through the exotic, which Huggan defines not as an 'inherent *quality* to be found "in" certain people, distinctive objects, or specific places', but as a mode of perception that 'effectively manufactures otherness'. In short Huggan sees the exotic as an integral filtering component of the Western perception of other cultures, a 'control mechanism of cultural translation',[34] that makes the other familiar, but not completely so, because then a crucial, 'mysterious' aspect of the exotic would be lost.

For Huggan, the most noticeable feature of writing by authors such as Rushdie and Roy is the way they manipulate the expectations and commercial literary codes of the 'alterity industry'. This is marked in *TGST* by a 'strategic exoticism',[35] and an ironic display of 'lushly romantic images',[36] which are designed to appeal to the fantasies and imperial fixations of its international audience. Huggan's argument is not that cosmopolitan authors simply 'sell themselves' to the West in their elaboration of certain literary styles and tropes. Instead, he makes the point that authors such as Rushdie and Roy exploit an unstable intermediary position. Their ostensibly anti-colonial politics have to be balanced against their commercial viability as globally successful postcolonial novelists (which may depend on their 'manipulative' use of colonial conventions), and their work 'is designed as much to challenge as to profit from consumer needs'. Huggan goes on to warn that this ironic, self-conscious design may be 'precisely the commodity form – the symbolic capital on which [these] writers have made their reputations as reader-friendly, but also wryly sophisticated, Indo-Anglian novelists'.[37] Like Mongia, Huggan reveals how easily *TGST* became embedded in pre-existing global networks of cultural consumption and challenges still further the presumption that Roy was unaware of the tastes and predilections of a potentially international readership for her debut novel.

While Mongia and Huggan investigate the cover design and cosmopolitan textual content of *TGST*, Petri Pietiläinen concentrates on promotional details

---

32  Timothy Brennan, *At Home in the World: Cosmopolitanism Now*, Cambridge, Mass.: Harvard University Press, 1997.
33  Graham Huggan, *The Postcolonial Exotic: Marketing the Margins*, London: Routledge, 2001, p. 12.
34  Huggan, *The Postcolonial Exotic*, p. 14.
35  Huggan, *The Postcolonial Exotic*, p. xi.
36  Huggan, *The Postcolonial Exotic*, p. 77.
37  Huggan, *The Postcolonial Exotic*, p. xi.

and Roy's 'discovery story', reviewed earlier, in an essay entitled 'The American Dream as Authentic Experience: The Reception and Marketing of Arundhati Roy as a Post-Colonial Indian Writer'. Here, Pietiläinen argues that there are three interrelated ways to understand Roy's success: through an awareness that she caters for a form of 'suitable otherness'; through an understanding of the role of her novel as a form of Indian national allegory[38] and Roy herself as an 'authentic' cultural representative; and, most importantly, in a realization of the novel's sophisticated marketing. Having examined numerous interviews and reviews in major British, American, Indian and Finnish newspapers in 1997, Pietiläinen makes some perceptive points about tendencies amongst reviewers to produce author profiles so that on 'a number of occasions the novel itself was of minor importance'.[39] In these 'Cinderella-story' accounts, 'Arundhati Roy becomes a young beautiful rebel, an outcast despised by her family [who] wins against all the odds'.[40] Pietiläinen's analysis of the Roy phenomenon is sometimes under-theorized, and there is scant discussion of how, specifically, it relates to the 'American dream'. The essay does, however, provide a useful review of the pro-motion of Roy and her novel and suggests, persuasively, that the marketing of TGST reflects an increasingly planned and rationalized publishing industry.

Marta Dvorak, in her paper 'Translating the Foreign into the Familiar: Arundhati Roy's Postmodern Sleight of Hand', which appears in Durix and Durix's collection, concurs with Huggan's view that 'even though Roy's appeal lies to a great extent in her oppositional discourse [. . .] this very discursive field is complicitous with the increasingly globalized ["exotic"] commodity culture within which it is contained'.[41] Of all the discussions of the marketability of Roy's novel, Dvorak's is the least forgiving and, as her title indicates, she interprets TGST almost wholly in terms of its formal 'mimicry' of modernist – rather than postcolonial – authors, such as Joyce and Borges. (Rushdie, who is cited as an important influence, is also treated as postmodern.) While she admits that TGST exposes 'the neocolonial commodification of native [sic] Indian culture, from the point of view of both supply and demand',[42] Dvorak also accuses Roy of employ-ing the very practices she condemns in TGST: 'With its domesticated mythological sensibility, its topographical details, its interpolation of Malayalam words, and descriptions of every sphere of social life [. . .] the novel also satisfies the western reader's taste for the exotic.'[43] Dvorak is refreshingly critical of postcolonial read-ings that 'gleefully' search for signs of resistance in Indian fiction, but in stressing TGST's 'postmodern' strategies she underemphasizes Roy's interrogation of the effects of colonialism and neo-colonial corporate power in India. More worryingly, she also misrepresents the novel's cultural contexts, arguing that contemporary *kathakali* is an 'arcane' elite Sanskrit drama which cannot be

38 See Jameson, 'Third-World Literature in the Era of Multinational Capitalism', pp. 65–88.
39 Pietiläinen, 'The American Dream as Authentic Experience', p. 110.
40 Pietiläinen, 'The American Dream as Authentic Experience', p. 111.
41 Marta Dvorak, 'Translating the Foreign into the Familiar: Arundhati Roy's Postmodern Sleight of Hand', in C. Durix and J.-P. Durix (eds), *Reading Arundhati Roy's The God of Small Things*, Dijon: Éditions Universitaires de Dijon, 2002, pp. 41–61, p. 43.
42 Dvorak, 'Translating the Foreign into the Familiar', p. 49.
43 Dvorak, 'Translating the Foreign into the Familiar', p. 50.

understood by Kerala's 'vernacular masses'.[44] (*Kathakali* combines Sanskrit and Malayalam and is not as elite a form as Dvorak claims; see Text and contexts, pp. 40–4.)

A much more positive critical view of Roy's cosmopolitanism is provided in Bishnupriya Ghosh's monograph *When Borne Across: Literary Cosmopolitics in the Contemporary Indian Novel*. Using Bruce Robbins and Pheng Cheah's term 'cosmopolitics' to describe Roy's political agenda, Ghosh counters earlier critiques of 'Third World' cosmopolitan writing to show how 'despite the glare of international visibility', certain contemporary Indian writers still 'engage in a literary politics that interrupts their own global circulation and rejects an over fetishistic localism'.[45] In Ghosh's rewarding study, Arundhati Roy is read alongside contemporaries such as Salman Rushdie, Upamanyu Chatterjee, Vikram Chandra and Amitav Ghosh as part of a 'progressive discursive formation' that challenges the reductive identity politics of nationalism and the 'pernicious globalism' that imposes a Western culture (and Western political and social ideals) on the rest of the world.[46] Like Huggan, Ghosh covers the 'renaissance' of Indian English literature in 1997 and carefully examines language and 'linguistic migrations' in recent fiction.

Recalling Huggan's claim that Roy anticipates, and plays on, the tastes of an international audience, but also remembering the centrality of concept terms such as hybridity in the development of more psychological and subjective models of postcolonial agency (formulated by Bhabha), it is also possible to ask how far *TGST* could be read as a novel that anticipates some of the theoretical preoccupations of its critics. My article '*The God of Small Things*: Arundhati Roy's Postcolonial Cosmopolitanism'[47] tries to answer this question and builds on Huggan's work on the exotic by tracing themes of classification and hybridity in *TGST* and relating these to some key concerns in Homi Bhabha's essays, especially his interest in a subjective, 'liminal' politics that blurs the boundaries of larger formations of 'racial' or national identity. Central to my argument is the concern that, by relating Roy's novel so closely to accepted theories of postcolonial identity or by seeing it as a reflection of exotic postmodern effects, as Dvorak does, we may be ignoring its more difficult, 'dissonant' representational strategies. These strategies, which displace or unsettle the reader, have been noted by other critics such as Elleke Boehmer (see Critical history, **p. 79**), and they remind us that the question of how far Roy's work conforms to Western literary *or* theoretical expectations is also potentially reductive, since it reproduces a conceptual framework in which the West remains the final arbiter of value for the postcolonial text – a situation that postcolonial critics routinely seek to challenge.

A further related objection which can be made to critical approaches that concentrate on the marketing of *TGST* for a 'Western' audience is that they may not accurately reflect newer, more complicated global geographies of cultural production and consumption. This is something Saadia Toor investigates in her original

44 Dvorak, 'Translating the Foreign into the Familiar', p. 51.
45 Bishnupriya Ghosh, *When Borne Across: Literary Cosmopolitics in the Contemporary Indian Novel*. New Brunswick, NJ: Rutgers University Press, 2004, p. 20.
46 Ghosh, *When Borne Across*, p.5.
47 Tickell, '*The God of Small Things*: Arundhati Roy's Postcolonial Cosmopolitanism', pp. 73–89.

essay 'Indo-Chic: The Cultural Politics of Consumption in Post-Liberalisation India'. Rather than revealing processes of literary consumption (reminiscent of older modes of colonial economic exploitation) in which contemporary Indian fiction is 'exported' and consumed overseas, Toor argues that Roy's success owes as much to the tastes of an emergent Indian middle-class which is young, urban and 'self-consciously cosmopolitan in orientation'.[48] As a product of India's economic liberalization in 1991–2, this new urban elite has strong connections with the Indian diaspora in Europe and North America. At the same time, as a class, it is newly able to consume aspects of its own culture – even though these may already have been sanctioned as 'exotic' in the West. Thus, in Toor's view, the popularity of Roy's novel depends as much on the cultural politics of India in its liberalized phase and the growing consumer power of Indian readers themselves as it does on the neo-colonial fascinations of the Western publishing industry.

Another searching contribution to the debate over the politics of postcolonial marketing and consumption surrounding Roy's debut novel is Elleke Boehmer's carefully historicized essay 'East is East and South is South: The Cases of Sarojini Naidu and Arundhati Roy',[49] which asks whether postcolonial criticism is compromised in some of its approaches to Indian women authors. Comparing Roy with the poet Sarojini Naidu,[50] who visited London in the 1890s and was championed by the critic Edmund Gosse, Boehmer argues that there are striking continuities between an orientalist colonial appreciation of the exotic 'enticements and intensities' of Naidu's work (and Naidu herself) and a contemporary fascination for 'stylistic whimsicality' and lyrical sensuality in TGST. She goes on to state: 'Despite postcolonialism's anti-colonial agenda, and its intersection with other liberatory theories such as feminism and minority discourses, forms of criticism [. . .] appear to have inherited still unexamined categories of the past, and to be reiterating, certainly in their journalistic manifestations, its objectifications of otherness.'[51] As Boehmer points out, although Roy's lyrical narrative is an artistic achievement in its own right, its reception, and Roy's presentation as a personification of her own work, has tended to reinforce older oriental projections of 'India as multiple, extreme, scented, sensual, transgressive'.[52]

## Marxist criticism

Indian Marxist critics have also noted the commercial success of TGST, although their readings have tended to focus more on the novel's anti-communism and its

---

48 Saadia Toor 'Indo-Chic: The Cultural Politics of Consumption in Post-Liberalisation India', *SOAS Literary Review*, 2, 2000, p. 4. Online. Available HTTP: <http://www.soas.ac.uk/soaslit/2000_index.htm>.

49 Boehmer, 'East is East and South is South', pp. 61–70, at p. 63. Boehmer develops her comparative reading of TGST in *Stories of Women: Gender and Narrative in the Postcolonial Nation*, Manchester: Manchester University Press, 2005.

50 For a similarly angled comparative approach, see Melissa Purdue's 'From Sarojini Naidu's "Curved and Eloquent Little Mouth" to Arundhati Roy's "Mass of Untamed Curls and Smouldering Dark Eyes": Stereotypical Depictions of Female Indian Authors in Reviews of Their Work', *Atenea*, 23(2), 2003, pp. 87–103.

51 Boehmer, 'East is East and South is South', p. 63.

52 Boehmer, 'East is East and South is South', p. 66.

sexual content than on formal elements that reflect particular literary tastes. As we might expect from our earlier discussion of his views on postcolonial theory, the critic Aijaz Ahmad, in his essay 'Reading Arundhati Roy *Politically*' (reproduced in the Critical readings section, **pp. 110–19**), associates Roy's work with a type of transnational 'postcolonial' politics, inimical to Marxist theorizing. In Ahmad's view, Roy's 'ideological opposition to Communism is not in itself surprising; it is very much a sign of the times, in the sense that hostility toward the Communist movement is now fairly common among radical sections of the cosmopolitan intelligentsia, in India and abroad'.[53] Ahmad is especially angered by what he calls the 'spiteful' satire on actual communist leaders such as E. M. S. Namboodiripad in *TGST* and is equally unimpressed by references to 'Naxalite' politics, which he regards as 'something of an all-purpose term in Roy's fiction'.[54]

But even if Roy presents us with a bourgeois cosmopolitan politics masquerading as radicalism, she does not, in Ahmad's opinion, enter into a creative negotiation with her own 'exoticism' in the way that Huggan suggests. Indeed, Ahmad is quick to praise the language of *TGST* and notes that while Roy has a tendency to repetition and sentimentality, 'she is the first Indian writer in English [for whom] a marvellous stylistic resource becomes available for provincial, vernacular culture without any effect of exoticism or estrangement'.[55] In Ahmad's article, *TGST*'s most serious 'failing' after its anti-communism and its stylistic unevenness is its treatment of caste and 'female sexuality'. These are issues on which the novel 'stake[s] its[. . .] radical claim',[56] and the fact that the erotic is the 'real zone of rebellion'[57] in the text is something that Ahmad sees as a major problem, because it unrealistically confines the political to the personal and replays a well-worn literary trope of fatal romantic attraction.

A less sophisticated Marxist response to Roy's novel comes from the politician E. M. S. Namboodiripad, one of the main satirical targets in *TGST*, who responded to Roy in an article entitled 'In Defence of Kerala's Communists' in 1997, shortly before his death. Far from addressing the accusation implicit in *TGST* that the Communist Party exploited existing inequalities of caste and class in Kerala,[58] Namboodiripad concentrates instead on what he sees as the novel's 'deviant sexuality' and its misrepresentation of party workers. As he argues, 'There is nobody in our party who resembles "Comrade Pillai" created by Arundhati Roy [. . .] the degeneration that has affected all bourgeois parties is something alien to us.'[59] In a manoeuvre reminiscent of some Marxist responses to the postcolonial outlined above, Namboodiripad concludes his defence by stating: 'I am not surprised that Arundhati Roy's novel is greatly appreciated [. . .] since the ideology of "world literature", dominated by the bourgeoisie is, by its very

53  Aijaz Ahmad, 'Reading Arundhati Roy *Politically*', *Frontline*, 8 August 1997, pp. 103–8, at p. 103. See Critical readings, **p. 112**.
54  Ahmad, 'Reading Arundhati Roy *Politically*', p. 104. See Critical readings, **p. 112**.
55  Ahmad 'Reading Arundhati Roy *Politically*', p. 108.
56  Ahmad 'Reading Arundhati Roy *Politically*', p. 104.
57  Ahmad 'Reading Arundhati Roy *Politically*', p. 108.
58  See Dilip Menon, 'Being a Brahmin the Marxist Way: E. M. S. Nambudiripad and the Pasts of Kerala', pp. 55–87.
59  E. M. S. Namboodiripad, 'In Defence of Kerala's Communists', *Frontline*, 5 September 1997, p. 110. See also <http://www.rediff.com/news/nov/29roy.htm>.

character, anti-Communist.'[60] Not all Marxist criticism has been this negative, however, and Kalpana Wilson's essay (see Critical history, **p. 90**) challenges Ahmad's assessment of *TGST*. Moreover, as we shall see shortly, certain critical ideas adopted from Marxist thought have informed debates about the representation of women, untouchables and other marginalized figures in postcolonial literature and theory and have, therefore, a direct relevance to our discussion of Roy's novel.

## The subaltern

Since the publication of *TGST*, Roy has often emphasized the growing distance between the powerful and the powerless in contemporary India. 'At some point,' she argues, 'we have to [. . .] realize that the inequity in our society has gone too far. Take for instance the refrain that India is a country of one billion people [. . .] the truth is that we are a nation of 50 million people and the rest are not treated as people.'[61] Alongside the oppression of women, the most enduring form of social inequity in India is the caste system (see Text and contexts, **pp. 22–8**), and Roy's sophisticated critique of caste in *TGST* encompasses both the social history of its proscriptive 'walking backwards' rules and its latter-day perpetuation in the prejudices of characters such as Mammachi and Inspector Thomas Mathew. Mammachi, we are told, displays an 'impenetrable touchable logic' (Ch. 2, p. 75) in her blindness to the inhumanity of caste, something which is evoked in her chronic short-sightedness. In fact, this blindness is shared by older untouchable Paravan characters such as Velutha's father, Vellya Paapen, whose mortgaged glass eye symbolizes his loyal acceptance of the world view of his 'touchable' employers.

As well as forming one of the central themes of *TGST*, caste inequality is implicated in the politics of the Narmada river dam schemes condemned by Roy in *The Cost of Living*. Many of those displaced by the construction of the dams are untouchables and tribal peoples, and, characteristically, Roy uses architectural metaphors to describe how the social 'design' of the caste system ensures that sections of the Indian population have become expendable in the workings of the state:

> What percentage of the people who plan these mammoth [dam] projects are [untouchable or tribal . . .] or even rural? Zero. There is no egalitarian social contact whatsoever between the two worlds. Deep at the heart of the horror of what's going on lies the caste system: this layered horizontally divided society with no vertical bolts, no glue – no intermarriage, no social mingling, no human – humane – interaction that holds the layers together. So when the bottom half of society simply shears off and falls away it happens silently. It doesn't create the torsion, the

---

60 Namboodiripad, 'In Defence of Kerala's Communists', p. 110.
61 Arundhati Roy, 'There Is a Need To Redefine the Artist's Role in Society', *Culture: An Interview with Arundhati Roy*. Online. Available HTTP: <http://38.200.221.50/culture/literate/aroy1.html> (Accessed 24 April 2001).

upheaval, the blowout, the sheer structural damage that it might, had there been the equivalent of vertical bolts. This works perfectly for the supporters of these projects.[62]

The representation of marginalized individuals and communities in both *TGST* and Roy's journalism is something which has prompted a number of important critical essays, but before we examine these readings we should consider how Roy's preoccupation with oppressed social groups in India poses questions to do with the conceptual figure of the 'subaltern', which have concerned Indian historians and postcolonial critics for some time.

Originally a word that denoted a junior officer in the British army, 'subaltern' was coined as a political term in the 1930s by the Italian Marxist thinker Antonio Gramsci, who used it in his *Prison Notebooks* to describe 'groups or classes' which were socially inferior and had no ideological power. Gramsci initially used the term instead of 'proletarian' in order to escape censorship, but it soon came to designate less organized working-class groups such as peasants and farm labourers.[63] The term was later taken up by the so-called 'Subaltern Studies' group, a number of largely India-based Marxist historians (many of whom were students during the 1967 Maoist Naxalbari uprising; see Text and contexts, **pp. 32–5**), who extended Gramsci's definition beyond a purely economic one and used 'subaltern' as 'a name for the general attribute of subordination in South-Asian society, whether this is expressed in terms of class, caste, age, gender and office or in any other way'.[64] The Subaltern Studies group was dissatisfied with both colonial and Indian nationalist historiography and what they saw as a failure, in these traditions, to represent the political struggles of peasants, women and low-caste groups. Their solution was to return to the historical texts of colonialism and Indian nationalism and to read them against the grain, thereby uncovering traces and overwritten signs of 'subaltern' resistance. In doing so, they challenged the very basis of academic historiography in India.

The postcolonial theorist and translator Gayatri Spivak, a fringe member of the Subaltern Studies project, subsequently questioned some of the group's assumptions, and revised the concept of the subaltern. In her essay 'Subaltern Studies: Deconstructing Historiography',[65] Spivak suggested that the methodology of the Subaltern Studies historians might not be adequate to the task in hand and warned that the self-determining consciousness of the subaltern could never be retrieved fully from colonial or nationalist archives. In trying to restore the historical 'agency' of peasants and tribal peoples from these documents, argued Spivak, the Subaltern Studies group was actually in danger of objectifying them in the same way as earlier historians had done. Spivak's aim was to underline the need for a 'deconstructive' self-awareness in the group's work. This awareness would

62  Arundhati Roy, 'Scimitars in the Sun', *Frontline*, 6–19 January 2001. Online. Available HTTP: <http://www.thehindu.com/fline/fl1801/18010040.htm> (Accessed 19 June 2006).

63  Gayatri Spivak, 'The New Subaltern: A Silent Interview', in Vinayak Chaturvedi (ed.), *Mapping Subaltern Studies and the Postcolonial*, London: Verso, 2000, p. 234.

64  Ranajit Guha, 'Preface', in R. Guha and G. Spivak (eds), *Selected Subaltern Studies*, Oxford: Oxford University Press, 1988, p. 35.

65  Gayatri Spivak, 'Subaltern Studies: Deconstructing Historiography', in R. Guha and G. Spivak (eds), *Selected Subaltern Studies*, Oxford: Oxford University Press, pp. 3–32.

acknowledge the power involved in the act of historical representation, as a process of *speaking for* minorities, and would result, ideally, in a 'strategic essentialism'[66] in which the retrieved subaltern consciousness is recognized as a politically expedient but unrepresentative image of intending identity rather than the true thoughts and wishes of subalterns themselves.

While she critiqued the Subaltern Studies project, Spivak also developed her ideas about subaltern representation in what is possibly her most famous essay 'Can the Subaltern Speak?'[67] Here Spivak questioned similar assumptions in the work of radical French theorists such as Michel Foucault and Gilles Deleuze that the opinions or needs of the oppressed (even though they are the subjects of 'discursive' ideological conditioning) can be transparently represented. Spivak's other fundamental qualification to the concept of the subaltern was to suggest that it was, necessarily, a gendered category, and while the essays outlined above deal with the effective erasure of the subaltern voice by historians and critics who claim a representative knowledge of them, in other pieces such as 'The Rani of Sirmur',[68] Spivak shows how different ideological systems such as colonialism and patriarchy combine to doubly erase women as subalterns. (This point has also been explored by other feminists critical of 'First World feminism'; see Text and contexts **p. 37**.) As Spivak argues: 'Within the effaced itinerary of the subaltern subject, the track of sexual difference is doubly effaced [. . .] if, in the context of colonial production, the subaltern has no history and cannot speak, the subaltern as female is even more deeply in the shadow.'[69]

A potential problem with Spivak's theorizing is that it seems to shift, as Bart Moore-Gilbert notes, between 'conceptual' and 'concrete' definitions of the subaltern.[70] These shifts reflect changing critical emphases in Spivak's ongoing 'subaltern' analyses, and there is not enough space to speculate on them fully here. What must be noted, in relation to Roy's political concerns, are Spivak's recent suggestions that developments in technology and global capitalism have changed the conditions of subalternity, especially the idea (outlined by Spivak in earlier essays)[71] that subalterns are excluded from wider networks of capital. Today, claims Spivak, 'the subaltern must be rethought. S/he is no longer cut off from lines of access to the centre'.[72] This is because transnational corporations, operating from the centres of European and American power, are now interested in the specialist environmental knowledge of rural South-Asian subalterns in order to develop new pharmaceuticals and patented crop strains. As Spivak argues, the

---

66  Spivak, '*Subaltern Studies*', p. 13.
67  Gayatri Spivak, 'Can the Subaltern Speak? Speculations on Widow-Sacrifice', *Wedge*, 7/8, (winter/spring), pp. 120–30; reprinted in Cary Nelson and Larry Grossberg (eds), *Marxism and the Interpretation of Culture*, Urbana, Ill.: University of Illinois Press, 1988, pp. 271–313, and in Patrick Williams and Laura Chrisman, eds, *Colonial Discourse and Post-Colonial Theory: A Reader*, Hemel Hempstead: Harvester Wheatsheaf, 1994, pp. 66–111.
68  Gayatri Spivak 'The Rani of Sirmur: An Essay in Reading the Archives', *History and Theory* 24(3) 1985, pp. 247–72; reprinted in F. Barker et al. (eds), *Europe and its Others*, Vol I. Colchester: University of Essex Press, 1985, pp. 128–51.
69  Spivak, 'Can the Subaltern Speak?' in Williams and Chrisman, pp. 82–3.
70  Bart Moore-Gilbert, *Postcolonial Theory: Contexts, Practices, Politics*, London: Verso, 1997, pp. 101–3.
71  See Gayatri Spivak, 'Supplementing Marxism', in Bernd Magnus and S. Cullenberg (eds), *Whither Marxism? Global Crises in the International Context*, London: Routledge, 1995, pp. 109–19.
72  Spivak, 'The New Subaltern', p. 327.

emergence of genetic patenting means that the knowledge and livelihood of the subaltern can now be 'owned' by patent-holding corporations: 'The issue [. . .] is one of property – and the subaltern body as *bios* or subaltern knowledge as (agri-) or (herbi-)culture is its appropriative object.'[73] These issues are equally pressing for the Indian environmentalist movement,[74] and coincide closely with Roy's concerns about 'development' and the impact of corporate investment in contemporary India.

This is, necessarily, a very basic approximation of the complexities of Spivak's notion of the subaltern, but even from this rough outline, a number of key points emerge which are relevant to *TGST*. In the figure of Velutha (as an untouchable), we might be tempted to see a fictional representation of the subaltern, especially as the social structures he inhabits only allow him to 'speak' in limited ways, and he often simply appears in the novel as a body, or as the object of other characters' fears and desires.[75] However, some reviewers see this lack of articulacy as an imaginative failure on Roy's part and describe Velutha as 'a wretched stick of a character, a good-hearted prole with a six-pack for a stomach'.[76] Putting these objections to one side and reminding ourselves of Spivak's discussions of subaltern figures in literature,[77] we could also argue that Roy's 'limited' representation of Velutha is a creative choice (rather than an obvious failure) and emphasizes the lack of political 'agency' available to the subaltern. Indeed, in looking for instances of subaltern resistance in *TGST*, Velutha's chimerical appearances and disappearances, his quiet suggestions and his bold technical 'design aesthetic' can be interpreted, more hopefully, as an evasive protest at the 'touchable logic' that confines him. This is the view taken by Anuradha Dingwaney Needham in her essay ' "The Small Voice of History" in Arundhati Roy's *The God of Small Things*' when she states: 'What makes Velutha *dangerous* so far as touchables *and* untouchables are concerned is his refusal to be interpellated [or addressed] as a Paravan [. . .] Within the governing logic of Roy's novel it is precisely this out-of-placedness [. . .] that makes Velutha a likely agent of the possibility of social change.'[78]

Our reading of Velutha is complicated, however, if we recall Spivak's definition of the 'subaltern' as a *gendered* female category that includes women from India's middle and upper classes. This qualification points us towards Ammu as the more obvious subaltern figure in the novel, locked in her stultifying social role as a divorced woman in the highly patriarchal Syrian-Christian community. Nevertheless, by staging Ammu and Velutha's affair as one of the central events of *TGST*,

73  Spivak, 'The New Subaltern', p. 327.
74  See Vandana Shiva, *Biopiracy: The Plunder of Nature and Knowledge*, Boston, Mass.: South End Press, 1997, and Vandana Shiva (ed.), *Closer to Home: Women Reconnect Ecology, Health and Development*, London: Earthscan, 1994.
75  See Vinita Bhatnagar, 'Fictions of Caste: Dalit Characters in the Modern Indian Novel', in J. Dodiya and J. Chakravarty (eds), *The Critical Studies of Arundhati Roy's The God of Small Things*, New Delhi: Atlantic, 2001, pp. 93–107, at p. 97.
76  Philip Hensher, 'Eastern Promise', *Mail on Sunday*, 8 June 1997.
77  See, especially, Gayatri Spivak, 'Versions of the Margin: J. M. Coetzee's *Foe* Reading of Defoe's *Crusoe/Roxana*', in Jonathan Arac and Barbara Johnson (eds), *Consequences of Theory: Selected Papers of the English Institute, 1987–88*, Baltimore, Ind.: Johns Hopkins University Press, 1990, pp. 154–80.
78  Needham, ' "The Small Voice of History" in Arundhati Roy's *The God of Small Things*', p. 374.

Roy seems to suggest a possible commonality in their – differently experienced – subalternity (something which sparks a heated debate about the novel's 'realism' in Aijaz Ahmad's and Brinda Bose's essays in the Critical readings section, pp. 110–19 and 120–31, and which is taken up in more detail in relation to the Subaltern Studies project in Anuradha Dingwaney Needham's essay mentioned earlier[79]). Interestingly, neither character is as 'doubly effaced' as some of the female tribal and low-caste characters such as Jashoda or Draupadi, whom Spivak discusses in her translations of Mahasweta Devi's short stories in *In Other Worlds*.[80] Together, however, the lovers in *TGST* figuratively represent the oppressive intersection of historically sanctioned forms of subordination (in this case caste *and* gender) that make up the theoretical category of the subaltern.

As an approach that takes account of how intellectuals and specialists (however well meaning) inadvertently silence subalterns by 'speaking for' or romanticizing them, Spivak's work should sensitize us to the tendency amongst her reviewers to present Roy as a subaltern herself. As Spivak warns: 'Often what happens is that [. . .] intellectuals [. . .] who become spokespersons for subalternity are taken as token subalterns.'[81] This brings us, in turn, to a related problem, that of Roy's power to represent and thus potentially silence the subaltern herself – an issue which is taken up by some critics who suggest that her depiction of Velutha is elitist.[82] In 'Can the Subaltern Speak?' Spivak's major objection to Foucault and Deleuze's claim to know the truth of the oppressed (in terms of the experience of what they call 'the worker's struggle') is that it masks their own role as academic 'representers' and conflates two types of representation, differentiated in German as *darstellen* (representation in the artistic form of a 'likeness' or picture) and *vertreten* (representation as 'standing for' a group politically). For Spivak, it is only by reminding ourselves of the different 'effects of the real' produced by these two types of representation that we can be sensitive to the political implications of representing minority groups. And this is why, in Spivak's theorizing, literature (in contrast to other forms of writing) can offer 'an alternative rhetorical site for articulating the histories of subaltern women'.[83]

Spivak's argument here is that authors of politically committed fictions are not hobbled by quite the same ethical constraints as political historians or activists, because we know that their work is a different, more imaginative kind of representation. On these terms, it is in 'factual' forms of writing such as her prose essays, rather than *TGST*, that we should be most wary of Roy's potentially 'assimilative' articulations of subaltern concerns. Roy's comments in interview suggest that she is unwilling to discuss, or consider, questions of subaltern representation in either her fiction or her essays – especially as they have been used to discredit the NBA:

> When dam proponents in India say, 'You know, these middle class people, they are against development and they're exploiting illiterate

79  Needham, ' "The Small Voice of History" '.
80  Gayatri Spivak, *In Other Worlds: Essays in Cultural Politics*, London: Routledge, 1988.
81  Gayatri Spivak, 'Subaltern Talk: Interview with the Editors', in Donna Landry and Gerald MacLean, eds, *The Spivak Reader*, London: Routledge, 1996, pp. 287–308, at p. 292.
82  Bhatangar, 'Fictions of Caste', p. 96.
83  Stephen Morton, *Gayatri Chavravorty Spivak*, London: Routledge, 2003, p. 55.

farmers and Adivasis', it makes me furious ... You can't expect the critique [of the Narmada Project] to be just rural or Adivasi. People try to delegitimize the involvement of the middle class, saying 'How can you speak on behalf of these people?' No one is speaking on behalf of anyone. The criticism of middle-class dam opponents is [just] an attempt to isolate the Adivasis, the farmers, and then crush them.[84]

While the accusation of 'speaking on behalf' of subaltern groups (and therefore 'silencing' them) is a tactic used by conservative political opponents of the NBA, the careful representational differentiation that Spivak insists on in 'Can the Subaltern Speak?' is blurred by Roy's refusal to distinguish between her fiction and prose, even though 'representing' Velutha and Ammu fictionally and 'representing' the Narmada communities in essays and public statements clearly involve different social expectations and commitments to truth. If we look at this problem from a different angle, we could argue that Roy is simply insisting on her right to make political claims in the 'alternative rhetorical site' of fiction and explore different kinds of political truth-telling. However, as we saw in the Text and contexts section (p. 16) her own journalistic attack on Shekhar Kapur's film *Bandit Queen*, which she claimed misrepresented its protagonist, Phoolan Devi, shows how keenly aware she is of the politics and pitfalls of representation, and in an interview with N. Ram she stresses, 'When I was writing *The Greater Common Good*, I was acutely aware [...] that I was not going to write on "behalf" of anyone [...] in our society particularly, the politics of "representation" is complicated and fraught with danger and dishonesty.'[85] Whether Roy can actually insulate herself from the pressures to represent India's dispossessed (as her profile as a social justice campaigner and activist grows) remains to be seen, and this may become an issue she will have to address more comprehensively in future work.

Although Doreen D'Cruz steers around the theoretical debates over representation summarized above, she conducts a searching comparative examination of caste in her essay 'Configuring the Dynamics of Dispossession in Rohinton Mistry's *A Fine Balance* and Arundhati Roy's *The God of Small Things*'.[86] Mistry is the only other contemporary Indian novelist in English to engage as closely with caste inequality as Roy, and, in her reading, D'Cruz reviews the cultural history of 'pollution' as an aspect of Hindu social law in the *Dharmashastras* and carefully traces the politics and representation of untouchability in both novels. Vinita Bhatnagar also discusses the *dalit* politics of both novels in 'Fictions of Caste:

84  Arundhati Roy, *The Chequebook and the Cruise Missile*, p. 16.
85  Arundhati Roy, 'Scimitars in the Sun', Interview with N. Ram. *Frontline*, 2 February, 2001. Available HTTP: <http://www.thehindu.com/fline/fl1801/18010040.htm>. (Accessed 5 June 2006). For further discussion of Roy and representation, see Julie Mullaney ' "Globalising Dissent?" Arundhati Roy, Local and Postcolonial Feminisms in the Transnational Economy', *World Literatures Written in English*, 40(1) (2002–3) pp. 56–70. Both interview and article are reproduced in Murari Prasad (ed.), *Arundhati Roy: Critical Perspectives*, New Delhi: Pencraft International, 2006.
86  Doreen D'Cruz, 'Configuring the Dynamics of Dispossession in Rohinton Mistry's *A Fine Balance* and Arundhati Roy's *The God of Small Things*', *New Zealand Journal of Asian Studies*, 5(2), 2003, pp. 56–76.

Dalit Characters in the Modern Indian Novel',[87] and a less extensive comparative analysis of Roy's treatment of caste is provided in Nirmala C. Prakash's 'The Twice Damned God of Arundhati Roy',[88] in which Velutha is compared with Bakha, the protagonist of Mulk Raj Anand's novel *Untouchable*. Pumla Dineo Gqola, on the other hand, skilfully nuances the issue of caste in her paper ' "History Was Wrong-Footed, Caught Off Guard": Gendered Caste, Class and Manipulation in Arundhati Roy's *The God of Small Things*'.[89] In Gqola's view, caste regulation operates hand in hand with other forms of oppression such as patriarchy in *TGST*, allowing Chacko to satisfy his 'Men's Needs' with lower-caste women, but punishing Ammu for a similar cross-caste affair. Gqola argues that Roy thus reveals how caste distinctions are maintained through the regulation and policing of female sexuality, and also how caste, class and patriarchy combine in the fatal 'official' response to Ammu and Velutha's liaison.

The oppressive conjunction of caste and gender is also something that Émilienne Baneth-Nouailhetas discusses in her monograph on *TGST*. Citing Patrick Williams and Laura Chrisman's point that because women are the biological 'carriers' of culture, 'discussion of ethnicity is always also by implication a discussion of gender and sexuality',[90] Baneth-Nouailhetas reinforces the link between these two expressions of power in *TGST*, stating: 'Issues of Untouchability and of sexuality are intimately connected, through the traditional concern of patriarchal discourse with the preservation of values and privilege through lineage, and therefore an obsession with the exclusive use of women as property.'[91] Furthermore, the fact that characters like Mammachi are obsessed with untouchability, something which is ridiculed by Roy in the reverse term 'touchability', transforms 'the simple question of touching into a power-issue, but also into a highly dangerous and sensual obsession: even the most casual "touch" is oversaturated with symbolic meaning'.[92] Finally, a further sub-category of the subaltern that we have not considered in as much depth, children, is the subject of Sujala Singh's comparative essay 'Postcolonial Children', which briefly critiques Graham Huggan's work on the exotic and touches on *TGST* alongside novels by Bapsi Sidhwa and Shyam Selvadurai.[93]

For readers interested in the portrayal of subaltern figures in Roy's later non-fiction, a useful point of orientation is Rashmi Varma's 'Developing Fictions: "The Tribal" in the New Indian Writing in English',[94] which compares Roy's

---

87 Vanita Bhatnagar, 'Fictions of Caste: Dalit Characters in the Modern Indian Novel' in J. Dodiya and J. Chakravarty, eds, *The Critical Studies of Arundhati Roy's The God of Small Things*, pp. 93–108.
88 See Pathak, *The Fictional World of Arundhati Roy*, pp. 125–31.
89 Pumla Dineo Gqola, ' "History Was Wrong-Footed, Caught Off Guard": Gendered Caste, Class and Manipulation in Arundhati Roy's *The God of Small Things*', *Commonwealth Essays and Studies*, 26(2), 2004, pp. 107–19.
90 Patrick Williams and Laura Chrisman (eds), *Colonial Discourse and Post-Colonial Theory: A Reader*, Hemel Hempstead: Harvester Wheatsheaf, 1994, pp. 17–18.
91 Baneth-Nouailhetas, *The God of Small Things: Arundhati Roy*, p. 100.
92 Baneth-Nouailhetas, *The God of Small Things: Arundhati Roy*, p. 102.
93 Sujala Singh, 'Postcolonial Children: Representing the Nation in Arundhati Roy, Bapsi Sidhwa and Shyam Selvadurai', *Wasafiri*, 41 (spring), 2004, pp. 13–18.
94 Rashmi Varma, 'Developing Fictions: The "Tribal" in the New Indian Writing in English', in Amitava Kumar (ed.), *World Bank Literature*, Minneapolis, Minn.: University of Minnesota Press, 2003, pp. 216–33.

essay on the Narmada Dam project, 'The Greater Common Good', and Sohaila Abdulali's novel *The Madwoman of Jogare* (1998). Responding to Spivak's 1991 essay 'How to Teach a "Culturally Different" Book',[95] in which Spivak argues that the 'tribal' (a term used to describe India's aboriginal inhabitants) has been subsumed in a universalizable, cosmopolitan Indian cultural identity in Indian writing in English, Varma contends: 'Recent writing from India, especially that which focuses on issues of economic and social development, has in fact recuperated the figure of the tribal, constructed it anew, and mapped onto it new anxieties and desires about the future of Indian identity in the globalizing world economy.'[96] Varma's essay does not continue its theoretical engagement with Spivak after the first page, nor does it consider whether this contemporary 'recuperation' of the tribal might involve new forms of erasure and 'silencing'. Nevertheless, Varma notes astutely how Roy represents subaltern groups in the Narmada valley, using 'the classic anthropological gesture that displaces the time of the Other onto some prehistoric moment', while simultaneously rejecting binary oppositions such as 'tradition/modernity' and eschewing romantic assumptions that tribal people embody a 'superior environmental consciousness'.[97] Varma's analysis also reasserts the inclusiveness of Roy's anti-dam politics, which calls for a coalitional 'rag-tag army of warriors' in which middle-class urban intellectuals and subaltern groups are allied in the struggle for social justice.

## Feminist readings

Feminist readings have provided some of the most rewarding insights into *TGST* so far, and the subheading above does not imply that essays discussed in other parts of this guide do not also engage closely with issues of gender. Similarly, Spivak's work on the subaltern must be seen as part of her wider project to re-establish the importance of cultural specificity, and representational care, in feminist thought. Both Spivak and Chandra Talpade Mohanty have taken issue with European and American feminism for assuming that the oppressions faced by women might be identical to those faced by 'First World' feminists.[98] In other words, by claiming to speak for women in India, 'First World' feminism has betrayed an in-built ethnocentrism (a prioritizing of one's own culture), which some Indian feminists see as a form of ideological colonialism. As we found in the discussion of gender politics earlier (Text and contexts, **pp. 35–40**), this interrogation of Western feminism is closely linked to a historical awareness of the 'double colonization' of Indian women under both colonial rule *and* indigenous patriarchy.

However, these warnings do not mean that we should reject 'First World'

---

95  Gayatri Spivak, 'How to Teach a "Culturally Different" Book', in Peter Hulme (ed.) *Colonial Discourse/Postcolonial Theory*, Manchester: Manchester University Press, pp. 126–50.

96  Varma 'Developing Fictions', p. 217.

97  Varma 'Developing Fictions', p. 228.

98  See Chandra Talpade Mohanty, 'Under Western Eyes: Feminist Scholarship and Colonial Discourses', *Feminist Review*, 30 (autumn), 1988, pp. 65–88; reprinted in Patrick Williams and Laura Chrisman, eds, *Colonial Discourse and Postcolonial Theory: A Reader*, pp. 196–220.

feminist theory out of hand as a way of reading *TGST*. Several critics reviewed below have drawn very usefully on European (and particularly French) feminism in their discussions of Roy's novel. Developed in the work of Julia Kristeva, Luce Irigaray and Hélène Cixous, this feminist tradition can be characterized by its concentration on the way language excludes woman from active, political subject positions and therefore perpetuates patriarchal power. This has led, in French feminist theory, to an interest in childhood language acquisition and mother–daughter relationships, as places where a viable linguistic counter-system, which escapes or precedes the representational authority of patriarchal language, might be found. Given the predominance of children's speech patterns in *TGST*, the relevance of these approaches is very clear, and we will encounter them again in connection with Cixous's work in the next section (see Critical history, **p. 92**).

Roy's statements in interview reveal her own early awareness of the 'brutalizing' treatment of Indian women and show how the politics of gender precluded any other political struggle in her growing consciousness of social injustice:

> In college in New Delhi I first encountered people who were actively committed to Marxist politics. But the talk of a noble working class seemed very very silly to me. Every time I stepped out of my college campus I would be brutalized [. . .] by men. It made no difference whether they were proletarian or not [. . .] The only real [political] conflict seemed to me to be between women and men.[99]

As we noted earlier (Text and contexts, **pp. 49–50**), Roy's portrayal of Ammu's growing desperation, which skirts the edge of madness in the title chapter (Ch. 11, p. 223), is reminiscent of a similar focus on domestic confinement and psychological stress in contemporary Indian women's writing. In response to this emphasis on psychological states, and also because of a strong disciplinary link between psychoanalytic thought and French feminism, a number of Roy's critics have drawn on psychoanalysis in their examinations of *TGST*. A good example of the psychoanalytic (originally Freudian) association of desire, mortality and the gaze in feminist readings of Roy's novel is Catherine Lanone's 'Seeing the World through Red-Coloured Glasses: Desire and Death in *The God of Small Things*',[100] and psychological connections between language, subjectivity and sexual taboos such as incest (theorized in the work of the French psychoanalyst Jacques Lacan), are carefully considered in Janet Thormann's paper 'The Ethical Subject of *The God of Small Things*'.[101]

The linking of sexual transgression and mortality is also the subject of Brinda Bose's elegant essay, 'In Desire and in Death: Eroticism as Politics in Arundhati Roy's *The God of Small Things*', which forms an important feminist riposte to Aijaz Ahmad's 'political' reading of *TGST*. (Both are reproduced here, Critical

---

99 Arundhati Roy, 'When You Have Written a Book You Lay Your Weapons Down', pp. 106–7.
100 Catherine Lanone, 'Seeing the World through Red-Coloured Glasses: Desire and Death in *The God of Small Things*' in C. Durix and J.-P. Durix (eds), *Reading Arundhati Roy's The God of Small Things*, pp. 125–44.
101 Janet Thormann, 'The Ethical Subject of *The God of Small Things*', *Journal for the Psychoanalysis of Culture and Society*, 8(2), fall 2003, pp. 299–307.

readings, **pp. 110–19**, and **pp. 120–31**.) In Bose's essay, Ahmad's assessment of *TGST* is criticized for its bias towards the public political sphere and its judge-ment that, while Velutha's violent death is realistic, Ammu's is a contrivance. For Bose, this distinction is unaccountable: 'One is a trifle confused,' she states, 'as to why, in an act of transgression that involves both Velutha and Ammu equally [. . .] his "fate is entirely credible and even ordained in the scheme of things" while hers is "arbitrary" and "astonishing". If we are referring here to (caste) lines that cannot be crossed, is it politically daring to be upwardly mobile but not so in reverse?'[102] Because, as Bose emphasizes later, the politics of desire in Roy's novel is intimately linked with the love laws and the power to tell certain narratives, 'to read her novel *politically* one may need to accept that there are certain kinds of politics that have more to do with interpersonal relations than grand revolutions, that [. . .] personal dilemmas can also become public causes, that erotics can also be a politics'.[103] The political dynamism of *TGST*, Bose goes on to argue, lies in the choices that Ammu willingly makes, choices in which the momentary freedom of the fatal, transgressive sexual act outweighs any possible penalties.

Interestingly, Ahmad's essay drew a similar response from the far left in Kalpana Wilson's article 'Arundhati Roy and the Left: For Reclaiming "Small Things" ', which appeared in the January 1998 edition of *Liberation*, the official publication of the Naxalite CPI(M-L) (see Text and contexts, **pp. 32–5**). In her essay, Wilson challenges Ahmad's claim that the novel sidelines politics, pointing out that it is about Ammu's struggle against sexist social mores and that Roy's 'anger at the crushing and destructive effects of patriarchal oppression runs through the novel, making it explicitly political'.[104] Bose's and Wilson's arguments that Ammu's act of sexual transgression should be seen as a matter of 'public' politics is comple-mented in Susan Stanford Friedman's extensive article 'Feminism, State Fictions and Violence: Gender, Geopolitics and Transnationalism'.[105] Recalling demands made by 'First World' feminists in the late 1960s that 'politics' refers to power relations within both the public and private spheres, Friedman argues that Roy's novel encourages a similar feminist rethinking of the term 'geopolitics' (which describes the geographical and spatial expression of politics), because her fictional critique of power is never restricted to a single point of identification such as gender, ethnicity or national identity. Instead,

> Roy's integration of gender and caste into the story of the nation – particularly as this story involves violence performed, tacitly sanctioned, or ignored by the state – demonstrates how feminist geopolitics engages locationally – that is to say *spatially* – with power relations as they operate both *on* the nation and *within* the nation.[106]

---

102 Brinda Bose, 'In Desire and Death: Eroticism as Politics in Arundhati Roy's *The God of Small Things*', *ARIEL*, 29(2), 1998, pp. 59–72, at p. 63. (See Critical readings, **pp. 120–31**.)
103 Bose, 'In Desire and Death', p. 68.
104 K. Wilson, quoted in Pathak, *The Fictional World of Arundhati Roy*, p. 110. Online. Available HTTP: <http://www.cpiml.org/liberation/year_1998/january/books.htm>. (Accessed 15 June 2006).
105 S. S. Friedman, 'Feminism, State Fictions and Violence: Gender Geopolitics and Transnationalism', *Communal/Plural*, 9(1), 2001, pp. 111–129.
106 Friedman, 'Feminism, State Fictions and Violence', p. 117.

Friedman goes on to examine settings in *TGST*, looking at 'historically over-determined' architectural sites, such as the History House, and discussing the theoretical tension between claims to 'global sisterhood' and located, culturally defined feminisms. In the midst of these debates, Roy's *TGST* represents, in Friedman's view, a 're-singularisation of feminism that is both "locational" [and] informed by the broadened understanding of the geopolitical'.[107] The intersection of the local, the national and the global in feminist politics is also one of Elleke Boehmer's concerns in *Stories of Women: Gender and Narrative in the Postcolonial Nation*,[108] which deftly locates Roy's work alongside fictions by a number of other postcolonial women writers.

From its punning allusion to Toril Moi's *Sexual/Textual Politics* (1985), we might expect Tirthankar Chanda's essay 'Sexual/Textual Strategies in *The God of Small Things*' to deal with feminist critical theory in its approach to Roy's fiction. In fact, Chanda passes over finer distinctions within feminist criticism (such as differences between Indian feminism and its French and Anglo-American counterparts), preferring to work in broader conceptual brush strokes and generalized categories such as 'feminist discourse' and 'patriarchal oppression'. Covering feminism, history and intertextuality in *TGST*, but with little reference to secondary material, Chanda's discussion is confined to the subject of history as 'HIS/story', and the patriarchal complicity of female characters such as Mammachi who, 'by facilitating the sexual exploitation of women by her son [. . .] accepts the tenets of a male dominated society where women are the marginalized Other, the eternal victims of an unfavourable *rapport de force*'.[109] Chanda also notes the power of Roy's fictional act of psychic 're-memberment' which she likens to similar techniques in Aimé Césaire's poem 'Le cahier d'un retour au pays natal'.

In Indira Bhatt and Indira Nityanandham's collection, *Explorations: Arundhati Roy's The God of Small Things*, several critics discuss the presentation of women and the effects of patriarchal oppression in *TGST*. These include Madhumalati Adhikari's 'Enclosure and Freedom: Arundhati Roy's *The God of Small Things*', Ranjana Harish's 'Her Body Was Her Own: A Feminist Note on Ammu's Female Estate' and Nirzari Pandit's 'Societal Oppression: A Study of *The God of Small Things*'.[110] One of the most interesting of these essays is Adhikari's, which examines the various unhappy marriages in *TGST* as forms of enclosure and then extends its discussion of confinement to include larger power structures such as caste and class. Adhikari concludes that, although gender-based 'confinements' predominate, 'role-reversals, situational challenges, traditional social norms [and] moral codes' all contribute to the social restrictions in Roy's novel.[111]

107 Friedman, 'Feminism, State Fictions and Violence', p. 124.
108 Elleke Boehmer, *Stories of Women: Gender and Narrative in the Postcolonial Nation*, Manchester: Manchester University Press, 2005.
109 Tirthankar Chanda, 'Sexual/Textual Strategies in *The God of Small Things*', *Commonwealth Essays and Studies*, 20(1), autumn 1997, pp. 38–44, at p. 40.
110 Madhumalati Adhikari, 'Enclosure and Freedom: Arundhati Roy's *The God of Small Things*, in Indira Bhatt and Indira Nityanandam (eds), *Explorations: Arundhati Roy's The God of Small Things*, New Delhi: Creative, 1999, pp. 39–46. Ranjana Harris, 'Her Body Was Her Own: A Feminist Note on Ammu's Female Estate', pp. 42–50. Nizari Pandit, 'Societal Oppression: A Study of *The God of Small Things*', pp. 168–77.
111 Madhumalati Adhikara, 'Enclosure and Freedom, pp. 39–46, p. 46.

Feminist readings of *TGST* also merit a section in R. K. Dhawan's *Arundhati Roy: The Novelist Extraordinary*, which includes several essays, the most notable of which are: Madhumalati Adhikari's 'Power-Politics in *The God of Small Things*', Mohit Kumar Ray's ' "Locusts Stand I": Some Feminine Aspects of *The God of Small Things*', and N. P. Singh's 'Women in *The God of Small Things*'.[112] Among these, Adhikari takes a non-partisan view, arguing that Roy 'has desisted from making a woman's powerlessness the central crisis [of *TGST* . . .] Both men and women are projected as victim and tyrant'.[113] Mohit Kumar Ray, whose essay is reproduced in a slightly edited form in R. S. Pathak's collection, examines the novel 'from a feminist perspective' and draws briefly on Luce Irigaray's work, which we have already encountered in our discussion of French feminism, in order to argue that Roy's 'spellings, syntax and sentence patterns' reflect an authentically 'feminine [*sic*] sensibility'.[114]

## Language and narrative structure

In her essay 'When Language Dances: The Subversive Power of Roy's Text in *The God of Small Things*', which appears in R. K. Dhawan's collection, Cynthia vanden Driesen considers the 'musical' structure of Roy's fiction, with its repeated motifs, flowing images and counterpoint techniques, and suggests that her prose is a model of women's writing that rejects conventional form: 'In [her . . .] reinventing of the traditional linear novelistic structure, Roy's text presents us with a mode of female écriture.'[115] The idea that certain kinds of experimental, linguistically inventive writing or *écriture féminine* can challenge the (oppressive) binary structures of patriarchal language is associated with the French feminist Hélène Cixous, and vanden Driesen gestures towards Cixous's work in her reference to female *écriture*. In a theoretical elaboration of the term, Cixous warns that she does not link gender and writing exclusively in her concept of *écriture* – only certain types of (experimental, modernist) literature can be described as *écriture féminine* and may be written by male *or* female authors, a point which should be remembered in comparisons between Roy's writing and that of modernists such as James Joyce. In vanden Driesen's view, Roy's language actually combines several modes of subversion, and her 'feminist' musicality and choreography operate alongside a child-centred linguistic resistance both to the adult world and to English as a colonial tongue. The critical attention to Roy's linguistic ingenuity continues in Dhawan's collection, which boasts a subsection on the language of *TGST* and includes a paper by Alessandro Monti entitled 'A(n) (En)Viable Idiom: Lexical Hybridizations and Speech Acts in Arundhati Roy', which deals with

---

112 Madhunalati Adhikari, 'Power-Politics in *The God of Small Things*', in R. K. Dhawan (ed.), *Arundhati Roy: The Novelist Extraordinary*, New Delhi: Sangam, 1999, pp. 41–8, Mohit Kumar Ray, ' "Locusts Stand I": Some Feminine Aspects of *The God of Small Things*', pp. 49–64 and N. P. Singh 'Women in *The God of Small Things*', pp. 65–70.
113 Dhawan, *Arundhati Roy: The Novelist Extraordinary*, p. 42.
114 Kumar Ray, ' "Locusts Stand I" ', p. 62.
115 Cynthia vanden Driesen, 'When Language Dances: The Subversive Power of Roy's Text in *The God of Small Things*', in Dhawan (ed.), *Arundhati Roy: The Novelist Extraordinary*, pp. 365–76, at p. 366.

Roy's dextrously 'hybridized' lexical structures and her use of neologisms and portmanteau words.[116]

Anna Clarke, in her insightful paper, 'Language, Hybridity and Dialogism in *The God of Small Things*' (see Critical readings, **pp. 132–41**), makes a distinction, like Vanden Driesen, between the authoritarian response to language represented by colonial mimic-man characters such as Pappachi – in his classifying will to 'pin down' meaning – and the more subversive, flexible language use of his grandchildren. Clarke, too, sees in Roy's more experimental poetic effects a choreographic dance of language, but relates this not to feminist models of *écriture* but to concepts of writing developed by the Russian critic Mikhail Bakhtin, who is principally famous for his theory of the novel as a modern, hybrid literary form in which a multiplicity of voices coexist and intermix 'dialogically', in contrast to 'monologic' writings which reflect a single, authoritarian viewpoint. Clarke's reference to Bakhtin is highly relevant to a reading of *TGST* since, as she points out, 'in cultural and literary criticism ideas are often adopted from a range of disciplines' and concepts such as hybridity, which originally referred to biological intermixtures, have been appropriated, through their use in Bakhtin's thought, to denote linguistic and cultural heterogeneity in postcolonial theory. Clarke's essay thus takes account of the conceptual precursors of the current postcolonial interest in hybridity (primarily in Homi Bhabha's writing) and identifies linked concepts of linguistic play, hybrid identities and dialogic variety in *TGST*.

Nishi Chawla also explores Bakhtinian approaches to *TGST* in her essay 'Beyond Arundhati Roy's "Heart of Darkness": A Bakhtinian Reading of *The God of Small Things*',[117] and hybridity provides the subject of Cécile Oumhani's 'Hybridity and Transgression in Arundhati Roy's *The God of Small Things*'.[118] Relying on a somewhat cautious understanding of Bhabha's conceptual use of hybridity, Oumhani argues that the Ipe twins occupy a liminal zone in *TGST*, reminiscent of the 'interrogatory, interstitial space between the act of representation [. . .] and the presence of community'.[119] Considering Roy's literary interest in connections, the structure of the novel as a whole could also be read as a continual intertwining of liminal viewpoints and marginal details, and this 'interlaced' aesthetic form is the focus of another worthwhile essay in Durix and Durix's collection, Elsa Sacksick's 'The Aesthetics of Interlacing in *The God of Small Things*'.[120]

Émilienne Baneth-Nouailhetas's careful analysis of 'language and perception' and 'poetic pleasure' in her monograph on *TGST* sheds considerable light on the interplay between the knowing adult narrative tone of the novel and the

116 Alessandro Monti, 'A(n) (En)Viable Idiom: Lexical Hybridizations and Speech Acts in Arundhati Roy', in Dhawan (ed.), *Arundhati Roy: The Novelist Extraordinary*, pp. 377–84.
117 Nishi Chawla, 'Beyond Arundhati Roy's "Heart of Darkness": A Bakhtinian Reading of *The God of Small Things*', in Dhawan (ed.), *Arundhati Roy: The Novelist Extraordinary*, pp. 342–55.
118 Cécile Oumhani, 'Hybridity and Transgression in Arundhati Roy's *The God of Small Things*', *Commonwealth Essays and Studies*, 22(2), spring 2000, pp. 85–91.
119 Bhabha, *The Location of Culture*, p. 3.
120 Elsa Sacksick, 'The Aesthetics of Interlacing in *The God of Small Things*', in Durix and Durix (eds), *Reading Arundhati Roy's The God of Small Things*, pp. 63–73.

children's unpredictable, often comic, manipulation of linguistic codes and conventions. In her argument, Estha and Rahel's language use not only provides the 'main support of narrative description' but also crucially undermines 'the legitimacy of official order and language'.[121] As Baneth-Nouailhetas warns, it is impossible to chart all the manifestations of linguistic rebellion in *TGST*. Nevertheless, she points to some instances that are exemplary. These include the twins' trademark habit of reading backwards and their affection for palindromes, which is interpreted as an analogue for one of the main concerns of the novel: time. Here, reversing words becomes, in effect, a way of turning back the clock:

> reading a word or a phrase both ways allegorizes the universal desire for the reversibility of action. In this sense, language is the children's own field of power in which they can bring forth their fantasies – and for that reason, characters like Miss Mitten or Baby seek to confiscate it from them.[122]

Like vanden Driesen, Baneth-Nouailhetas sees Roy's 'childish' narrative as a response to the world on a number of different levels and warns against ascribing 'a single, simple reason or motivation to the self-conscious elaboration of language in the text'.[123] Indeed, she goes on to argue that: 'Linguistic idiosyncrasies in the narration have similarly multiple functions: they signal its cultural hybridity, its status as a postcolonial text, and its poetic and ideological impact.'[124]

Roy's evocative portrayal of children's language use has further important implications for our understanding of the style and form of *TGST*. The twins' experimental narrative, as Baneth-Nouailhetas points out, brilliantly evokes their understanding of the events in which they are trapped and traces their growing disappointment that language does not 'reflect' reality. Instead the world is continually 'named', and imperfectly shaped, by language, which leads to some deep ironies, such as the 'old' bellboy at the Hotel Sea Queen: 'The bellboy who took them up wasn't a boy and hadn't a bell' (Ch. 4, p. 114) – an observation that prompts Rahel to consider the cruelty of making old men wear undignified uniforms. The gap between linguistic signs and their signification[125] recalls another feature of Roy's language use noticed by Elleke Boehmer – its ability to shock: 'Most predominantly,' argues Boehmer, 'the childish play on language of the seven-year-old twins at the centre of the story shockingly literalizes conventional actions and sayings [. . .] exposing hidden cruelties.'[126]

Lastly, in a comparative essay that examines 'language relations' in Roy's *TGST* and Jaishree Misra's *Ancient Promises* (2000), Christine Vogt-William

---

121  Baneth-Nouailhetas, *The God of Small Things: Arundhati Roy*, p. 106.
122  Baneth-Nouailhetas, *The God of Small Things: Arundhati Roy*, p. 109. On narrative and memory see also Aïda Balvannanadhan, 'Re-membering Personal History in *The God of Small Things*', *Commonwealth Essays and Studies*, 25(1), 2002, pp. 97–106.
123  Baneth-Nouailhetas, *The God of Small Things: Arundhati Roy*, p. 110.
124  Baneth-Nouailhetas, *The God of Small Things: Arundhati Roy*, p. 110.
125  These terms derive from Ferdinand de Saussure's concept of linguistic meaning as a product of patterns of signification in language. For Saussure, all language involved, at its most basic level, the operation of signs made up of a signifier (or word for something) and signified (the referent).
126  Boehmer, 'East is East and South is South', p. 70.

considers how the use of language deprives certain characters of their rights in both novels. Concentrating mainly on the subtle language usage of families in both texts rather than exploring abstract questions about linguistics and ethics, Vogt-William makes some perceptive points about the manipulation of English in *TGST*. In particular, she notes that Roy 'reports' Velutha's speech in a neutral English that lends him a dignity which is refused to higher-caste characters whose prejudices are satirized in their eccentric Indian-English. This is a technique which Roy has also used in her non-fiction to ridicule the legal charges brought against her for 'public-order' offences.[127] Vogt-William also discusses Roy's frequent capitalizations and vernacular transcriptions in *TGST* and concludes that the use of untranslated Malayalam words in the novel 'does not just assert a cultural distinctiveness but also present[s] a form of resistance to demands that [Roy's] literature conform to either accepted varieties of American or British English or the diverse regional languages of India'.[128]

## Genre, religion and ecocriticism

The linguistic complexity of *TGST* is matched by the way in which Roy blurs the boundaries between genres and gestures beyond her own text towards other kinds of narrative. This is clearest in Roy's interest in the older forms of epic and myth, which are represented (as 'Great Stories') in the *kathakali* performances watched by Estha and Rahel, and which Roy's pared-down romantic epic seems to mirror on a structural level. Drawing on the Marxist critic and social theorist Walter Benjamin's distinction between 'storyteller' and novelist, my essay 'The Epic Side of Truth: Storytelling and Performance in *The God of Small Things*' (see Critical readings, see **pp. 155–66**), looks at the cultural politics of Roy's use of pre-novelistic, orally transmitted narratives. As well as reflecting the commercial position of the postcolonial novelist in new, highly reflexive ways, Roy's narrative investment in the 'storyteller' forms of myth, epic and fable allows her to engage, symbolically, with the cultural histories of the subaltern communities she supports in her political activism. At the same time, she has to negotiate the contemporary politicizing of myth in Hindu nationalism, and the legitimization of social order, as *dharma*, in epics such as the *Mahabharata*. Ultimately, Roy's interest in the 'Great Stories' is also formal, and her own fiction can be seen as an attempt to 'miniaturize' the conventions of the national epic and to re-articulate the social and political commitments of the postcolonial author.

Deepika Bahri covers similar issues in her book *Native Intelligence: Aesthetics, Politics and Postcolonial Literature* where she reads *TGST* (and Roy's presentation of *kathakali*) via the work of Walter Benjamin and other Frankfurt School theorists such as Theodor Adorno and Herbert Marcuse. The Frankfurt School – a group of intellectuals based at the German university of Frankfurt am Main in the 1930s – used Marxist thought to pioneer the study of mass culture and were

---

127 See Roy, *Power Politics*, p. 91.
128 Christine Vogt-William, ' "Language is the skin of my thought": Language Relations in *Ancient Promises* and *The God of Small Things*', in Christian Mair (ed.), *The Politics of English as a World Language*, Amsterdam: Rodopi, 2003, pp. 393–404, at p. 402.

generally highly critical of popular culture and consumerism. We have already encountered one of their key works, Adorno and Horkheimer's *Dialectic of Enlightenment* (1944) in our discussion of the marketing of *TGST* (see Critical history, **p. 70**). For Bahri, in a contemporary world 'that subjugates story to information, tradition to novelty, and geography to globalization', Roy's narrative strategies and her focus on the *kathakali* actor as storyteller 'revivify the relation of the novel form to the fecund tradition of Great Stories' and 'short-circuit [. . .] simple reductions, reconfiguring the relation between the particular and the universal'.[129] Bahri is especially acute in her discussion of the Great Stories as a narrative presence that allows Roy to concede the end of a rich 'storytelling' tradition in Kerala while also denying the modern impulse to abbreviate in her own work.[130] Few other critics have examined *TGST*'s ancient narrative subtexts so extensively, although Urbashi Barat (see Critical history, **p. 97**) notes the way in which Roy's novel draws deeply on the 'little traditions' of sacred sites and village deities that constitute popular Hindu religion.[131]

The fact that *TGST* touches on two major world religions, Christianity and Hinduism, as well as critiquing what Roy ironically calls a third 'faith', Marxism, has prompted essays such as Chelva Kanaganayakam's 'Religious Myth and Subversion in *The God of Small Things*' and Suguna Ramanathan's 'Where is Christ in *The God of Small Things*?'. In the former, Kanaganayakam makes some important connections between Roy's treatment of religion and a 'much broader framework of myth' and gives an insightful account of the novel's Syrian-Christian contexts.[132] The essay also notes Roy's appropriation of Christian tropes such as the abandoned garden and the motif of mythical return and suggests that her objective 'is not so much to play off Christianity against Hinduism as to suggest that orthodox religions collude in preserving the status quo'.[133] Kanaganayakam goes on to argue that, as it reworks Christian myth, *TGST* forms a 'radical critique of religious practice' and reveals 'the collective ideology of an [elite] group that refuses to accommodate the margins except in very limited terms'.[134] Suguna Ramanathan's paper,[135] in Bhatt and Nityanandam's collection, interrogates the (Christian) ethic of suffering which pervades *TGST* and traces Roy's use of Christian imagery while also showing how the novel challenges the moral orthodoxies of the Syrian-Christian Church.

In her essay 'Arundhati Roy's *The God of Small Things*: Great Stories and Small Ones' (also in Bhatt and Nityanandam's collection), Urbashi Barat emphasizes

129  Bahri, *Native Intelligence*, pp. 202–12.
130  Bahri, *Native Intelligence*, p. 206.
131  For a detailed discussion of narrative aspects of this tradition, Romila Thapar's essay 'A Historical Perspective on the Story of Rama', in Sarvepalli Gopal (ed.), *Anatomy of a Confrontation: Ayodhya and the Rise of Communal Politics in India*, London: Zed, 1993, pp. 141–63, provides an invaluable account of the spread of the Hindu religious epic into multiple regional variations.
132  Chelva Kanaganayakam, 'Religious Myth and Subversion in *The God of Small Things*', in Erik Borgman, Lea Verstricht and Bart Philipsen (eds), *Literary Canons and Religious Identity*, Aldershot: Ashgate, 2004, pp. 141–9, at p. 142.
133  Kanaganayakam, 'Religious Myth and Subversion in *The God of Small Things*', p. 146.
134  Kanaganayakam, 'Religious Myth and Subversion in *The God of Small Things*', p. 147.
135  Suguna Ramanathan, 'Where is Christ in *The God of Small Things*?', in Indira Bhatt and Indira Nityanadam (eds), *Explorations: Arundhati Roy's The God of Small Things*, New Delhi: Creative, 1999, pp. 63–8, p. 63.

the centrality of religious and mythical tropes in Roy's novel and discusses both its Christian imagery and archetypes from classical Greek drama such as Sophocles' *Antigone*. For Barat, *TGST* can be read as a 'modern bourgeois epic' that mixes a close focus on social relations with mythical subtexts drawn from numerous sources. Thus, in the novel: 'Mythical patterns lie [so] deeply embedded in its structure and have integrated so many disparate elements within them that they seem to create new myths even as they reinforce [. . .] old ones.'[136] Barat is especially interested in the role of Velutha within the context of the little traditions of popular Hindu faith already mentioned. Like the handsome flute-playing figure of Krishna in devotional *Bhakti* poetry, Velutha is, in Barat's view, a 'lover and surrogate-father on one hand and the way to salvation and selfhood and the ideal human being on the other, and as such is the nearest approximation to the Little Gods [of devotional folk-Hinduism] that Indian fiction has imagined'.[137]

The last two essays discussed in this section, by Peter Mortensen and Graham Huggan, hint at important new directions in Roy criticism, representing approaches that focus on environmental themes in her fiction and non-fiction. The literary critical interest in the environment and green politics is a comparatively recent development and dates from the early 1990s when a critical approach known as 'ecocriticism' was pioneered in the USA. A central concern of this movement is the relationship between literature and the environment, and ecocritics generally share the assumption that culture and nature are interconnected. In their view: 'Literature does not float above the material world in some aesthetic ether, but, rather, plays a part in an immensely complex global system in which energy, matter and *ideas* interact.'[138] The first law of ecology states that 'everything is connected to everything else',[139] and, given Roy's interest in 'connections' and her warning of the dangers of severing 'the link [and] – the *understanding* – between human beings and the planet they live on [. . .] the intelligence that connects eggs to hens, milk to cows, food to forests, water to rivers, air to life and the earth to human existence'[140] and her vocal support for various environmentalist causes in India, it is surprising that this aspect of her writing has received such scant attention.

Having emphasized the relevance of these approaches, we find that Peter Mortensen's ' "Civilization's Fear of Nature": Postmodernity, Culture and Environment in *The God of Small Things*' largely ignores ecocriticism in favour of more established critical paradigms, in spite of his essay title. However, Mortensen is careful not to place Roy's novel too firmly within the ranks of either the postcolonial or the postmodern. Like some of the critics discussed earlier, Mortensen notes Roy's reflexive awareness of a self-promoting postcolonial exoticism but also suggests that, while juxtaposing high and low cultural forms, Roy's novel actually 'flies in the face of postmodern sensibilities, insofar as it

---

136 Urbashi Barat, 'Arundhati Roy's *The God of Small Things*: Great Stories and Small Ones', in Bhatt and Nityanadam (eds), *Explorations*, pp. 69–82, p. 71.
137 Barat, 'Arundhati Roy's *The God of Small Things*', p. 71.
138 Cheryll Glotfelty and Harold Fromm (eds), *The Ecocriticism Reader: Landmarks in Literary Ecology*, Athens, Ga.: University of Georgia Press, 1996, p. xix. See also Laurence Coupe, *The Green Studies Reader: From Romanticism to Ecocriticism*, London: Routledge, 2000.
139 Glotfelty and Fromm, *The Ecocriticism Reader*, p. xix.
140 Roy, *The Cost of Living*, p. 101.

recognizes the inseparability of nature and culture'.[141] Mortensen makes this claim because, in his view, the postmodern, although enshrining the possibility of new relationships between humans and the natural world in its more radical forms, has a strong tendency to subsume nature *within* culture and to see the natural word as a cultural construct. Roy, on the other hand, subversively yokes nature and culture together in *TGST*, where various forms of patriarchal and governmental power are reflected, in multiple ways, in 'civilization's fear of nature'.

Mortensen carefully plots these civilizational fears in the rest of his essay and finds, in the Ipe family's exploitative interpersonal relationships an extension of their appropriative attitude to the natural world, epitomized in 'Pappachi's moth' and Chacko's jealous references to '*my* factory, *my* pineapples, *my* pickles' (Ch. 2, p. 57). Significantly, Mortensen also argues that *TGST* does more than simply chart the negative ecological impact of 'development' and globalized (post-)modernity in Kerala. In the novel: 'Nature, is not so much absent as simply repressed, and the brilliance of Roy's approach consists precisely in showing that the postmodern denial of nature produces a threatening return of the repressed.'[142] Echoing the 'unpunished crime that contaminates the collective unconscious' in the novel, this environmental 'return of the repressed' (a concept invented by Freud to explain certain types of neurosis), takes place on many levels: from the smell of raw sewage that the hotel guests try to ignore, to the filth and weeds that lay siege to the Ayemenem house.[143] Throughout, Roy's 'toxic discourse toys with the notion of eco-apocalypse to test the limits of postmodern irony and detachment' reveal 'hidden or forgotten relations that render the "unthinkable [. . .] thinkable" '.[144] Comparisons between the presentation of Ammu and Velutha's affair and D.H. Lawrence's sense of the transcendent power of human sexuality are also ventured, but these are less convincing than Mortensen's environmental insights. In his assessment, there is little hope of returning to unspoiled nature in the text. Instead, Roy constantly reasserts the ecological networks and fragile natural systems in which humans are involved.

A more closely theorized discussion of ecocriticism and postcolonial studies is provided in Graham Huggan's essay ' "Greening" Postcolonialism: Ecocritical Perspectives', in which he argues that the two critical approaches have important points of intersection. However, Huggan also warns that ecocriticism remains a 'predominantly white movement, arguably lacking the institutional support-base to engage fully with multicultural and cross-cultural concerns', and that postcolonialism's ecological focus has, in the past, been too restricted in its concentration on settler colonies and issues of indigenous land rights.[145] Unlike his earlier work on exoticism and *TGST*, Huggan deals here with 'The Greater Common Good', Roy's 1998 essay on the Narmada dam schemes. Nevertheless, the essay

141  Peter Mortensen, ' "Civilization's Fear of Nature": Postmodernity, Culture, and Environment in *The God of Small Things*', in Klaus Stierstorfer (ed.), *Beyond Postmodernism*, New York: Walter de Gruyter, 2003, pp. 179–95, at p. 186.
142  Mortensen ' "Civilization's Fear of Nature" ', p. 188.
143  Mortensen ' "Civilization's Fear of Nature" ', p. 188.
144  Mortensen ' "Civilization's Fear of Nature" ', p. 189.
145  Graham Huggan, ' "Greening" Postcolonialism: Ecocritical Perspectives', *Modern Fiction Studies*, 50(3), 2004, pp. 701–33, at p. 703.

has significant bearing on Roy's novel because it traces some of her influences in the work of the Indian environmental sociologist Ramachandra Guha and the eco-feminist thinker Vandana Shiva (see Text and contexts, **pp. 34–5**). Of course, any comparison between Guha and Roy should take into account the former's criticism of Roy's political essays – which drew an infuriated response from Roy in her 'Scimitars in the Sun' interview with N. Ram. Less contentious is Vandana Shiva's influence, and recalling Roy's 'aesthetic of connection', we find in Shiva's work a strikingly similar emphasis on reconnection as a political process. In her view, 'separatism is patriarchy's favoured way of thought and action [. . .] the externalization of women's work and nature's work from dominant economic thought has allowed [. . . their] contributions to be used but not recognized'.[146]

As Huggan points out, both Guha and Shiva are aware of the political and ecological legacy of colonialism (and wary of the universalizing, neo-colonial tendencies of First World models of environmentalism), but are just as concerned about the damaging 'developmental' policies of the Indian state: 'For Shiva, there are [. . .] two symbiotically related crises in postcolonial India: an ecological crisis brought about by the use of resource-destructive technological processes and a cultural/ethnic crisis emerging from an erosion of social structures that make cultural diversity and plurality possible.'[147] (Like Shiva, Roy also underlines the social impact of industrial development and privatized resources in the figures of the 'fisher folk' and *kathakali* men in *TGST*.) Lastly, Huggan notes the stylistic unevenness of Roy's essay, which remain an 'unresolved mixture – part hard-headed investigative report, part sentimental political fable, part historically situated postcolonial allegory, part universal Green manifesto and call to arms'.[148] Returning us to some of the issues to do with representation and the subaltern discussed above (see Critical history, **pp. 81–8**), Huggan indicates that the stylistic merging of fiction and non-fiction in Roy's work 'raises the larger question of how to harness the resources of aesthetic play to reflect on weighty philosophical/ ethical issues as well as to serve a variety of "real world" needs and "direct" political ends'.[149] This is a pressing question for future critics of Roy's writing, and an in-depth comparative study of her fiction and non-fiction, and how these two bodies of work relate to one another aesthetically, remains to be written.

---

146 Shiva, *Close to Home*, pp. 4–5.
147 Huggan ' "Greening Postcolonialism" ', pp. 704–5.
148 Huggan ' "Greening Postcolonialism" ', p. 708.
149 Huggan ' "Greening Postcolonialism" ', p. 709.

# 3

# Critical readings

# Padmini Mongia, 'The Making and Marketing of Arundhati Roy'

The critical text that starts this section discusses the marketing of *TGST* and examines the promotion of Roy and her novel as a type of exotic postcolonial commodity or 'product'. Padmini Mongia was one of the first critics to investigate the cultural politics behind Roy's literary celebrity, and her perceptive essay 'The Making and Marketing of Arundhati Roy' was first presented at the 'India: Fifty Years After' conference in Barcelona in 1997, an event which is discussed by Graham Huggan in his influential work *The Postcolonial Exotic: Marketing the Margins* (2001). Mongia's 1997 essay – part of a longer study in progress titled *Indo Chic: Marketing English India* – is published here for the first time and examines both the cover design of the novel (an aspect of the production process over which Roy had considerable control) and the promotional myth of Roy's discovery, both of which rework colonial tropes of exploration as acts of dis/uncovering and sexual possession. In her discussion of the media construction of a new 'Indo chic', Mongia goes on to contextualize Roy's discovery story in terms of the global economic climate of the mid- to late 1990s, during which India was increasingly portrayed, in the West, as a new investment opportunity and a place of untapped financial promise.

## From Padmini Mongia, 'The Making and Marketing of Arundhati Roy'

For about six months or more in 1997, it was difficult to get away from the attention surrounding Arundhati Roy and her novel, *The God of Small Things*. Both the novel and its author were fêted – in the English-speaking world and more widely in translation – as the novel was sold in eighteen different countries, within weeks of being finished.[1] Whatever the merits of the novel, the attention Roy received wasn't commensurate with them and was certainly unprecedented for an

---

1   Michael Kenny, 'Novelist Arundhati Roy Finds Fame Abroad, Infamy at Home', *The Boston Globe*, 5 August 1997, E01.

Indian novelist, arguably for any contemporary novelist. Not only that, there was a large myth-making machine that nurtured and sustained the Roy phenomenon. Nor was this phenomenon restricted to a mythical 'West';[2] in fact, the media machines had been very much in motion in India and elsewhere for months preceding the publication of the novel, and they did their part in the myth-making and marketing of Roy and *The God of Small Things*. However, given the limited interests – a decade ago – of the Western market and media in Indian cultural artefacts, it was particularly striking that a first novel by an unknown writer should generate the kind of response it did. How, then, should we understand the interest Roy commanded?

It is, of course, true that for a certain readership and clientele Indian writers had been making a secure space for themselves ever since Salman Rushdie published his *Midnight's Children* in 1981. However, within the arena of Indian writing in English, the publication of Roy's novel signalled the end of one era – the one which, we might say, had begun with *Midnight's Children*, and heralded the beginning of another very different era. India – a country only intermittently in the US consciousness prior to 1997 – had, it seemed, come to stay.[3] In order to understand the attention Roy received, I want to examine the marketing of Roy and her novel, which was part of the hype that attended – albeit briefly – the moment of India's fiftieth anniversary of independence in August 1997. I should clarify right away that I enjoyed Roy's novel immensely. Yet the story of the novel's dissemination is a different one from its literary merits, and it is part of this story I want to try to unpack.

Let me begin with a consideration of the novel's cover.[4] Most readers of this article are probably familiar with the cover, with its image of blurred lotus leaves within which one can find a single, surprising, small pink bougainvillea flower. Placed almost at the dead centre of the front cover, the small pink flower draws the viewer's eye both for its placement and for its colour. The flower is the more striking for being a small drop of colour amid the greenish gloom of the leaves and stems of the lotus plants. On the left of the front cover, though, another concentration of the same colour – partly a dead leaf and partly the bud of a lotus flower – draws the gaze. As the reader's eye follows the pink lotus on the side of the spine, an even fuller lotus appears on the back. Although not in full bloom and photographed from the side, the lotus on the back cover is the deepest concentration of colour on the book jacket. Following the path suggested by the colour red leads the reader to the inside jacket, where a winsome author photo greets the reader. Photographed against foliage, she too glows and is luminous. Just as the green lushness allows the flower on the front cover to be more striking, the blurred green background highlights the picture of the author with the

---

2    [Mongia's note.] The term 'West' evokes a figure of the imagination rather than a geographical space. This is the sense in which Dipesh Chakrabarty uses the term 'Europe' in his 'Postcoloniality and the Artifice of History: Who Speaks for Indian Pasts?', *Representations*. 37 (winter), 1992, pp. 1–26.

3    [Mongia's note.] Much has changed since 1997, and India is now more consistently of interest to the West than this article suggests.

4    [Mongia's note.] Throughout this section I refer to the hardback editions of the novel published in 1997 by India Ink in India, Random House in the USA and Flamingo in the UK. The Indian and US editions reproduce colour photographs of the author, although each uses a photograph with a different appeal. The Flamingo edition also uses a different photograph, but in black and white.

dreamy eyes. The circularity of Roy's narrative is mirrored in the images which adorn the cover of her book, where hints of red tinge all its sides, including the author photograph where the red band in her hair rounds out the use of red on the rest of the book jacket. Further, the entire book jacket glows and is iridescent.[5]

The cover of the novel is stereotypically evocative of the tropical: lushness, overgrowth, moisture and colour. Hardly different visually from a tourist brochure or travel guide, Roy's novel holds out the same sensual promise as those publications would. This book is an object to be desired; both the cover and the inviting author photograph beckon the reader to possess and enter the world of the book.[6] As Somini Sengupta succinctly puts it in an article in *The New York Times*, 'Roy is gazing dreamily, beckoning the reader to open her debut novel'.[7] Now, of course, books must be inviting and must sell, and dreamy photographs are part of the package. However, the tropes used in the aestheticization of the book are worth remarking on, especially since the work is clearly very skilfully put together and an enormous effort expended for its construction and marketing.

There are three conclusions I'd like to draw from a consideration of the novel's cover. First, we need to acknowledge all that is evoked in the picture of lotus flowers amongst dark gloomy leaves. The picture on the book jacket is a predictable one, amongst the commonest images used to evoke the 'tropical' and the 'exotic'. Second, the photographs used in the British and US editions of the novel are strikingly different from the one used in the Indian edition. In the Indian edition, Roy gazes directly at the camera, certainly inviting in her striking, photogenic beauty but not gazing dreamily in the distance as she's doing in the Random House edition. Further, in the US edition, she's several tones lighter than in the Indian edition. While Roy gazes directly at the camera in the British edition as well, the author photograph is not the same as the one in the Indian edition. More contemplative, the black-and-white photograph used by Flamingo tends towards sepiatone. Here, the dreamy appeal of the author photo relies on nostalgic softness, unlike the beckoning sensuality of the Random House edition. Third, the cover replays the story of the book's 'discovery'. The exquisite found object is itself, in part, the story of how the book came into being, a story which mirrors how the author emerged on the world literary scene.

In some of the earliest analyses of colonial discourse, much attention was paid to the ways in which fantasies of dis-covering and un-covering played into the construction of the colonial space. I am thinking here of the work done by Peter Hulme and Helen Carr, by Annette Kolodny and Edward Said, as they worked out in different ways the conflation of topography and the female body, of the colonial space with the feminine, of maps and the unknown with the female and

---

5   [Mongia's note.] Even covers of the paperback editions of the book, published since this essay was first written, have the glossy texture of the hardcover, although paperback editions reproduce the author photo in black and white rather than colour.

6   [Mongia's note.] Rukmini Bhaya Nair convincingly argues that Roy's novel has 'focused our attention on the book as an object of desire. A little Gutenberg has been enacted around it'; Rukmini Bhaya Nair, 'Twins and Lovers', *Biblio*, May 1997, pp. 4–6, at p. 6.

7   Somini Sengupta, 'The New Indo Chic', *The New York Times*, 30 August 1997, p. 13.

the Other.[8] The energizing of the white male adventurer was propelled in part by the urge towards dis- and un-covering, with all its fantasies of sexual possession. The trope of discovery also demanded that the colonial 'other' be unaware of the worth of the object discovered. In a fiction such as H. Rider Haggard's *King Solomon's Mines*, the natives are literally sitting on a mound of diamonds, unconcerned and unaware of their worth. The white male adventurer, in his greater wisdom, his access to technology, his access indeed to Time and History, discovers the native worth, grants it its fair price and then disseminates it. Time and time again, this tale was played out, particularly at the time of the New Imperialism and the scramble for Africa. And now, 100 years later, with Roy's enormously savvy novel marketed through enormously savvy marketing techniques, I'd like to suggest that the same tropes of discovery are employed and what is dis- and un-covered is that colonial space of lushness, excess and sensuality with which late-Victorian writers familiarized us. I am not talking about the story the novel tells, although many critics charged Roy with succumbing to 'orientalist' formulations. Rather, I am talking about the myth-making that propelled this particular novel to the kind of position it assumed.

The cover offers in miniature the many stories that were told of the book's inception and initial entrée into the world. The book itself was proffered to us as a 'found' jewel. Before it appeared in print, there were the blurbs advertising it, quoting the words of Philip Jones, the editorial director at Flamingo, as 'a masterpiece that has fallen out of the sky fully formed'.[9] Then there was the story of the manuscript's journey which has been told and re-told: Roy gave the book to Pankaj Mishra of HarperCollins, New Delhi. He loved the book so much that he jumped off a train at a remote station to call in his praise. He suggested sending the book to the agent David Godwin in London, who took the next plane out to New Delhi. And then the bidding wars began which culminated in Roy receiving over 1.5 million dollars for the novel. Now, in addition to the wonderful tale of the found object lying like a jewel out there in the 'colonies' is the concomitant story of Roy's writing. As she herself has described the process, she happened to get a Macintosh computer just as things with her screenplay with Channel 4 were not working out. And as she played with the computer, the story appeared. All of us familiar with stories of the Romantic gestation of novels are familiar with this story and indeed take it seriously. But add to this Roy's by-now-notorious claim that she never revises because it's like 're-breathing a breath',[10] and we have a tale that stresses perfection merely awaiting decipherment.

Discovered by the Western publisher, this masterpiece, having received its seal

---

8   [Mongia's note.] The proceedings of the Essex Conference on the Sociology of Literature, published as Francis Barker et al., *Europe and Its Others*, Vol. II, Colchester: University of Essex, 1984, offer instances of Carr's and Hulme's work (Helen Carr, 'Woman/Indian: "The American" and His Others', pp. 46–60; Peter Hulme, 'Polytropic Man: Tropes of Sexuality and Mobility in Early Colonial America', pp. 17–32). See also Annette Kolodny's *The Lay of the Land*; Chapel Hill, NC: University of North Carolina Press, 1975; Edward Said's introduction to *Kim* in *Culture and Imperialism*, New York: Vintage, 1994, pp. 132–62; and Anne McClintock's 'Maidens, Maps and Mines: The Reinvention of Patriarchy in Colonial South Africa', *South Atlantic Quarterly*, 87(1), winter 1988, pp. 147–92.

9   Quoted in Praveen Swami, 'A Tiger Woodsian Debut', *Frontline*, 8 August 1997, pp. 100–2, at p. 101.

10  Quoted in Anthony Spaeth, 'No Small', *Time*, 14 April 1997, pp. 46–7, at p. 46.

of academic and literary approval, could make its legitimate advent into the world. Not only that, Roy has no acknowledged literary antecedents, Indian or other, nothing at all by way of a tradition or its inheritance. Every time the question of influences has been posed to her, she has sidestepped it coyly by saying that she would respond at a later date.[11] This response only underscores the 'newness' and 'novelty' of this found object even though the novel, as those who have read it are aware, is not only consciously echoing so many writers but also completely aware of how it evokes colonial constructions of India and deliberately and self-consciously challenges those constructions. It is hard to subscribe to the fiction of Roy as unschooled genius, despite what the stories in the media repeatedly have been stressing.

Let me now turn to a quotation from Bill Buford's 'Declarations of Independence' in the 'Comment' section of the special issue of the *New Yorker* devoted to India in 1997. Comparing the common history of the USA and India as colonies, Buford recalls that an 'American language and an American literature are, historically, relatively recent: they came into being after Independence'.[12] Just as America had to appropriate English from the British, Buford suggests, so does India:

> we are witnessing a similar thing now, among Indian writers, fifty years after India's Independence: that in a land of eighteen languages and a seemingly infinite range of cultures, a new kind of English is finding its voice, a distinctly Indian English, one that is at once local and international, of its culture and of the globe.[13]

It is within the contours laid out by such a statement that we can understand the remarkable success of Roy's novel and the attention it has received. Prior to Roy, those Indian writers who had achieved success on the world scene had been diasporic or at any rate sufficiently polyglot not to be considered 'pure' products. So, Rushdie, Ghosh, Seth, Mistry, Iyer, etc., all of them have roots elsewhere. Roy, on the other hand, was presented as a home-grown product but one who partook of a cosmopolitan moment. Both in India and the West, Roy was very proudly defined as the indigenous writer. An article in a British newspaper claimed: 'Beautiful, outspoken and unconventional, Roy, 37, represents the spirit of the new India unfettered by [. . .] claustrophobic traditions.'[14] Just as India was taking its place as one of the nations on the semi-periphery rather than the periphery, Roy's success as a writer was created in similar terms.

In fact, her success was possible because of India's position as one of the largest emerging markets in the world. Let me turn to two articles published in the *New York Times* at roughly the same time as the attention lavished on Roy. The first, published on 30 August, and titled 'The New Indo Chic' by *New York Times* writer Somini Sengupta, addresses the new currency afforded to Indian cultural artifacts. Sengupta says:

11  Bhaya Nair, 'Twins and Lovers', p. 6.
12  Bill Buford, 'Declarations of Independence', *The New Yorker*, 23 and 30 June 1997, pp. 6–8, p. 8.
13  Buford, 'Declarations of Independence', p. 8.
14  Jan McGirk, 'Indian Literary Star Faces Caste Sex Trial', *Sunday Times*, 29 June 1997, p. 19.

perhaps the starkest example of Indo chic can be found in the new popularity of literature out of India and its diaspora. Flip through a major American magazine, for instance, and you are likely to encounter a photo of Arundhati Roy, gazing dreamily, beckoning the reader to open her debut novel, *The God of Small Things*, published with much fanfare this year by Random House.[15]

Probing answers for this interest in India, Sengupta offers several possibilities, including the flurry of activities surrounding celebrations of fifty years of Indian Independence, a 'bumper crop' of interesting writing, almost 1 million Indian immigrants in the USA, etc. But her analysis ends with the following insight:

> India's economic and political relationship to the US has changed radic-
> ally since the last round of Indo-mania in the mid-80's when the movie
> *Gandhi* was released. [. . .] India has embraced market capitalism, avidly
> promoting tourism and seeking American foreign investment. With the
> end of the cold war, India is aggressively seeking to be part of the global
> economy.[16]

According to Appadurai, quoted in the same article: 'India is now the jewel in the new US-centered crown whose key elements are capital, leisure and high technol-ogy.'[17] Sengupta savvily points out that understanding 'what Indo chic is requires understanding what Indo chic is not. For the most part, Indo chic is not about South-Asians in America'.[18] Although most writers who would fit under the bumper crop described above live outside India, their fictional worlds are rooted in India.

The second article, titled 'World Bank Report Sees Era of Emerging Econo-mies', was published on 10 September 1997. I quote from the article by Richard Stevenson: 'The World Bank forecast today that growth in developing countries would accelerate over the next decade, and that the five biggest emerging econ-omies – China, India, Indonesia, Brazil, and Russia – would become economic powerhouses in the next quarter-century.'[19] Although growth rates for these economies would be only slightly higher than those for developing nations over all, 'the sheer size [of these five countries] and their rapid integration into the global economy will have far-reaching consequences, the report predicted. The rapid emergence of those five nations is likely to "redraw the economic map of the world over the next quarter-century," it said.'[20] These changes would produce, according to the article, 'huge economic opportunities for both industrial and developing nations', by providing, according to Joseph E. Stiglitz, the bank's chief economist, opportunities 'both in terms of the growth of important export

15  Sengupta, 'The New Indo Chic', p. 13.
16  Sengupta, 'The New Indo Chic', p. 23.
17  Sengupta, 'The New Indo Chic', p. 23.
18  Sengupta, 'The New Indo Chic', p. 23.
19  Richard Stevenson, 'World Bank Report Sees Era of Emerging Economies', *The New York Times*,
     10 September 1997, D7.
20  Stevenson, 'World Bank Report', D7.

markets and as a source of exports'.[21] It is within the parameters established by these two articles that we can understand the enormous, unprecedented success of Roy's novel.

As India became and becomes of greater interest to US markets, a more positive image of the country needed to be produced. Sucheta Mazumdar, quoted by Sengupta, argues: 'As more US companies are interested in exploring the Indian market, there is also an effort to promote a more positive image of India in the media.'[22] Peppered through the many articles and reviews which attended the launch of Roy were comments helping to create this positive image. Kenneth Cooper's article in the *Washington Post* crowed: 'The award [the Booker] temporarily satisfied a hunger for international validation of the worthiness of India and things Indian.'[23] Further, as Cooper emphasized, quoting Shoba De, another Indian novelist: 'It is the first time a true Indian, a home-grown product who has not lived or worked in the West or looks to it for inspiration, has won.'[24] That Roy's novel was first published in India didn't go unnoticed by Cooper either.[25] The explicit linkage of Roy and Indian independence from the British is also worth noting. The 12 August 1997 radio show, *Morning Edition*, advertised a conversation with Roy on their web site as follows: 'This week, as India celebrates 50 years of independence from British rule, Indian women are celebrating the success of writer Arundhati Roy. Roy [. . .] is the latest of several Indian women whose literary works have earned international respect.' The year, 1997, needed a new symbol, a symbol of India's independence, and what better symbol than the woman who apparently lived defying convention, who had lived in a slum and sold cakes on a beach, who had trained as an architect only to become a writer?

The marketing of Roy's novel contributed to the domestication of India for the Western consumer. The story of Roy's fairy-tale success restores our faith that true genius will be recognized despite the increasingly competitive market-oriented world in which we live. Repeatedly stressing claims of an unknown writer making it big, the media largely ignored the fact that Roy was by no means an unknown, and in her connections and allegiances was very well connected to a powerful elite in New Delhi and in the UK. Unlike an earlier native, the native scrutinized by the ethnographic gaze, this native gazes at the West with the knowledge of its fictions so well absorbed that they do not even have to be stated. Even Rushdie, the so-called grandfather of contemporary Indian fiction in English, states his literary forebears and so claims both a high European and Indian tradition. But Roy emerged new out of nowhere – apparently ill read, unschooled and rebellious. The writer and her phenomenally successful debut novel seemed to be awaiting discovery, much like the small flower that glows on the cover. Could a better symbol have been created for the new India?

21  Stevenson, 'World Bank Report', D7.
22  Sengupta, 'The New Indo Chic', p. 23.
23  Kenneth J. Cooper, 'For India, No Small Thing: Native Daughter Arundhati Roy Wins Coveted Booker Prize', *Washington Post*, 20 October 1997, C01.
24  Cooper, 'For India, No Small Thing', C01.
25  Cooper, 'For India, No Small Thing', C01.

# Aijaz Ahmad, 'Reading Arundhati Roy *Politically*'

Aijaz Ahmad's article 'Reading Arundhati Roy *Politically*', which originally appeared in 1997 in the Indian current-affairs magazine *Frontline*, is a valuable addition to this guide because it represents a commentary on *TGST* by a leading Marxist literary critic and theorist. Ahmad is best known for his Marxist reorientation of the 'postcolonial' and his critiques of work by Edward Said and Fredric Jameson, but he has also published widely on Indian literature, especially Urdu fiction and poetry. Because of his Marxist approach, which concentrates on the political and ideological role of literature in relation to capitalism, Ahmad's reading is highly sensitive to the representation in *TGST* of actual communist leaders such as E. M. S. Namboodiripad, which he sees as defamatory and 'spiteful'. However, this does not stop him applauding Roy's linguistic and technical accomplishments and praising the novel almost against his political inclinations. In Ahmad's intriguing reading, *TGST* becomes a flawed masterpiece, a work that is 'a curious mixture of matchless achievement and quite drastic failings'. Ahmad finds three major failings in Roy's fiction: her sentimental over-written prose, her lack of 'realism' (primarily in her depiction of communists) and the focus on eroticism and sexual transgression in place of what he calls 'the actually constituted field of politics'.

In his conceptual reliance on realism as a literary form that must 'rise above' its author's ideological prejudices, Ahmad's commentary betrays the influence of the Hungarian Marxist critic and proponent of realism, Georg Lukács, and we might respond by asking whether realism itself is not also inevitably constructed and 'ideological'. As we will see (see Critical readings, **pp. 120–31**), other critics have also taken issue with Ahmad's remarks on the sexual/romantic content of *TGST* and have argued that the novel is no less 'political' for its focus on personal relationships. These debates aside, Ahmad's reading is acute, and he makes an important point about the structure of the novel, in which he sees parallel variants of a standard romance plot. On one hand, the narrative ends tragically, with the conventional death of Ammu and Velutha, but it also ends positively in the second 'romance' of Estha and Rahel's reunion. The taboo-breaking coupling of the twins, argues Ahmad, 'is thus depicted not only as the final end of a [shared] childhood [. . .] but also as private balm for emotional injuries once caused by various brutalities in the public domain'.

## From Aijaz Ahmad, 'Reading Arundhati Roy *Politically*', *Frontline* (8 August 1997), pp. 103–8

In *The God of Small Things*, Arundhati Roy may well have written the most accomplished, the most moving novel by an Indian author in English. *The Moor's Last Sigh*, which Rushdie published after 20 years of practising the art, compares credibly, [*sic*] and the ending in the two novels goes wrong equally. Hers is possibly the more distinguished *first* novel. The earlier half of *Midnight's Children* comes to mind but not the latter, and she gains in compactness and intensity what she shuns by way of scale. For anything truly comparable, one would have to go to a different Indian language, a different set of formal conventions, different sets of social and political convictions, a time zone earlier and different than this, the disastrous closing decade of our 20th century.

That is very high praise indeed. It is a difficult novel to write about, though, thanks to a curious mixture of matchless achievement and quite drastic failings. We shall first offer some detailed comment on the problematic aspects of the book. Later, then, we shall return to the more difficult question of how it is that, despite such consequential problems in the book, one can nevertheless safely think of it as possibly the most polished novel we have had in the language so far.

# I

All novels have failings. This one has three that matter. The easiest to ignore is that for a novel in which form and language are for the most part so expertly controlled, far too much is anxiously written, and therefore over-written. There *are*, as some reviews have said, far too many capitalisations! Her over-writing does not produce the effects so familiar from so much Indian fiction in English: stilted style, in the manner of composition classes, or, more damagingly, the kind of exoticism that is quite common in so much Indo-Anglian literature, even at times Rushdie's, because the non-Indian audience is so much on the writer's mind. Of the quaint, the cute, the exotic, she is free. But she can sometimes lose the battle, with herself, over sentimentality. Indeed, the work is so charged with emotion, is so very much about bad faith and emotional integrity, that it often seems to be a battle to educate oneself out of one's own sentimentalities. This battle she usually wins but sometimes loses, and the sign of losing usually is in the repetitions. Not that all her repetitions are sentimental! In most cases she has a flawless ear, and she basically knows how to draw the reader into intricate webs woven with little fragments of ordinary language that begin to sing in our ears as they gather, with each repetition, the whole emotional charge of the narrative. That, alas, does not always happen. Far too much of the prose in the middle sections, and some toward the end, tends to be, alternately, repetitive or monotonous or purplish.

That is still a minor flaw and one mentions it only because so much of the achievement is really in the formal construction. The relatively more serious failing is in the way the book panders to the prevailing anti-Communist sentiment, which damages it both ideologically and formally. A key strength of Arundhati Roy is that she has written a novel that has learned all that there is to be learned from modernism, magic realism, cinematic cutting and montage and other such developments of narrative technique in the 20th century, but a novel that nevertheless remains Realist in all its essential features. She knows what Realist fiction always knows: love, grief, remembrance, the absolute indispensability of verisimilitude in depiction of time, place and character, so exact that we who know it to be fiction can nevertheless read it as the closest possible kin of fact. She succeeds so long as she is telling the tale of private life in the form of what is basically a miniaturised family saga. But the limits of private experience seem also to be the limits of her Realism. Her ideological opposition to Communism is not in itself surprising; it is very much a sign of the times, in the sense that hostility toward the Communist movement is now fairly common among radical sections of the cosmopolitan intelligentsia, in India and abroad. The peculiarity is that, judging from the novel, she has neither a *feel* for Communist politics nor perhaps rudimentary knowledge of it. This is all the more surprising from someone who hails from Kerala and has such a fine feel for so much else there, from the landscape to modes of oppression or diffidence or intimacy; and one who is young enough to have lived more or less all her life since E. M. S. Namboodiripad, whom she merely lampoons, was first elected as Chief Minister of that State. This affective distance from the world of Communism cannot be because she lacks intelligence or imagination; of these she seems to have plenty for all else in the book. It is perhaps the settled ideological hostility which leads to an inherent incapacity to affectively imagine what she so passionately despises.

As an artist, though, she has paid dearly for a hostility so implacable. In three ways. First, there is the breakdown of Realism itself, which is the main formal virtue of the book. The only place where class conflict is portrayed with any real feeling for the situation is in chapter two, when the family car is stranded in the midst of a Communist demonstration. Significantly what she *can* depict imaginatively and with affect in this scene is the terror felt by the women inside the car; the other side of this conflict, the striking workers, remains for her an indistinct mass, except for the figure of Velutha whom Rahel fleetingly recognises. So indistinct is this mass that the reader is given to understand both that the demonstration has been organised by the ruling CPI(M) for the workers to demand only very pitiful little reforms *and* that the 'passion' that is swirling around is 'Naxalite', something of an all-purpose term in Roy's fiction. The same ambiguity is there about Velutha himself. We are told that he is a cardholding comrade of Pillai and thus a member of the CPI(M), which the book portrays as a party of traitors, more or less; but when Rahel tells Ammu of having seen him in that CPI(M)-led demonstration, the latter *hopes* that the child is right and that Velutha *is* a 'Naxalite' and thus a true revolutionary – a 'rumour' that Baby Kochamma also presents to the police officer, but with opposite sentiment. This breakdown of realism in depicting the Communist world, and the attendant rhetoric of sheer condemnation, takes peculiar shapes. The depiction of Comrade Pillai, presumably a fictional character who symbolises the corruptions of the CPI(M) and is complicit in the murderous assault on Velutha, borders on the burlesque. References to Namboodiripad, an actual historical figure and a towering presence in Kerala and beyond, belong straight in the realm of libel and defamation. It is simply not true that his ancestral home exists anywhere near Kottayam; or that it has been turned into a tourist hotel where Communists serve as waiters. Naming an actual historical figure and then ascribing to him degradations that bear no resemblance to actuality has nothing to do with artistic licence. It is spite, pure and simple.

These ways of depicting the world of Communism are of relevance to people on the Left. The anti-Communist radicals among the cosmopolitan intelligentsia no longer care for any line of demarcation between what can and should be criticised in the conduct of the Left parties, on the one hand, and on the other, that which is spiteful fabrication. What should be of concern to them as well, however, is that the virtue of good Realist literature is that it strives to portray the world realistically, so that the literary product *can* rise above the ideological prejudices of the author. In Arundhati Roy's case the opposite has happened. Her ideological prejudice masters and makes nonsense of the Realist's commitment to verisimilitude. It is significant that this is the only area where the commitment so dramatically falters.

Accurate depiction of Communists is in any case not a concern of either the author or her primary readership, here or abroad. From that perspective, the third major failing of the book, which has to do with the way it depicts and resolves issues of caste and sexuality, especially female sexuality, is the more damaging, since the novel does stake its transgressive and radical claim precisely on issues of caste and bodily love. It appears that an upright gentleman in Kerala has taken Roy to court on the charge that she has authored a pornographic book. Little does this citizen know that the problem with Arundhati Roy's handling of sexuality is not that it is pornographic but that it is so thoroughly conventional as not even to surprise anyone who reads English fiction with any degree of regularity.

The intermeshing of caste and sexuality is indeed the ideological centre of the book, and it is precisely the transgressive claim in this domain that will account for much of the popularity of the book. That inter-caste sex is neither a forbidden nor an entirely uncommon topic in Indian fiction in other languages is probably not known or relevant to the book's primary readership. What should detain us somewhat is the question of well-known conventions of European fiction on which Arundhati Roy's seemingly transgressive treatment of this theme relies almost entirely.

European modernity generally and more especially the post-Freudian world has seen an immense proliferation of discourses about sexuality as the final realm of both Pleasure and of Truth – as that zone of experience where human beings discover what they truly are. That is why sexuality has been a central preoccupation of much Euro-American fiction, especially since about the second decade of [the twentieth] century, with increasing degrees of frankness. This frankness has been identified as gain in artistic courage, realism, authentic experience, transgression of oppressive social fetters and so on. Key aspects of this preoccupation with sexuality Roy inherits.

There is, first, the theme of the privatisation of both pleasure and politics, which leads then to sheer aggrandisement of the erotic relation in human life, as a utopic moment of private transgression and pleasure so intense that it transcends all social conflicts of class, caste and race. Second, however, this aggrandisement of the sexual encounter as a zone of transcendent human authenticity is usually accompanied, as Lukács was the first to note, with an enormous 'reduction of affective and erotic relations to the pre-eminence of phallic sexuality', with its attendant theme of woman as a Sleeping Beauty waiting for Prince Charming to come and awaken her repressed sexuality. Third, this phallocentric utopia is of course all the more pleasurable if partners in it transgress such boundaries as those of class and caste, but in its deep structure this discourse of Pleasure is also profoundly political, precisely in the sense that in depicting the erotic as Truth it also dismisses the actually constituted field of politics as either irrelevant or a zone of bad faith.

In the tradition of such fictions *Lady Chatterley's Lover* is central, not because it was banned for so long on charges of pornography but because it brings together so many of the essential elements of the genre. There is Lady Chatterley herself, the upper-class woman with repressed sexuality; Mellors, the lower-class gamekeeper and keeper of phallocentric drives; the moment of encounter and awakening coming to them not as decision but as sudden explosion; the remark-able lack of intelligent speech between them as being absolutely essential to building the erotic utopia across class lines; the happy ending in which the Lady becomes a commoner and prepares to settle down to domesticity and erotic bliss. That novel is canonical but by no means unique. Variations are myriad. E. M. Forster, so well-known to us as author of *A Passage to India*, left behind him a novel, *Maurice*, made recently into a successful film, which replays a variation of that plot of cross-class erotic utopia for the world of the homosexual. Hanif Kureishi's famous film, *My Beautiful Launderette*, takes up all that but then, in the familiar triumphalist mode, depicts the homosexual utopia as the zone where social conflicts between black immigrants and white, racist skinheads are simply evaporated. These are random examples from British fiction and countless such examples could be given from American fiction as well, where inter-racial sex plays the same generic role.

Novels of this kind come to an end in one of two ways. The more pervasive in modern fiction is the characteristically 20th century, optimistic and ideologically permissive Conclusion in which the lovers walk away into the sunset, or at least find in each other the solace that the external world of social relations denies them. Cinema, from Hollywood to Bombay, is full of such endings, in which love conquers all and easy personal solutions are offered for intractable social con-flicts. But fictions of transgression, especially sexual transgression, also end in another way, very familiar since the 19th-century novel, in which the wages of sin are death and the individual is helpless against the overwhelming weight of social hypocrisy. *Anna Karenina* is the classic of this genre but much Victorian fiction ends this way, and the convention survives to this day. The same story can be told, in other words, in either the triumphalist or the tragic mode. Part of the reason why critics and readers who are steeped in conventions of modern fiction find *The God of Small Things* so very satisfying is that Arundhati Roy provides both of these possible endings, in ways at once compact and emphatic.

The novel has a tight thematic unity, condensed in those wonderfully sparse sentences that come at the end of the first chapter but then haunt the whole novel, and which tell us that the book is really about certain oppressive social structures that 'actually began thousands of years ago . . . in the days when Love Laws were made. The Laws that lay down who should be loved, and how. And how much' [Ch. 1, pp. 33]. These Laws rest on some taboos, the most ancient, the most universal and, according to Freud, the most pre-eminent of which is the taboo against incest. And, in the specific practices of the Indian 'Love Laws', prohibitions rest equally on ideas of purity and pollution, lineage and miscegenation, that constitute caste society. The novel's main claim to transgression is that it ends by violating both these taboos, but in ways that gives [sic] up parallel endings to a single story.

For, within the unity of a family chronicle, there are in fact two plot outlines: one that narrates the growing up of Rahel and the stunting of Estha, and the other which brings their mother so fatally close to Velutha. The parallel unfolding of these two strands of the story gives to Arundhati Roy the opportunity to end the novel not once but twice. In the plot line that is centred on Rahel, the growing girl goes out into the world, from her little village in Kerala to Delhi and into – then out of – a marriage with an American. The leaving of the family home and the sowing of the wild oats endows her with the autonomous self that would have been denied to her, as it was denied to her mother, in the stifling world of the provincial, caste-bound gentility of her family. Traumatised into silence by the horror of a childhood guilt, caused by a fatally false witness extracted from him in a police station, Estha meanwhile languishes in his poignant dumbness and immobility until Rahel returns, wiser and surer of herself, takes him into her arms and reaches out to heal his psychic wounds through the bereaved solace of incest. That coupling of twins, transgressive of the oldest taboo (the 'Love Laws' of who and how much), is thus depicted not only as the final end of a childhood shared earlier in some other ways, but also as private balm for emotional injuries once caused by various brutalities in the public domain. Whether or not the balm makes Estha more capable of confronting that public domain we are not told. This particular line of the plot simply ends at that eroticisation of sisterly mercy.

The greater is the pity. Some of the most assured, most nuanced prose in the novel is to be found in precisely the depiction of the childhood that is thus left behind. It is a very great pity that a tale so masterfully told should end with the author succumbing to the conventional idea of the erotic as that private transgression through which one transcends public injuries. In the larger scheme of the novel, though, this ending is probably the lesser flaw compared with the parallel ending that brings the story of Velutha and Ammu, mother of Estha and Rahel, to a close and in which sexuality is tied up with both caste and death.

Velutha is the Untouchable carpenter, the maker of little wonders in carved wood and thus 'the god of small things', whose tempestuous sexual encounter with Ammu, the upper-caste woman, toward the end of the story violates all the Love Laws laid down by caste boundaries and ideas of propriety as to who will love whom, and how. The wages of such sin are death, but the problem with that ending is not that Velutha is in return beaten to pulp by the police that is drawn from and serves the 'Touchables'. That is entirely likely. So is the idea that even some Communists drawn from the upper castes would find such a relationship intolerable, though it is quite implausible that a Communist trade union leader would actively conspire in a murderous assault on a well-respected member of his own union so as to uphold caste purity. This bit of anti-Communism notwithstanding, the real problem with that ending, *in the terms set by the author herself*, lies elsewhere.

The problem is that in order to construct eroticism as that transcendence which takes individuals beyond history and society, straight into the real truth of their beings, Arundhati Roy in fact reduces the human complexity of the characters she herself has created and whom she wishes to affirm and even celebrate, albeit in the tragic mode. Until then Ammu has been a woman who has fought hard to keep her dignity, to maintain reserve and calm contempt for her family's hypocrisies, to create an autonomous self in her own way, against all odds. Velutha has been affectionate in a variety of ways, humorous in conversation, intelligent, creative, a fighter in the political domain. All of that falls off as an inexorable sexual attraction overcomes them almost literally as a *mystery*; without a word spoken or any other indication passing between them, both arrive, in the thickness of the night, at the spot where they are to meet, as if by predestination. Night after night they return to the same spot, for a series of unions brief and utopic and so self-sufficient that the pasts simply fall away and the future is at once feared and ignored with all the terrors of the Romantic Sublime. They become pure embodiments of desire, and, significantly, not a word of intelligent conversation passes between them. They seem consumed by helplessness, twice over: before their own bodily desires, and in relation to the world that surrounds them and about which they appear to wish to do nothing.

What is most striking about that final, phallic encounter between Ammu and Velutha is how little it has to do with *decision* and how much it takes the shape of what the title of a recent movie calls *fatal attraction*. Now, the difference between decision and fatal attraction is that whereas decision, even the decision to accept suffering and/or death, is anchored in praxis, in history, in social relationships chosen and lived in a complex interplay of necessities and freedoms, fatal attractions can never cope with such complexities and must be acted out simply in terms of a libidinal drive. What we get, in other words, is a closed, fatalistic world at the heart of individual choice: deaths foretold, as the obverse of phallic ecstasy. One sins, and then one waits for the wages of sin, which is death.

While Velutha's fate is entirely credible and even ordained in the very scheme of things, the nullity that sets into Ammu's existence after his death and after a brief flicker of her own belligerence in the police station, which then culminates in her wasting herself away into an unnecessary death, is utterly contrived by the author. Ammu had been all through her adult life a woman of great grit, and this grit is what makes it possible for her to take the *initiative* in breaking the Love laws, even as Velutha hesitates. That she would not be able to face the consequences of her own grit is an odd decision that the author makes on her behalf, more or less arbitrarily. One reason is probably generic; it is one of the oldest conventions in fiction that women who live impermissibly must also die horribly. But there is something else as well. If Ammu were to live on, she would have to face the fact that the erotic is very rarely a sufficient mode for overcoming real social oppressions; one has to make some other, more complex choices in which the erotic may be an element but hardly the only one. For that, Arundhati Roy would have had to give Ammu a second chance, a grit beyond the fatal attraction, and thus shift the ideological centre of the novel as such. It is really quite astonishing how much fiction is littered with the corpses of characters who die quickly because authors do not know how to let them go on living.

## II

How, then, does one say that *The God of Small Things* may well be the most accomplished novel written by an Indian author in English?

Fictions can only be read within the conditions of their own possibility which are historical, ideological and formal. Once the Revolution divided the French between republicans and royalists, what is surprising about Balzac, Marx noted, is not that he was a royalist but that he could, despite his royalism and thanks to his commitment to Realism, give us accurate and enduring analyses of post-Revolutionary France. *Anna Karenina* is a great novel, Lenin claimed, not because we approve of its ideologies of Christian piety, rural romanticism and social conservatism but because of Tolstoy's accurate and elaborate understanding of the dominant ideologies of his time in which he himself was wholly complicit. To expect that literature would somehow transcend the conditions of its own possibility is to romanticise literary activity beyond measure. Within the possibilities available in Indo-Anglian literature at the present moment, Arundhati Roy is exceptional in the use of language and form as these have evolved so far in this literature, and she accurately and powerfully reflects the themes and ideologies that are currently dominant in the social fraction within which she seems to be herself located and which is in any case the primary readership for her fiction.

For all the claims that are made these days for Indo-Anglian writing, partly under pressures of the global market, this literature has until recently lived a peripheral and precarious existence. In the first, quite prolonged phase virtually all English writers in India – including the most prominent, such as Raja Rao, Mulk Raj Anand, Ahmed Ali, Khushwant Singh, Anita Desai – wrote in English what could easily have been written in another Indian language, and they did so simply because they lacked either the competence or the inclination to write in any other language. Even Vikram Seth's *A Suitable Boy* belongs essentially within this tendency, hence Rushdie's well-known contempt for it. Starting from my childhood, I read Mulk Raj Anand in Urdu for some 20 years before finding out that he wrote in English. Ahmed Ali made his literary debut as a writer of short stories in Urdu. Then he published *Twilight in Delhi* – with the ambition of making a mark in England, his critics say. The novel reads much better in the Urdu translation that was published some 30 years later, under his wife's signature; it is possible that the English is the translation and the Urdu the real original which the author withheld for so long, for reasons of ambition and eccentricity. Even the title, *Dilli Ki Sham*, reads better in Urdu, as its colloquial ordinariness comes trippingly off the tongue and as the preposition *ki* – which could mean 'of' or 'in' or 'from', depending on the usage – gives to the phrase a different resonance.

The formal originality of *Midnight's Children* was that it was the first novel written by an Indian writer which was in its sensibility, its linguistic competence, its formal construction, distant enough from other Indian languages to have been possible *only* in English. Rushdie's was so original a style precisely because he raised to high literary excellence the language of a very particular social fraction: those who could perhaps speak, undoubtedly understand the original language of their family but whose training in elite public schools had given them great inwardness toward English, which they inhabited the way one slips into one's favourite clothes. Hence the hybrid character of the style, where so much of the ingenuity reads like the translation of an absent text. If Conrad was preoccupied with leaving his Polishness behind and write [*sic*] an English more proper than the British themselves, Rushdie forged an English whose energy came precisely from his confidence that the language was so much his own that he could invent a high cosmopolitan style by bringing into it a whole range of resources from elsewhere.

In this line of evolution, Arundhati is an original. She knows about language and form what Rushdie knows. But with English she has even a greater inwardness and naturalness; the novel is actually *felt* in English. If Rushdie's prose signifies the ironical fact that cosmopolitan intellectuals among Midnight's Children were to be located in English far more briskly than was the case during the colonial period, Arundhati Roy's prose signifies that the culture that the public schools create is now, some years later, more widespread, more confident of itself, more constitutively a part of the very structure of feeling for this fraction. Roy's prose is not only superb but also representative. She is the first Indian writer in English where a marvellous stylistic resource becomes available for provincial, vernacular culture without any effect of exoticism or estrangement, and without the book reading as a translation. English is here to stay, much like Christianity, of which Roy writes that it 'arrived in a boat and seeped into Kerala like tea from teabag'.

We can turn, finally, to issues of affect and ideology. First, the ideology of form! She has written a Realist novel but not like Vikram Seth; her Realism folds into itself all the plenitude of narrative techniques that the 20th century has spawned. And she is too deeply committed to Realism to take flight into magic Realism; Rushdie has never written of vernacular culture with such assuredness of touch. In its affective structure, *The God of Small Things* is heartbreakingly tied to love, loss and remembrance; *Midnight's Children* and especially, *Shame*, are, by contrast, remarkable for their lovelessness, quite at par with Naipaul's fictions. Her novel is, as such novels usually are, about the need to take leave but she knows, as few novelists do, the ache and the vertigo of love for precisely that which must be left behind. This Realism, and the accompanying refusal to partake of either the sentimentality so common in Indo-Anglian literature or the cynicism that is characteristic of so much modernism, makes it possible for her, then, to depict a whole range of relationships and characters with extraordinary emotional depth. The love between Rahel and Estha, the twins who do not look alike but who dream each other's dreams, is so complete and so self-evident to both that it is often experienced not as love of one being for another but as the identity of a single existence, as if they had forgotten to evolve separate selves after being born merely 18 minutes apart. Rarely has a childhood, so favourite a theme of Realist fiction, been re-imagined so lyrically, with such ingenuity, power and precision. In a completely different register is the comedy of Chacko's absurd, priggish existence which finally knows its moment of assertion only in impotent rage against Ammu, in defence of caste purity and family honour; yet, however impotent the actual rage, it is made invincible through the power of property which he owns, against a divorced, defenseless sister who lacks rights of proprietorship in the home of her natal family. Or Baby Kochamma, whose girlhood was once marked by an unrequited infatuation and who lives a sterile, spinsterish existence, full of a malignity that is often motiveless but always conventional, caste-ridden and cruel. In the hands of a lesser writer, such characters, so well known from so much Realist fiction, could have become merely stereotypical. Instead, Arundhati Roy's flawless ear, her genius for the individuating detail, and the chiselled edge of her prose make them altogether memorable. If she can write about even the weather and vegetation of Kerala with such evocative force, she can also observe with devastating precision the malignant and manipulative inventiveness of Baby Kochamma as her will twists and turns in the police station, changing her tactics from one minute to next, until she gets what she wants. The range of registers in Roy's prose are by any standards impressive.

The ideology of form is her strength. The matter of political ideology is more complicated. The anti-communism of the novel's political ideology is disconcerting but not surprising; in this too, Arundhati Roy appears to be representative of the social fraction whose particular kind of radicalism she represents. And she is a representative intellectual of this particular moment in India in her preoccupation with the tie between caste and sexuality; in her portrayal of the erotic as the real zone of rebellion and Truth; in her sense that resistance can only be individual and fragile; in her sense that the personal is the only arena of the political, and therefore her sense of the inevitability of nullity and death. About caste she writes with devastating precision; about class she seems not to be particularly concerned with those aspects which are not tied to caste. In this too, she is representative of these times. ('Just forget mother-tongue and social class,' Salman Rushdie advises us in *India Today* of 14 July 1997). Some of this ideology one can take; much of it one may leave aside. But that her fiction gives us much insight into her world – the world she depicts in her novel, and the world she inhabits as author – is undeniable. This is Literature's central ideological vocation.

**Brinda Bose,** 'In Desire and in Death: "Eroticism as Politics in Arundhati Roy's *The God of Small Things*"'

Brinda Bose's article, first published in the Canadian critical journal *ARIEL* in 1998, is reproduced here not only as an exemplary feminist reading of *TGST* but also as a considered response to some of the critical assumptions made about Roy's politics in Aijaz Ahmad's essay 'Reading Arundhati Roy *Politically*'. In contrast to Ahmad's assumption that the sexual-transgression theme in *TGST* obscures more important political issues, Bose concentrates on the 'utopian' possibilities of eroticism and sexual experience, especially where this experience is socially forbidden. In doing so, she examines the politics of desire which, although they may evolve in the private 'erogenous' realm of personal sexual relations, are not divorced from the world of public politics. In fact, as Bose goes on to argue, a recognition of shared anger against their common subjugation is the very thing that catalyses Ammu's desire for Velutha (see **p. 125**):

> Ammu is not dismissive of Velutha's red politics, but sees in its inherent anger
> a possibility of relating to Velutha's mind [. . .] her own politics are embedded
> in her 'rage' against the various circumstances of her life, and it is through this
> sense of shared rage that she finds it possible to desire the Untouchable
> Velutha.

Elsewhere in Roy's novel, Ammu's 'rage' is described in singularly political terms – as that of a 'suicide bomber' – and Bose's article, which makes interesting comparisons between Roy's work and that of Milan Kundera, carefully delineates the political calculations and consequences of Ammu's courageous decision to allow herself to desire. Because it represents such a momentous transgression, the cross-caste affair goes beyond the commercial formulas of the exotic romance and develops into a daring political statement. In Bose's reading, Estha and Rahel's incestuous love-making is similarly political because it, too, represents a dangerous willingness to cross boundaries and turn desire into a form of rebellion.

**From Brinda Bose, 'In Desire and in Death: "Eroticism as Politics in Arundhati Roy's The God of Small Things"', ARIEL: A Review of International English Literature, 29(2) (April 1998), pp. 59–72**

Arundhati Roy's debut novel *The God of Small Things* depicts protagonists who are ready to break social laws and die for desire, for love. In doing so, the novel raises the question of whether there is a viable (rather than die-able) politics in Roy's construction of the erotic in her novel. It would be easy enough to read eroticism as an utopic indulgence; however, utopias are not devoid of politics, and a deliberate validation of erotic desire as an act of transgression probably cannot be dismissed as a momentary lapse from the politicization of one's being. Is the pursuit of erotic desire a capitalist preoccupation? Does this make its politics – assuming that we agree it has one – suspect and ultimately regrettable? Or could Roy have valourized sexuality – and preeminently female sexuality – as an acceptable politics with an agenda that can and does sustain itself in the tumult of sociocultural fluxes?

Roy's novel, even as it flits back and forth between childhood and a wiser, sadder adult existence, explores two dissimilar sexual transgressions. Ammu of the earlier generation catapults across caste/class divisions to pursue an erotic desire for the Untouchable carpenter, the 'God of Small Things', Velutha. Daughter Rahel, after a youth gone awry, returns to her childhood home and her soul-twin Estha to rediscover his pain and to offer him her body as an unnameable balm. Both violate the most basic 'love laws' that govern their social existence; the transgressions are the result of conscious decisions by the emotionally overcharged characters. The very circumstances of their choice(s) affirm the political judgment that surely it could not simply be bodily need; the sublimely erotic experience is also the pursuit of a utopia in which ideas and ideals, greater than what a momentary sexual pleasure offers, coalesce.[1]

Aijaz Ahmad, characterizing Roy's preoccupation with moments of private (sexual) pleasure as indulging in the theme of a 'utopic' transgression, concludes that

> in its deep structure this discourse of Pleasure is also profoundly political, precisely in the sense that in depicting the erotic as Truth it also dismisses the actually constituted field of politics as either irrelevant or a zone of bad faith.[2]

Ahmad's criticism of Roy's apparent lack of knowledge (let alone understanding and support) of the contemporary left-wing politics of Kerala within which her

---

1  [Bose's note.] Both First and Third World feminisms long have been exploring the political contexts of female sexuality. Since the Irrigarayan [sic] discourse of the early 1970s, sexual difference has been addressed and validated. Twenty years on, the task today is no longer that of rendering female sexuality visible; it is now, as Tharu and Niranjana have discussed in 'Problems for a Contemporary Theory of Gender,' the more complex one of investigating the contradictions of gender, caste, class, and community composition that works upon the 'subject' in the dominant order; Susie Tharu and Tejaswini Niranjana, 'Problems for a Contemporary Theory of Gender', in Shahid Amin and Dipesh Chakrabarty (eds), *Subaltern Studies IX*, New Delhi: Oxford University Press, 1996, pp. 232–60.

2  Aijaz Ahmad, 'Reading Arundhati Roy *Politically*', *Frontline*, p. 104. [See **p. 114.**]

story is constructed, is valid. However, one's personal politics is often an extension of, but always greater than, one's positioning – left, right, centre, or beyond – and a politics of desire, even if merely proclaiming 'the erotic as Truth', could certainly be considered as viable a politics as any other.[3]

Desires – particularly 'personal' ones – have always been severely underrated in comparison to revolutions, particularly those in which the underclasses unite to lose their chains. Perhaps the secret of the scale lies in the simplicity, the smallness of the former in relation to the epic sweep of mass movements. Yet Nancy Armstrong and Leonard Tennenhouse, writing in 1987 on the ideology of (sexual) conduct in literature and history, make what appears to be some basic claims for the political validity of sexual desire:

> the terms and dynamics of sexual desire must be a political language . . .
> we must see representations of desire, neither as reflections nor as consequences of political power but as a form of political power in their own right.[4]

Gilles Deleuze, theorizing the construction of the 'desiring machine,' has analyzed the tendency to read desire in some sort of minimalist measure:[5]

> Do you realize how simple a desire is? Sleeping is a desire. Walking is a desire . . . A spring, a winter, are desires. Old age is also a desire. Even death. Desire never needs interpreting, it is it which experiments.[6]

Deleuze, ironically anticipating Ahmad, goes on to say that

> we [then] run up against very exasperating objections. They say to us that we are returning to an old cult of pleasure, to a pleasure principle, or to a notion of the festival (the revolution will be a festival). . . . above all, it is objected that by releasing desire from lack and law, the only thing we have left to refer to is a state of nature, a desire that would be natural and spontaneous reality. We say quite the opposite: *desire only exists when assembled or machined.*[7]

---

3  [Bose's note.] What one is questioning here, in response to Ahmad's formulations, is not his analysis of Roy's anticommunism, which is obvious, but his charge against her 'sense that resistance can only be individual and fragile . . . that the personal is the only arena of the political' as well as 'her sense of the inevitability of nullity and death' (p. 108 [see Critical readings, **p. 119**]). Roy's novel could be validating the politics of the personal without insisting that it is the *only* arena of the political; it does not appear merely to accept the inevitability of death without recognizing the politics inherent to that end.

4  Nancy Armstrong and Leonard Tennenhouse (eds), *The Ideology of Conduct: Essays in Literature and the History of Sexuality*, London: Methuen, 1987, p. 2.

5  [Bose's note.] Deleuze reads desire through psychoanalysis. In talking about desire as a machine and an assemblage, he looks at the role of psychoanalysis in its regulation or even in staking out dominant positions in this regulation. His emphasis is on the multiplicity of experiences, of 'the field of desire crisscrossed by particles and fluxes' (Gilles Deleuze, 'Desire and Schizoanalysis', in Constantin B. Boundas (ed.), *The Deleuze Reader*, New York: Columbia University Press, 1993, pp. 112–13). Of course, desire as Deleuze defines it is larger and wider that the context of sexuality, which 'can only be thought of as one flux among others' (p. 140).

6  Deleuze, 'Desire and Schizoanalysis', p. 112.

7  Deleuze, 'Desire and Schizoanalysis', p. 136; emphasis added.

Assemblages and machinery are analogous with politics rather than with a natural state of being; the experience of desire – or desiring – in Roy's novel, contrary to the idea that it proclaims the 'erotic as Truth,' explores its many political possibilities and appears to reject finally any truth that would grandstand over and above the validity of the process in itself.

Roy's politics, it may be said, exists in an erogenous zone; the erotics, however, are not totally divorced from the world of 'actual' politik, though they do intervene in predictable ways, as Ahmad has alleged: 'this phallocentric utopia is of course all the more pleasurable if partners in it transgress such boundaries as those of class and caste'.[8] There is a suggestion in this allegation that Roy was looking for the most saleable formula of sexuality for her novel, which would then (v)indicate a capitalist politics. Roy's comments on the process of her composition, however, appear to foreground the politics of gender, the logic of basic, 'biological' difference:

> the talk of a noble working class seemed very, very silly to me . . . like other women I would be brutalised so much by men. It made no difference whether they were proletarian or not, or what their ideology was. The problem was the biological nature of these men. The only real conflict seemed to me to be between women and men.[9]

She talks of Kerala as a place where biology has been subdued, where, despite their obvious physical beauty, men and women cannot cross the barriers of caste and class in desiring one another. Roy's novel focuses on the lines that one cannot, or should not, cross – and yet those are the very lines that do get crossed, if only once in a while – and then that makes for the politics of those extra-ordinary stories. In *The Unbearable Lightness of Being*, another (though rather different) novel about communism and sexuality, Milan Kundera explores the experience of a moment of sheer ecstasy, in which happiness in its absolute weightlessness becomes 'unbearable' and must die. The essential philosophical question that his novel poses is applicable to Roy's central dilemma too:

> But is heaviness truly deplorable and lightness splendid?
> The heaviest of burdens crushes us, we sink beneath it, it pins us to the ground. But in the love poetry of every age, the woman longs to be weighed down by the man's body. The heaviest of burdens is therefore simultaneously an image of life's most intense fulfillment. . . .
> Conversely, the absolute absence of a burden causes man to be lighter than air, to soar into the heights . . . his movements as free as they are insignificant.
> What then shall we choose? Weight or lightness? . . . which one is positive, weight or lightness?[10]

If one reads lightness or absolute absence of a burden to mean a lack of

8   Ahmad, 'Reading Arundhati Roy *Politically*', p. 104. [See Critical readings, **p. 114.**]
9   Arundhati Roy, 'When You Have Written a Book, You Lay Your Weapons Down', p. 107.
10  Milan Kundera, *The Unbearable Lightness of Being*, New York: Harper, 1987, p. 5.

involvement – of politics, personal or 'actual,' sexual or communist – then Roy's protagonists, like Kundera's, finally choose to be political and burdened, and to die for it. The (Elizabethan) connotation of 'dying' as a consummation of the sexual act – linked to Kundera's passing reference to the weighing down of one body by another – is particularly relevant to this construction of absolute happiness as equivalent to the heaviest burden, which then becomes 'unbearable.' In light of this philosophical formula, the deaths of Velutha and Ammu in Roy's novel would be as 'ordained' as Tomas's and Teresa's in Kundera's: in desire, and therefore in death, they choose to be more heavily burdened than they are able to bear.

If one reads the erotic as apolitical (or politically-suspect) then one may condemn the double-death as 'utterly contrived by the author,' as Ahmad does:

> If Ammu were to live on, she would have to face the fact that the erotic is
> very rarely a sufficient mode for overcoming real social oppressions; one
> has to make some other, more complex choices in which the erotic may
> be an element but hardly the only one.[11]

Perhaps Ammu's death is in itself something of a political statement[12] – neither simply 'generic' ('it is one of the oldest conventions in fiction that women who live impermissibly must also die horribly'), nor merely the trick of a tired novelist who does not 'know how to let [her character] go on living'.[13] Surely, death as punishment for transgression is an accepted politics in every sphere of living; one is a trifle confused as to why, in an act of transgression that involves both Velutha and Ammu equally (though it is Ammu who actually takes the initiative in destroying the sexual taboo, as Ahmad himself points out), his 'fate is entirely credible and even ordained in the very scheme of things' while hers is 'arbitrary' and 'astonishing'.[14] If we are referring here to (caste) lines that cannot be crossed, is it politically daring to be upwardly mobile but not so in reverse? Or is it that Velutha's Naxalite convictions – indicative of the more complex choices that Ahmad has advocated – make him more deserving of a martyr's fate than Ammu's mere womanly eroticism?

Clearly, there is a tendency to read Ammu's single-minded commitment to her 'fatal attraction' for the Untouchable Velutha as lacking the true grit that her character had promised – true grit being equivalent to the truly political in an arena outside of the personal. Velutha, though nurturing anti-caste/class aspirations in love/desire, is seen as a more fully committed political being because of his participation in the communist uprisings in the state. In such readings, the politics of Ammu's position – and therefore perhaps her less 'complex' choices – in

---

11  Ahmad, 'Reading Arundhati Roy *Politically*', pp. 106–7 (Critical readings, **p. 116**).

12  [Bose's note.] Rukmini Bhaya Nair, in her review of Roy's novel, is possessed so completely of her thesis that it is the work of a 'narcissistic impulse' that she appears to discount the death of Ammu as tragedy. She berates Roy instead for failing to end the novel with the death of Rahel, which, she believes, would have raised the work to the status of a Great Story (a tragedy rather than a fairytale). This relentlessly pursued identification between Roy and Rahel leads Bhaya Nair to miss the centrality of Ammu to the novel and so the importance of her death in determining its tone. Rukmini Bhaya Nair, 'Twins and Lovers', *Biblio: A Review of Books*, 11(5), 1997, pp. 4–6.

13  Ahmad, 'Reading Arundhati Roy *Politically*', p. 107. (See Critical readings, **pp. 116–17**.)

14  Ahmad, 'Reading Arundhati Roy *Politically*', p. 106. (See Critical readings, **p. 116**.)

terms of her gender, is largely ignored. In any case, there are indications in the text that parallels can be drawn between the politics of Ammu and the rather more obvious Leftist leanings suspected of Velutha, and that hers are probably as viable, though more personal:

> Suddenly Ammu hoped it *had* been him that Rahel saw in the march. She hoped it had been him that had raised his flag and knotted arm in anger. She hoped that under his careful cloak of cheerfulness, he housed a living, breathing anger against the smug, ordered world that she so raged against.
> She hoped it had been him.
>
> [Ch. 8, pp. 175–6]

Apparently Ammu is not dismissive of Velutha's red politics, but sees in its inherent anger a possibility of relating to Velutha's mind, not just his body. Her own politics are embedded in her 'rage' against the various circumstances of her life, and it is through this sense of a shared raging that she finds it possible to desire the Untouchable Velutha. It is not only sexual gratification that she seeks; she seeks also to touch the Untouchable. There is then no reason why Roy's (personalized/individualized) interrogation of the caste/class/gender/sexuality nexus should necessarily be seen as soft politics, while an intervention of communist ideology into the same nexus should raise its status, in some kind of arbitrary measurement of radicality.

The perception that women tend to soft-pedal on issues of 'hard' or 'actual' politics is of course an old one. In an analysis of the significance of gender in the construction of militant and nationalist agendas,[15] Sylvia Walby has questioned the reasons for what is often seen as lesser commitment on the part of women:

> Women's greater commitment to peace and opposition to militarism might be thought to be linked to their lesser commitment to 'their' nation. Do women less often think war for nationalist reasons is worth the candle because they have fewer real interests in 'victorious' outcome, since it would make less difference to their place in society than that of men? . . . Conversely is the gap between women and men's militarism less marked in societies where women have a greater stake as a result of less gender inequality?[16]

---

15 [Bose's note.] The significance of gender/sexuality in nationalist and militant movements has been discussed in a variety of specific historical contexts. See, for example, Andrew Parker *et al.* (eds), *Nationalisms and Sexualities*, New York: Routledge, 1992; Chandra T. Mohanty *et al.* (eds), *Third World Women and the Politics of Feminism*, Bloomington, Ind.: Indiana University Press, 1991; Bishnupriya Ghosh and Brinda Bose (eds), *Interventions: Feminist Dialogues on Third World Women's Literature and Film*, New York: Garland, 1997; Kumkum Sangari and Sudesh Vaid (eds), *Recasting Women: Essays in Colonial History*, New Delhi: Kali for Women, 1989; Partha Chatterjee, *The Nation and its Fragments*, Princeton, NJ: Princeton University Press, 1993; and the Subaltern Studies volumes. The question has been raised as to whether women are indeed less involved/interested, or whether they are deliberately silenced for the containment of women's agency. If one accepts that Roy's disinclination for the Marxist politics of Kerala is in itself political, is her politics capitalist, or gendered, or both?

16 Sylvia Walby, 'Woman and Nation', in Gopal Balakrishnan (ed.), *Mapping the Nation*, London: Verso, 1996, pp. 235–54, at p. 248.

This appears to be somewhat in keeping with Roy's own impression that talk of a noble working class seems 'silly' when the only real conflict seems to her to be between women and men, and the contention is always the woman's subject position in relation to the biological nature of men, which tends toward domination and subjugation. In asserting her own 'biological' desire for a man who inhabits a space beyond the permissible boundaries of 'touchability,' it appears that Ammu attempts a subversion of caste/class rules as well as the male tendency to dominate by being, necessarily, the initiator of the sexual act. Further, Rahel and Estha's incestuous lovemaking as the culmination of a 'dizygotic' closeness that transcends – and violates – all biological norms, is proof once again of the subversive powers of desire and sexuality in an arena that is rife with the politics of gender divisions and the rules that govern them.

In the politics of literature and culture, we are now cognizant of the 'new historicist' position that

> there is no transhistorical or universal human essence and that human subjectivity is constructed by cultural codes which position and limit all of us in various and divided ways ... that there is no 'objectivity', that we experience the 'world' in language, and that all our representations of the world, our readings of texts and of the past, are informed by our own historical position, by the values and politics that are rooted in them.[17]

It is true that Roy's own (historical) experience of communism in Kerala has been subjectivized in her fictional (re)constructions, which in itself constitutes a conscious act that is essentially political. However, by deliberately undermining the prevalent Leftist politics of the state, Roy also appears to be questioning the efficacy of a perception that always categorizes politics by colour (not of the skin but of the flag):

> He tried to hate her.
> *She's one of them*, he told himself. Just *another one of them*.
> He couldn't.
> *She had deep dimples when she smiled. Her eyes were always somewhere else.* Madness slunk in through a chink in History. It took only a moment.
>
> [Ch. 10, p. 214][18]

If Madness is erotic desire, its slinking in through a chink in (Touchable-Untouchable, gendered), History is no momentary aberration. Even if it takes only a moment, these chinks abound in History and they are the sources of alternative revolutions.

---

17 Judith L. Newton, 'History as Usual? Feminism and the "New Historicism" ', in H. Aram Veeser (ed.), *The New Historicism*, New York: Routledge, 1989, pp. 152–67, at p. 152.
18 In *TGST* the last sentences actually read: 'Madness slunk in through a chink in History. It only took a moment.'

Therefore, though it would be fairly easy to dismiss the beautifully-written erotic passages of the novel as necessary ingredients of marketability, or the formula of desire-into-death as the chosen path of a fledgling novelist taking recourse to tested narrative strategies, it would be more worthwhile to examine them for their inherent politics. For all the drama contained in either the inter-caste/class, or the incestuous carnalities, the question we keep returning to is that of the 'Love Laws'. It is not just the matter of transgression but, as Roy puts it evocatively, of *who* and *how much* [Ch. 1, p. 33]. Society and government make rules and define boundaries; many of these are continuously transgressed. But there are some who are allowed to transgress more than others, and there are some rules that are (acceptably) transgressed more often. Women's transgressions are generally more easily condemned, as are those to do with the 'Love Laws'. When women seek to transgress the rules that govern love and desire, the penalty is death. Knowing this, to desire (sexually) what one cannot have may be seen as indulging in a death-wish.

Such a formula – for desire, for death – is as easily constructed as it can be condemned. It can be condemned, both for lack of a viable politics (it becomes only a die-able one), and for an easy authorial escape. Not necessarily, however, is the pursuit of desire – in the context of sexuality – analogous with a desire for self-annihilation. Death being a penalty one is willing to pay for a realization of desire, it is indistinguishable from wishing for death as one wishes for the sexual fulfilment of one's desires. Deleuze has also made this distinction between desire and the death-drive.[19] The implication that desire as a process is disconnected from the death-drive is central to a reading of eroticism as politics in this text because it is an endorsement of the process itself rather than a recognition of it as a conduit to a more overwhelming culmination – that of physical death.

This is not to say that desire and death are completely de-linked in Roy's novel but to suggest that they are two separate processes, and that the politics of each are distinguishable. To desire (sexual fulfilment) is an end in itself, and the process of it a wholly positive movement.

> Desire: who, except priests, would want to call it 'lack?' Nietzsche called it 'will to power'. There are other names for it. For example, 'grace'. Desiring is not at all easy, but this is precisely because it gives, instead of lacks, 'virtue which gives'.[20]

Whatever one lacks, wishes, misses, or desires constitutes its positivity, and 'even individually, the construction of the plane is a politics; it necessarily involves a "collective", collective assemblages, a set of social becoming'.[21] According to Deleuze then the process of (sexual) desiring is not confined to being a personal politics because it does not enact itself in isolation; this is so not even simply because it desires (an)other, but because it involves an entire set of social codes in its process of (re)construction.

The codes of death as penalty are, of course, socially constructed and enacted.

---

19 Deleuze, 'Desire and Schizoanalysis', p. 113.
20 Deleuze, 'Desire and Schizoanalysis', p. 114.
21 Deleuze, 'Desire and Schizoanalysis', p. 114.

However, to conceive of a particular desire as worth 'dying for' is not equivalent to wishing for death as one wishes for the fulfilment of that desire. In any case, there are two distinct cases of sexual desire that are important to Roy's novel, though the Ammu-Velutha union may easily be read as the central relationship. The relation of each of these cases to a probable death (as penalty/punishment) is different. For its eventual social visibility (despite the secrecy with which the affair is conducted), the Ammu-Velutha relationship is preordained to die. For the fact that the Rahel-Estha incest is conducted in the (social) invisibility of a family home, and indeed involves a partner who has ceased to speak and to be noticed in/by society at large, the sexual experience here may evade the punishment it apparently would deserve within the same set of social codes. However, if one were to link desire to the death-penalty, then on some sort of measuring scale the Ammu-Velutha union would be positioned higher – viable because die-able – than the process by which the closeness of the twins' 'Siamese souls' culminates in the sexual solace that Rahel offers Estha for his unspeakable pain. Clearly such a measure of erotic validity would be useless, and once again, de-emphasizes the centrality of the process (of desire and desiring) to the politics of the novel.

*The God of Small Things* delineates a politics of desire that is vitally linked to the politics of voice. The key is offered even before the novel is launched, in Roy's epigraph from John Berger: 'Never again will a single story be told as though it's the only one.' Since the novel is a tale not merely of transgressions – and there are so many of them – but also of the processes of desiring that lead to those acts of rebellion, the re-construction of the stories that Roy wants to tell can only be validated by their various tellings. All histories, as we all know now, are re-told in various ways. There is no one story that endures; *who* tells the tale and *who* listens is almost as important as *who* broke the Laws in the first place. However, Roy wants to take us back to that particular time when the Laws were made – a Time that pre-dates all the histories she knows and will re-tell

> [l]ittle events, ordinary things, smashed and reconstituted. Imbued with new meaning. Suddenly they become the bleached bones of a story.
>     . . . to say that it all began when Sophie Mol came to Ayemenem is only one way of looking at it.
>     Equally, it could be argued that it actually began thousands of years ago. Long before the Marxists came. Before the British took Malabar . . . It could be argued that it began long before Christianity arrived in a boat and seeped into Kerala like tea from a teabag.
>     That it really began in the days when the Love Laws were made. The laws that lay down who should be loved, and how.
>     And how much.
>
> [Ch. 2, pp. 32–3]

The politics of (her) desires, therefore, has to do with cultural histories, with the ways in which sexuality has been perceived through generations in a society that coded Love Laws with a total disregard for possible anomalies. This is a society, Roy believes, that bypassed the very efficacy of Love by laying down Laws that dictated who to love, and how much. Roy takes on the histories that perpetuate such Laws, and to read her novel *politically* one may need to accept that there are certain kinds of politics that have more to do with interpersonal relations than with grand revolutions, that the most personal dilemmas can also become public causes, that erotics can also be a politics.[22]

It is not as if this in itself is a novel construct, but clearly it is a premise that is still reiterated, as is seen in contemporary analyses of women's writing, particularly from the postcolonies:

> In literary representations of 'the personal as political', postcolonial women writers explore the personal dimensions of history rather than overt concerns with political leadership and nation-states as in the work of their male counterparts. This does not make women writers' concerns any less political; rather, from a feminist standpoint of recognizing the personal, even the intimate and bodily as part of a broader sociopolitical context, postcolonial women writers enable a reconceptualization of politics.[23]

There is a generalization at work here which is potentially dangerous, but in the Indian (postcolonial/Third World) context, the reconceptualization of politics through 'the intimate and bodily' is perhaps a much more radical act than it would be in Western (neocolonial/First World) perception and can therefore least afford to be dismissed as disassociated from hardcore politics. Recent debates in the arena of cultural studies have been addressing the question of whether it is enough just to globalize the local or whether one must now step out further to look and recognize the *singular* politics of the individual:

> Politics of identity are synecdochal, taking the part (the individual) to be representative of the whole (the social group defined by a common identity). Such a logic not only too easily equates political and cultural identities, it makes politics into a matter of representation (or its absence). . . . Challenging culture's equation with and location in an identity (even when defined within a logic of difference) may enable us to think about the possibilities of a politics which recognises the positivity or singularity of the other.[24]

Without detracting from the importance of a common cultural identity, Grossberg's highlighting of an individualized politics that challenges – even while emerging from within – the same equations, is a timely intervention into (re)reading

---

22 [Bose's note.] See, for example, Young, who discusses the development of literary theories that seek to 'cross the boundary to the social . . . by using history . . . or the history and culture of colonialism, or sexuality'; theories of sexuality, according to this model, necessarily invoke 'the notion of "transgression", the crossing of the law as a supremely human and therefore political act'; Robert J. C. Young, *Torn Halves: Political Conflict in Literary and Cultural Theory*, Manchester: Manchester University Press, 1996, p. 12.

23 Ketu H. Katrak, 'Post-Colonial Women Writers and Feminisms', in Bruce King (ed.), *New National and Post-Colonial Literatures*, Oxford: Clarendon Press, 1996, pp. 230–44, at p. 234.

24 Lawrence Grossberg, 'The Space of Culture, The Power of Space', in Iain Chambers and Lidia Curti (eds), *The Post-Colonial Question*, London: Routledge, 1996, pp. 169–88, at p. 169.

feminisms for our particular context.[25] Indulging in an erotic utopia – as Ammu is charged with doing, and perhaps even Rahel maybe accused of – is neither too personal nor too utopic for political consideration; to argue for its politics, however, is not to demand a validation of their very individual responses to specific sociocultural pressures, as representative of an entire group of (sexually) repressed women of a given location and time. It is merely a substantiation of the many different kinds of politics that an individual may propose in response to 'laws' that are obviously culturally promulgated and sustained.

This proposal of a logic of singular difference, however, does not accept that an erotic utopia is necessarily elitist. It is, of course, an argument of long-standing that economics determines one's responses to such indulgences as love – or sexual desire; and that coterminously love and desire are indulgences when pursued by the elite but 'political'/radical when sought by the poorer masses (which is what makes Velutha's death-by-desire credible and Ammu's arbitrary). Alternatively, it is argued that the poorer masses have no time in their daily grind against overwhelming poverty to seek love and sexual fulfilment as a means of alleviating their despair. However, fictional responses aside, sociological studies have repeatedly proven that the idea that love and desire are elitist indulgences is a myth.[26] It is true, however, that class differences do generate their own compulsions that may override certain ideals and prescriptions of a traditional culture – but this is to assume that there does exist a monolithic 'traditional culture', which all classes are then expected to adopt and pursue. In reality, the traditional cultures that prescribe social existence are varied to suit a classist/casteist society such as India's, which is what made it possible in the first place to view Velutha's sexual transgression as revolutionary and Ammu's as an elitist indulgence.

There is much sadness in Arundhati Roy's novel, and not least to do with the desire-death nexus. It is this very sadness, perhaps, that stands as eloquent proof of the fact that the sexuality which forms the core of the novel is not dismissible, either as a non-politics or as a profoundly capitalist one that validates an eroticism divorced from any other social reality. John Updike analyzes Roy's Faulkner-like torturous story-telling as a method that responds to 'a chord in stratified, unevenly developed societies that feel a shame and defeat in their history';[27] one cannot quite agree. There is an exploration of shame and defeat here, certainly, but the politics of the novel is contained in the subversion of this shame and defeat through the valourization of erotic desire. To lunge, knowingly and deliberately, for what one must not have – for what will result in shame and defeat – is to believe that the very process of the pursuit would render the ultimate penalty worthwhile. To know that there may be death at the end of it – and still to

---

25 [Bose's note.] Grossberg confronts the limitations of contemporary theories in cultural studies that are organized around notions of globalization, identity, and difference. He argues that there is now a new 'spatial economy' that does not adhere to simple geographical dichotomies (First/Third, Centre/Margin, Local/Global) but transcends the category of identity and implies a new organization/orientation of power and space.

26 [Bose's note.] See, for example, Kakar, who profiles the personal lives of slum women to contradict the myth that love/sexual desire are elitist indulgences; Sudhir Kakar, *Intimate Relations: Exploring Indian Sexuality*, New Delhi: Penguin, 1989.

27 John Updike, 'Mother Tongues: Subduing the Language of the Colonizer', the *New Yorker*, 23 June 1997, pp. 156–61, at p. 156.

desire – is not necessarily to accept a just punishment but to believe that such a death is not a shame and a defeat. There are repeated indications in the novel that the choices of those who desire (and perhaps, die for it) are deliberate; the options have been weighed, and the transgressive experience valued above its possible penalty. The politics lie in the choices: 'If he touched her, he couldn't talk to her, if he loved her he couldn't leave, if he spoke he couldn't listen, if he fought he couldn't win' [Ch. 11, p. 217].[28]

28  In italics in the original.

# Anna Clarke, 'Language, Hybridity and Dialogism in *The God of Small Things*'

In an essay specially commissioned for this guide, Anna Clarke addresses the complexities of Roy's language use and explores two key approaches to *TGST*, based on the concept terms 'hybridity' and 'dialogism'. Hybridity, an idea which is most frequently associated with the theorist Homi Bhabha, has a formative place in postcolonial theory because it has been used to explain (and explore) the cultural intermixtures that result from the historical experience of colonialism. As Clarke points out, hybridity can also be seen as a subversive force because it undermines hierarchical power structures and blurs the boundaries of language and culture. Clarke carefully traces the contemporary postcolonial interest in hybridity back to the 1920s and 1930s in the work of the Russian critic Mikhail Bakhtin, whose study *The Dialogic Imagination* proposes a model of the modern novel form that is 'dialogic' (characterized by a constant play of different voices), as well as inherently hybrid in its incorporation of other earlier narrative genres.[1]

Drawing on these ideas and demonstrating how they can be applied in a close reading of *TGST*, Clarke comments on the variety of linguistic and narrative effects in Roy's fiction and shows how the authority to classify and define social, cultural and scientific boundaries intersects with similar rules about language, rules that Roy's child-protagonists consistently undermine. Thus, for Clarke, the linguistic playfulness and the lack of narrative certainty in Roy's novel can be read as a radical literary strategy that evades and challenges society's 'mono-logic' tendency to control narrative meaning, and structure our perception through forms of linguistic order.

---

1  Mikhail Bakhtin, *The Dialogic Imagination: Four Essays*, ed. Michael Holquist, trans. Caryl Emerson and Michael Holquist, Austin, Tex.: University of Texas Press, 1994.

## From Anna Clarke, 'Language, Hybridity and Dialogism in *The God of Small Things*'

> Pappachi had been an Imperial Entomologist at the Pusa Institute. After Independence, when the British left, his designation was changed from Imperial Entomologist to Joint Director, Entomology. The year he retired, he had risen to a rank equivalent to Director.
>
> His life's greatest setback was not having had the moth that *he* had discovered named after him.
>
> (Ch. 2, pp. 48–9)

In the narrative of *TGST*, and for the characters represented in the novel, language matters. As the passage quoted above from Chapter 2, 'Pappachi's Moth', illustrates, language does not simply matter because it indicates who we are in the world; it is also significant because of our ability to name and give meaning to things. Precise designations and titles denote identity and social standing. Thus the tragedy of Pappachi's life is the fact that the moth he discovered did not bear his name.[2] In this instance the enormity of 'tragedy' juxtaposed with the seeming insignificance of a small insect creates an ironic effect, which the narrator encourages the reader to note. However, this apparently simple passage, conveyed in deceptively effortless prose, offers an important figurative representation of complex issues regarding the ownership of language.

As I have already noted, what upsets Pappachi more than anything is that his discovery is not *named* after him. To pin down and immobilize a once lively, fluttering insect is like pinning down and deciding the shifting, mobile meaning of words, and in its references to Pappachi the text develops a metaphor in which an act of fixing, constraining and thus controlling the meaning and form of language is comparable to the task of an entomologist or lepidopterist who takes a living organism as ephemeral it would seem as a butterfly or a moth, 'mount[s] it, measure[s] it and [. . .] place[s] it in the sun for a few hours for the alcohol to evaporate' (Ch. 2, p. 49), thus transforming it into a lifeless, classified, named object of study. On these terms, to classify something by its only correct name is also to 'kill' it.

A strikingly similar critical differentiation between a mummified, inert, authoritative word and a living, dialogic word was developed in the 1930s by a Russian critic Mikhail Bakhtin, to whose ideas I will return later in this essay. Suffice it to say here that Pappachi's approach to language seems to indicate his approach to life: both are governed by an authoritarian impulse which admits no challenge or denial. The narrative description of his working life in immobilizing, mounting and naming delicate insects, is followed by an account of his attempt to immobilize and stifle the creativity and talents of his wife whom he stops from playing the violin. Throughout *TGST*, figures of authority and control are juxtaposed with those of movement and play.

---

2   Only from the press note reporting his death do we learn that Pappachi's name was Shri Benaan John Ipe (Ch. 2, p. 50).

This essay draws on concepts of hybridity and dialogism in a reading of the function of language in *TGST*. The passage with which I opened the discussion already hints at the importance of historical contexts of language use, here highlighting the presence of a colonial legacy in the novel. As Pappachi is an *Imperial* Entomologist, the practice of fixing meanings and living organisms is presented in the context of imperialism. Imperialism underpins practices of colonization,[3] and, like patriarchy, can be interpreted as a discourse, or a way of using language which reinscribes or indicates relationships of power. In its focus on discourse, postcolonial theory is particularly sensitive to issues of who has the power of speech in colonial and postcolonial contexts. In the world of the novel, it is, for instance, the indigenous elites which include family elders, members of the upper castes, police, and men who are represented as having the power of speech in the society to the extent that their words can decide the fate of Ammu, the Untouchable Velutha, or the children. Conversely, as the novel lays bare the relationships of power in society, it also adopts a strategy of deliberately foregrounding and allowing us to hear the voices of some of those marginalized, 'subaltern' figures.

In addition to Pappachi being a patriarchal figure, his social standing and position of power seem to derive at least in part from his associations with the imperialist British. Pappachi, we soon learn from his son, was 'an incurable British CCP, which was short for *chhi-chhi poach* and in Hindi meant shit wiper. Chacko said that the correct word for people like Pappachi was *Anglophile*' (Ch. 2, pp. 51–2). The description, which highlights the contrasts between the italicized Hindi colloquial epithet and the English, sanitized term of Latin and Greek origin, marks the existence of multiple linguistic legacies of colonialism in the novel. Clearly, though, the preoccupation with the authority of speech and deciding the meaning of language is not restricted to the colonial historical context. Following India's gaining of independence in 1947, the 'struggle for the sign'[4] has continued, in the language politics of the postcolonial state, as different social groups have jostled for supremacy and as regional governments have come into conflict with the federal administration.

However, the novel also suggests another, markedly different approach to language. The fixed method of rigid classification associated with Pappachi is contrasted with an uninhibited, playful and highly creative attitude adopted by Rahel and Estha. Roy's choice of child protagonists and focalizers (characters through whose eyes we perceive the world of the novel) is a highly effective strategy in representing this mode. The twins, like most children, play with language; they enjoy making up words and breaking rules of grammar, and they cherish the sound of words without even knowing their meaning. Critics, early reviewers and readers have responded strongly to the use of language in the novel and arguably, next to the fragmented, cyclical narrative structure of the novel, its linguistic idiom is the first thing we notice when we come to read the text. Roy's use of language strikes some readers as innovative, fresh and certainly memorable. This effect is achieved partly through the author's typographic arrangement of words on the page, which often resembles poetry rather than prose, and the

---

3   Edward Said, *Culture and Imperialism*, p. 8.
4   Valentin Voloshinov, *Marxism and the Philosophy of Language*, trans. Ladislav Matejka and I. R. Titunik, New York: Seminar Press, 1973, p. 23.

narrative voice which draws on a range of poetic devices. Let me illustrate this point with a passage from the opening sections of the novel:

> Edges, Borders, Boundaries, Brinks and Limits have appeared like a team of trolls on their separate horizons. Short creatures with long shadows, patrolling the Blurry End. Gentle half-moons have gathered under their eyes and they are as old as Ammu was when she died. Thirty-one.
> Not old.
> Not young.
> But a viable die-able age.
>
> [Ch. 1, p. 3]

The wealth of stylistic devices: unusual capitalization of words, similies, metaphors, personification, and imagery ('Edges ... like a team of trolls', 'Gentle half-moons'), the typography, internal rhyme (viable, die-able), repetition and the fragmentation of semantic unity and syntax so that single phrases or compounds are offered as complete grammatical structures (e.g., 'Not young.'), are all features of language which one would more often expect to encounter in a poem, rather than a passage of prose. Prose, obviously, does use many poetic devices, but it is their intensification and recurrence in the novel which is unusual.

The French poet Paul Valéry famously made an analogy of prose being like walking and poetry being like dancing.[5] You walk to get from A to B but dance for pleasure of movement. Indeed, the entire narrative structure of Roy's novel lacks the straightforward progression associated in this metaphor with the 'walking' from A to B of prose. Events are not narrated chronologically, in the order in which they occur. Instead, the memory of the past returns in a cyclical, circular manner, haunting the present. As we read, we gradually learn of events through the repetition of images, snippets of sensory associations (such as an image of a sky-blue Plymouth family car, or the taste of Estha's tomato sandwiches on the Madras Mail to Madras).[6] Part of the repetition which structures the novel is the recurrence of choric-like phrases, such as those of the last three lines of the previous quotation. The cyclical, imagistic structure of the narrative is consistent with the focalization of adult Rahel and Estha who return to the location of events from their childhood which have haunted them throughout their lives. If the use of language by the narrative voice seems 'poetic', it is also consistent with the use of child focalizers. Poetry, after all, seems the opposite of a scientific impulse to allocate and fix correct meanings and relies on semantic variation and linguistic ambiguity; in other words, like Estha and Rahel, it plays with language.

All the instances of the children's play with language diametrically oppose the attitude displayed by their grandfather. There is nothing solidified, final or fixed

---

5   Paul Valéry, 'Remarks on Poetry', in T. G. West (ed.), *Symbolism: An Anthology*, London: Methuen, 1980, pp. 50–2; first published as 'Propos sur la poésie', in *Oeuvres Complètes* ed. Hytier, Paris, 1957; reproduced in Dennis Walder (ed.), *Literature in the Modern World*, Oxford: Oxford University Press, 1990, pp. 138–42.
6   For further discussion of the workings of memory which structure the narrative, see Émilienne Baneth-Nouailhetas's chapter on 'The Structures of Memory', in *The God of Small Things: Arundhati Roy*, pp. 49–74. (Reproduced in Critical readings, **pp. 142–54**).

about the meanings and experience of words for Rahel and Estha. The twins frequently break the connections between signified (object or concept referenced) and signifier (the word used for it); terms associated with the work of the linguist Ferdinand de Saussure.[7] They enjoy the sound of the word in dissociation from its meaning; indeed, they use the sound as a building block for a development of a complex image, markedly divorced from the primary meaning of the signifier.

> The luggage would be in the boot.
> Rahel thought that *boot* was a lovely word. A much better word, at any rate, than *sturdy*. *Sturdy* was a terrible word. Like a dwarf's name. *Sturdy Koshy Oommen* – a pleasant, middle-class, God-fearing dwarf with low knees and a side parting.
>
> [Ch. 2, p. 46]

The narrative style ensures that we are certain we are privy to a child's experience of language here. An objective, external observation in the first sentence moves to Rahel's focalization in the second sentence, only to be replaced with the use of free indirect speech (a device which allows the narrative voice to take on an intonation, vocabulary and syntax of a character without differentiating the character's voice through quotation marks). The added visual effect of italics foregrounds the arbitrariness of the relationship between signified and signifier. 'Boot' and 'sturdy' are experienced independently of contemplating the objects or conditions which they denote in the world.

The twins also play with language by breaking semantic unity (Lay Ter, A Live, A Lert, A Wake), as well as forging and shifting grammatical categories and innovating words (Bar Nowl, for barn owl, and Stoppited, as a past tense of an imperative verb with its object 'stop it').

One of the twins' favourite language games is reading backwards.

> The red sign on the red and white arm said STOP in white.
> 'POTS,' Rahel said.
> A yellow hoarding said BE INDIAN, BUY INDIAN in red.
> 'NAIDNI YUB, NAIDNI EB,' Estha said.
>
> [Ch. 2, p. 58]

The example again signals the legacy of colonial, pre-independence India in the world of the novel. The 'Be Indian, Buy Indian' slogan which the children turn on its head, so to speak, recalls the *swadeshi* movement,[8] but is also a reference to the economic self-reliance of the Nehru era. This is hardly, however, to the forefront of Rahel and Estha's concern as they practise their trademark skill. For the children, political slogans, city signs, or an English 'baby book – *The Adventures of*

---

7    Ferdinand de Saussure, *Course in General Linguistics*, trans. Roy Harris, London: Duckworth, 1986.
8    *Swadeshi* (meaning the use of things 'belonging to one's own country') had its genesis in the anti-partition movement in Bengal in 1903 and was later adopted by Gandhi in his call for self-sufficiency, including economic self-sufficiency, as a strategy for opposing the British intervention in India.

*Susie Squirrel'* (Ch. 2, p. 59) – all represent a rich linguistic archive which they can draw on, freely play with and make their own.

In the meantime, in the world of the adults, games with language are hardly as innocent. The rules of language, which we obey every time we communicate, are part of the 'Edges, Borders, Boundaries, Brinks and Limits' which are yet to appear on the horizons of children's lives (Ch. 1, p. 3). Breaking the rules, however they manifest themselves, is a highly subversive and politicized act. It is also an act which invariably has social and political repercussions. The children's mother, Ammu, and her lover, Velutha, cross the boundaries of caste segregation and, as a result, lose their families and ultimately their lives. The twins break the rules and unsettle the certainties of the knowable order of grammar and, as a consequence, are declared by the upset Australian missionary Miss Mitten to have 'Satan in their eyes'. It would be impossible to miss one of the key stylistic devices used in the novel, irony, as the narrative immediately transposes the accusation in a typically Satanic gesture: *'nataS in their seye'*, only to follow it with the reporting of how, 'A few months later Miss Mitten was killed by a milk van in Hobart, across the road from a cricket oval. To the twins there was hidden justice in the fact that the milk van had been *reversing*' (Ch. 2, p. 60).

The subtleties of the novel's use of language can be further probed with the deployment of two important critical terms: hybridity and dialogics. The first of these concepts, hybridity, has been a central concern of postcolonial studies and derives from the word 'hybrid' which is defined in the *Oxford English Dictionary* as 'the offspring of two animals or plants of different species, or (less strictly) varieties: a half-breed, cross-breed, or mongrel'. The term has been used in reference to humans at least since 1630 and, as the postcolonial critic Robert Young notes, applied to 'the crossing of people of different races' as early as 1861.[9] Since in cultural and literary criticism ideas are often adopted from a range of disciplines, the term with originally biological connotations has been transposed into discussion about culture and language. Thus hybridity is now widely taken to refer to 'something or someone of mixed ancestry or derived from heterogeneous [i.e., of diverse, different origins] sources.'[10] To that end one could argue that there is nothing new about hybridity as a cultural phenomenon: surely languages and cultures have been traditionally made up of heterogeneous elements to the extent that it would be difficult to find a 'pure' example of linguistic or cultural homogeneity, or uniformity.[11]

Hybridity as a critical concept has had a privileged place in postcolonial studies. This is because contact and intermixture between different cultural groups have often taken place in the historical context of colonization. Since colonial relationships were relationships of power between what the colonizers saw as the privileged 'enlightened', 'civilized', 'rational' and 'advanced' colonizer and the

9  Robert J. C. Young, *Colonial Desire: Hybridity in Theory, Culture and Race*, London and New York: Routledge, 1995, p. 6.
10  Julian Wolfreys, Ruth Robbins and Kenneth Womack, *Key Concepts in Literary Theory*, Edinburgh: Edinburgh University Press, 2002, p. 43.
11  Let us think, for instance, about a range of words from the languages of India that are now part of the repertoire of English: anaconda, bangle, catamaran, cot, jungle, pyjamas, bungalow, Raj, yoga, loot, mango, panda, sugar, rogue, thug, veranda, to name but a few. See Nigel Hankin, *A Treasury of Indian Words in English*, New Delhi: Penguin Books India, 1998.

subaltern 'barbaric', 'superstitious', 'backward' colonized, hybridity in such contexts has often taken on a politicized dimension. For example, in the colonial discourse of early nineteenth-century British colonialism in India, the historian and politician Thomas Babington Macaulay advocated the introduction of English education in India for the creation of 'a class of persons, Indian in blood and colour, but English in taste, in opinions, in morals, and in intellect'.[12]

Thus, the object of such a colonial educational mission would clearly not be a homogenous, but a heterogeneous, hybrid entity: persons Indian in 'blood and colour' but English in tastes.[13] This controlled hybridization, however, would be far from value-free: elements of English literature and culture were to be introduced into India for the purposes of elevating and civilizing the natives. Their hybridity would set them apart from other Indians but would also ensure that they could never usurp the place of their 'pure' colonial masters. In *TGST*, Chacko, himself an Oxford graduate, explains to Rahel and Estha that they are a family of Anglophiles, a product of the legacy of such colonial endeavour. From Chacko's disillusioned perspective, cultural hybridity is seen as emphatically negative as it alienates the subject from both cultures, making closer identifications on which identity so strongly depends ultimately impossible: 'We belong nowhere. We sail unanchored on troubled seas. We may never be allowed ashore' (Ch. 2, p. 53).

Postcolonial theorists, while remaining aware of the dislocating effects of colonialism, have tended to view hybridity more positively than Chacko does. Homi Bhabha, in particular, famously privileges hybridity as the 'Third Space', an in-between or interstitial space between cultures that carries the burden of the meaning of culture. In his seminal collection of essays, *The Location of Culture*, Bhabha writes of:

> an *inter*national culture, based not on the exoticism of multiculturalism or the *diversity* of cultures, but on the inscription and articulation of culture's *hybridity*. To that end we should remember that it is the 'inter' – the cutting edge of translation and negotiation, the *in-between* space – that carries the burden of meaning in culture.[14]

To put it simply, the location of the meaning of culture is the contact zone between cultures: the space of culture's hybridity. There is a strong connection here between Bhabha's ideas and those of Ferdinand de Saussure, who argued that *meaning in language is created in the relationship between words*.

In insisting on the importance of cultural hybridity in the production of (relational) meaning, Bhabha focuses specifically on its subversive potential. Hybridity is seen as offering a space from which one can subvert and challenge the power structures of homogenous, unified discourses and hierarchies: 'The interstitial passage between fixed identifications opens up the possibility of a cultural

---

12  Thomas Babington Macaulay, 'Minute dated 2nd February 1835, Department of Public Instruction in Calcutta', in H. Woodrow (ed.), *Macaulay's Minutes on Education in India, Written in the years 1835, 1836 and 1837*, Calcutta: The Baptist Mission Press, 1862, p. 115.
13  The 1835 Minute has been famously taken up by the critic Homi Bhabha in his discussion of the subversive potential of colonial mimicry in the seminal essay 'Of Mimicry and Man', *The Location of Culture*, London: Routledge, 1988.
14  Bhabha, *The Location of Culture*, p. 38.

hybridity that entertains difference without an assumed or imposed hierarchy'.[15] To entertain difference is not to allow an imposition of an order which assumes that it is exclusively right, natural or privileged. Quite how dangerous such a stance of entertaining difference, abiding in a space of interstitial hybridity can be, is amply illustrated in Roy's novel.

We can gauge how unsettling hybridity is seen to be in the novel from the fact that all the central instances of hybridization, where characters try to breach the established hierarchies (of colonizer and colonized, touchable and untouchable, grammatical order and 'disorder') and 'entertain the difference' of hybridity are punished, criticized or controlled within the narrative. Ammu, who does not obey the rules of caste segregation, and defies patriarchal structures of society, is said to have an 'Unsafe Edge [. . .] An unmixable mix', as she lives 'in the penumbral shadows between two worlds, just beyond the grasp of their power' (Ch. 2, p. 44). The twins, as a prime example of biological hybridization, are castigated and ostracized by their great-aunt Baby Kochamma as 'Half-Hindu Hybrids whom no self-respecting Syrian Christian would ever marry' (Ch. 2, p. 45), while, as I have already mentioned, their playfulness with fixed systems of language provokes an accusation of 'Un-Godly' behaviour. The most violent and brutal social reaction, however, is reserved for Velutha who breaks the Hindu taboo of caste segregation.

Hybridity, then, or the state of 'entertaining difference', whether biological, cultural, linguistic or conceptual, is represented in the novel as something that engenders responses of fear, hatred, even violent retribution. The reason for those responses is the perception of hybridity as a threat, on the grounds of its capacity to challenge, subvert and oppose the prevalent structures of power. It is an important point to grasp that hybridity is not, though, *inherently* seditious. Children play with language not with a conscious, explicit intention to challenge a world order. Velutha and Ammu, even if they, as adults, are conscious of the repercussions of their act, enter into a love relationship in an expression of love and sexual desire for each other, not in simply some sort of joint manifesto against the religious rules of Hinduism. What makes hybridity dangerous is its social perception; that is, what the novel explores is the social functioning of hybridity, which includes its simultaneous perception as a threat and a subversive tool in relation to established hierarchies of language and culture.

There is, however, a much more positive perception of hybridity in the novel, manifesting itself in the novel's use of language. The Indian novel in English is itself a hybrid, the novel form 'arriving' in India with the British in the nineteenth century. Since Bankimchandra Chatterjee's pioneering *Rajmohan's Wife* (1864),[16] Indian novelists continue to write in English, which is now seen as one of many languages of India. *TGST* is obviously written in English but also uses Malayalam words and phrases, only some of which are translated for the benefit of non-Malayalam readers. Let us compare, for instance, 'In Malayalam Mol is Little Girl and Mon is Little Boy' with ' "*Aiyyo*, Rahel Mol!" Comrade K. N. M. Pillai said, recognizing her instantly, "*Orkunnilley*? Comrade Uncle?" "*Oower*," Rahel said' (Ch. 2, p. 60 and Ch. 5, p. 128). English-speaking readers are thus

15  Bhabha, *The Location of Culture*, p. 4.
16  Bankimchandra Chatterjee, *Rajmohan's Wife: A Novel*, Delhi: Ravi Dhayal, 1996. First published 1864.

forced to confront their ignorance, caricatured in the text in the figure of Miss Mitten who thinks that in Kerala people speak Keralese (Ch. 2, p. 60). Much of the text's linguistic and cultural hybridity – the presence of Malayalam and English, elements of Western high and popular culture, Hindu and local traditions – merges kaleidoscopically in the world of child focalizers. If the twins read *The Jungle Book* and quote from *Julius Caesar*, they are equally at home with the spectacle of the Hindu ritual recitation of the narrative of the *Mahabharata* in the local performance of *kathakali* dancers. The family's regular outings to see *The Sound of Music*, and Estha's impersonation of Elvis Presley coexist alongside the linguistic inscription of the local tradition in the many words in Malayalam pertaining to family relations (e.g., Ammu, Kochamma), social interactions, as in the quoted exchange between Comrade Pillai and Rahel, or everyday familiar items, such as food (e.g., *avalose oondas*).

This operation of somewhat undifferentiated hybridization of cultural and linguistic influences in the children's lives seems to represent a model suggestive of what Mikhail Bakhtin identified as unconscious 'organic' hybridity: 'a mixing of various "languages" co-existing within the boundaries of a single dialect, single national language', 'an encounter, within an arena of an utterance, between two different linguistic consciousnesses'.[17] This model of linguistic hybridity is one of amalgamation rather than contestation. To that end, the novel posits a productive and positive model of existence in between different cultures based on a notion of syncretism as a 'confluence of cultures whose inherently *contradictory forces are kept in a playful balance*',[18] just as they are in the world of the children.

This, however, is far from saying that *TGST* displays an ignorance of contestatory and politicized uses of language. Those come into play when English or Malayalam is used to assert social power or status. Characteristically, perhaps, the text does not miss such an opportunity to ridicule social pretensions, here embodied in the figure of a communist-party member, Comrade Pillai. As Pillai attempts to impress a visitor with his son Lenin's knowledge of Shakespeare and English classics, the initially reluctant child finally manages to gather his courage in a 'breathless, high-kneed gallop' accompanied by the shouting of clearly incomprehensible-to-him lines '*lend me yawYERS* [. . .] *I cometoberry Caesar, not to praise him*' (Ch. 14, pp. 274–5).

Bakhtin's understanding of hybridity as a way in which language, and even a single sentence, mixes different voices, takes me to my final point in considering the language in *TGST*: the concept of dialogism. In a series of essays, collected and translated into English in a volume *The Dialogic Imagination*, Bakhtin developed highly influential theories of language, and of the novel form in particular. For the critic, language, and especially the language of the novel, is inherently dialogic, that is, characterized by the constant play of different discourses, without necessarily an assumption of authorial control by any of them. Bakhtin associates this multiplicity of fictional voices (something he called heteroglossia), with the hybrid nature of the novel form: 'The novel permits the incorporation of

---

17  Mikhail Bakhtin, *The Dialogic Imagination: Four Essays*, (ed.) Michael Holquist, trans. Caryl Emerson and Michael Holquist, Austin, Tex.: University of Texas Press, 1981, pp. 358–9.
18  Monika Fludernik, *Hybridity and Postcolonialism: Twentieth-Century Indian Literature*, Freiburg: Stauffenburg Verlag, 1998, p. 19; my emphasis.

various genres, both artistic (inserted short stories, lyrical songs, poems, dramatic scenes, etc.) and extra-artistic (everyday, rhetorical, scholarly, religious genres and others). In principle, any genre could be included in the construction of the novel.'[19]

*TGST* indeed presents us with many different discourses, genres and types of speech: as we read the text we can encounter the voices of different characters and that of the narrator, the utterances of children and adults, English and Malayalam, songs, poems, dictionary definitions, recipes, political slogans, quotations from plays, snippets of newspaper cuttings, etc., each of them carrying a particular set of beliefs. All those voices, with their different value systems, are set against one another dialogically – 'one point of view opposed to another, one evaluation opposed to another, one accent opposed to another'.[20] Bakhtin calls this interaction 'dialogic tension' between different languages and belief systems. The juxtapositioning of different languages is thus a characteristic of the novel as it 'orchestrates all its themes, the totality of the world of objects and ideas depicted and expressed in it, by means of the social diversity of speech types and by the differing individual voices that flourish under such conditions'.[21]

Because, for Bakhtin, these different voices coexist in a state of constant play or productive tension, his writing gives the word the qualities of a living organism: 'The word, directed towards its object, *enters* a dialogically *agitated* and *tension-filled* environment of alien words, value-judgments and accents, *weaves in and out* of complex interrelationships, *merges* with some, *recoils* from others, *intersects* with yet a third group.'[22]

The mobility, restlessness, and liveliness of this word strongly resembles the creative way Rahel and Estha use language in the novel. There is no impulse to rigidly classify, fix and solidify meaning. Consequently, this way of thinking about language could not be further removed from Pappachi's approach, with which I have opened my discussion. Moreover, one could argue that the novel favours precisely this dialogic, mobile and innovative use of language.

Thus, *TGST* takes up John Berger's statement 'Never again will a single story be told as though it's the only one', using multiple focalizers and a complex narrative structure to bear out its relevance as a fitting epigraph for the novel. Instead of a single story told as though it's the only one, what we get in the novel are several stories affording insights into different perceptions of the same events. This insistence on multiple perspectives in the novel's structure, or perspectivalism, is closely related to Bakhtin's view that just as no single viewpoint can be adequate in the comprehension of an object, no single voice can create a multiplicity of voices, or polyphony. The creative orchestration of voices in the novel allows for an ending that defies the tragic conclusion to the narrative events. Holding out a promise that gestures towards the future, the novel's orchestration of voices lets the sound in Ammu's ' "*Naaley*." Tomorrow' reverberate in our ears (Ch. 21, p. 340).

19  Bakhtin, *The Dialogic Imagination*, pp. 320–1.
20  Bakhtin, *The Dialogic Imagination*, p. 314.
21  Bakhtin, *The Dialogic Imagination*, p. 263.
22  Bakhtin, *The Dialogic Imagination*, p. 276; my emphasis.

# Émilienne Baneth-Nouailhetas, 'The Structures of Memory'

The passages excerpted as follows, from Émilienne Baneth-Nouailhetas's critical study of *TGST*, are a key addition to this guide because they offer us a reading of Roy's novel which is not principally informed by 'political' critical strategies drawn from Marxist, feminist or postcolonial theory. Baneth-Nouailhetas is keenly aware of the contexts of *TGST*, and an initial chapter section in her book deals with the novel's colonial heritage and its postcolonial characteristics, but her analysis is more strongly informed by narratology – a type of literary study that explores forms of narration and narrative construction. In contrast to the other critical methods featured in this section, narratology does not concern itself with issues of ideology and cultural/gender difference, but instead looks for narrative components which are common to all stories. In this, it is influenced by a linguistics-based critical theory called structuralism, which deals with the grammar-like structures and codes that underlie cultural forms such as myths, fairy tales and novels.

The extract takes its title from a larger chapter section on 'the structures of memory', in which Baneth-Nouailhetas painstakingly traces the narrative patterning of *TGST* – which she envisages as cyclical rather linear – and reveals how the story is assembled around the process of recollection and 'rememoration'. She goes on to relate this memory-based (mnemonic) narrative structure to general themes of transgression in the novel and contrasts it with the more oppressively selective ordering of the past in official history. In doing so, she draws on the work of the narratologist critic Gérard Genette, who examines one of the most important French fictional explorations of time and memory, Marcel Proust's *À la recherche du temps perdu* (1913–27; translated as *Remembrance of Things Past*), in his well-known critical study *Narrative Discourse: An Essay in Method* (1980).[1] Because of her interest in narratology, Baneth-

---

1  Gérard Genette, *Narrative Discourse: An Essay in Method*, trans. Jane E. Lewin, New York: Cornell University Press, 1983.

Nouailhetas uses a specialized critical vocabulary that describes different levels and mechanisms of narrative very precisely. Some readers may find this off-putting, but it is worth persevering with the essay, especially when we keep in mind that all the technical terms relate to details of narrative structure (and are often paraphrased or explained as part of the discussion). In the opening section of the extract, the term 'focalizer' is used to differentiate characters who provide the narrative perspective (in this case mostly Estha and Rahel) from Roy's more 'omniscient' third-person narrative position. In structuralist criticism, 'paradigmatic' refers to a series of words that have a similar grammatical function, therefore denoting a common idea or mood. The term is connected in this extract with 'semantic', an expression that simply refers to the meanings generated by words. Lastly, Baneth-Nouailhetas's use of the narratological term 'diegesis', to describe the 'diegetic present' of *TGST*, differentiates the level of the story that encompasses Rahel's return to Ayemenen from the earlier, 'recollected' story line.

## From Émilienne Baneth-Nouailhetas, 'The Structures of Memory', in *The God of Small Things: Arundhati Roy* (Paris: Armand Colin/VUEF-CNED, 2002), pp. 49–60, 66–9

*The God of Small Things* develops around a highly complex and sophisticated narrative structure, based on the combination of digression and anachrony. Digressions, that cause the narrative to recurrently side-track the central story, are effected mainly through the recollections or musings of various characters, whose thoughts are followed by the narration as they lead away from, or back to, the principal events of the story. The narrative follows the threads picked up by the focalizers, and in so doing stretches back into the past events that have led to the shattering of the twins' family, before reverting to a fragmentary diegetic present. And in the narration of this 'present', the time of the twins' reunion in Ayemenem, hints are dropped, images sown, that become clear only when the story of, the past unravels. The narration spins a thread of significance across the two levels of the story, aiming at conveying a sense of doom-laden expectation: minute, almost negligible details, recur hauntingly as if to prod the reader into flipping back the pages of the book to understand the paradigmatic impact of semantic echoes. The narrative thus stretches in two directions, first towards the past and reminiscence, then towards the outcome of the story, constantly referred to through proleptic hints, that ultimately come together like the pieces of a puzzle.

Therefore memory is a relationship to the past, imitated in the novel's structure which reproduces the piecemeal, tentative process of rememoration, by relying on mnemonic triggers, objects, places, ('small' things); but it is also fragile and easily interrupted. The retrospective narration is not linear, but circular, constructing meaning by going over and over the same field, collecting different elements and points of view at each revolution; similarly, memory itself may focus on disconnected recollections, details which then coalesce into significance and shed a light not only on the past, but also on the interpretation of present and future.

Remembering is also an effort that is forced upon the reader through the system of repetitions and echoes that characterize the text, both on a semantic and on a diegetic level, as characters return to certain places that are inhabited by memories, or as they are involved in situations that cause them to recall circumstances of their past. These recollections are frequently inserted in the narrative *before* the related events in the story are actually evoked: thus the reader is frequently in a situation of apparent technical amnesia, as the focalizer embarks on the recollection of a fact that the narrative has not yet revealed. This provokes, in narratological terms, a combination of paralipsis (the withholding, by the narrator, of some key information), of prolepsis (the reference to some future event of the story by the omniscient narrator), and analepsis (a retrospective narration[2]).

Memory in the singular is tightly bound to the narrative structure as it is in itself a process of narration, which strives towards the organization of the past as meaning, on the one hand; but *memories* in the plural, which are isolated events that can be summoned up as separate episodes or images of the past, are active elements of the story, inasmuch as the characters self-consciously seek them, collect them or distort them. In this sense, memories are in fact one of the faces of forgetfulness, as they obliterate the past to replace it with the throbbing sense of what has been lost: thus Sophie Mol fades away to be replaced by the active presence of the 'Loss of Sophie Mol' [Ch. 1, p. 15], and is, in a way, killed twice in the process. Such memories are impositions, violent or pathetic, as destructive as they are creative, and can be associated with the artificiality of memorization, a mental exercise often derided in the novel . . .

The importance of memory, recollection and their corollaries (the sense of foreboding or of 'déjà vu', of expectation or of familiarity) is somehow hammered into the reader through the stylistic characteristics of this text: mainly, the unabashed, sometimes disconcerting use of repetition, semantic and structural, in a spiralling narration that brings the past to bear on the future, and the present to reconstruct the past. It is both the process of recollection that transforms a character's past into a narrative, and the process of investing all familiar places and objects with an identity-constructing recognition: the meaning of the present comes together through the action of remembering the past. The circular effect is enhanced in the narration by the recurrence of phrases, expressions or songs, apparently out of context sometimes, but which point out a web of connections that retrospectively confer significance on dispersed recollections. In opposition to the linearity of time, memory as a wheel relentlessly goes over the same places and collects even the smallest details in its spin of significance.

This process is one of the corollaries of the structuring oppositions between 'Big', associated with official history that abandons so much on the sides of its sanctioned narratives, and 'small', the realm of individual memory and imagination. Small words, snatches of songs or refrains, quasi-onomatopoeic, childish idioms ('dum dum' [Ch. 4, p. 98; Ch. 18, p. 310; Ch. 19, p. 319; Ch. 20, p. 325]) all appear as icons of the significant smallness that from one repetition to the next, spirals into a narrative or into symbols: repetition is also the mode through which the characters are constructed in the novel, each one being associated with a cluster of words or phrases, which the narrator summons to accompany their

---

2    [Baneth-Nouailhetas's note.] Cf. Gérard Genette, *Figures III*, Paris: Seuil, 1972.

presence, just as each character of Prokofiev's *Peter and the Wolf* is announced by an individual instrument and specific tune.

## *Echoes and recollections*

Whereas time seems to pull forward, erase traces, and work in favour of what the narrator qualifies as the 'Official Version' [Ch. 17, p. 303] of power and history, memory is on the contrary invested in the novel with the qualities of clarification and creativity. Through memory emerges the attention to detail that characterizes the children and of course, Velutha, the God of Small Things, but also the narrator. In a movement that imitates the heuristic aim of Rahel and Estha's wanderings around Ayemenem after their return there, the narration shuns the linearity of chronology in order to construct layers of recollections around places, objects, words, or minute details, that plunge into the core events of the focalizers' childhoods like the spokes of a same wheel. The narration seems to slide from one spoke to the next, until it has completed a spiral, and continues the process, each time repeating, and adding some elements, to the wheel of the story.

### The mnemonic narrative: wheels within wheels

Memory as a process of reappropriating the past begins in the novel with space: it is Estha's (re)return, followed by Rahel's, that is the trigger of the recollections to follow. At first, these recollections seem disconnected, isolated as plural memories, and it is precisely the hypnotic work of the narrative that brings them together and organizes them as a significant whole. Places are the material link of present with past and future, as they are invested with significance in the story through the characters' recollections of the past, and significance in the narrative through the narrator's prophetic hints. Descriptions of places and objects allow the narrative to bridge the different time zones covered by the story, from the twins' adulthood, to the moment of Sophie Mol's funeral, to the weeks that precede it and back. The moment of Rahel's return is clearly underscored as the beginning of a process of rememoration that will progressively lead the story to unravel:

> Heaven opened and the water hammered down, reviving the reluctant old well, greenmossing the pigless pigsty, carpet bombing still, teacoloured puddles the way memory bombs still, tea-coloured minds.
> [Ch. 1, p. 10]

In this simile memory is an active and aggressive protagonist, is endowed with quasi-divine abilities, that put it at the centre both of the narrative itself, and of the almost exclusively mnemonic action that characterizes the diegetic present. In a few pages at the opening of the novel, several places are evoked, and in the wake of their description, they bring forward not only scenes of the past, but memories that have already modified them in the characters' perception during those scenes. These topoi are clearly marked for their mnemonic function, as spaces where the passage of time is incarnated by change or decay, but also as settings in which the past can be conjured up.

The house, to begin with, is immediately described in terms of ageing and lasting: it bears both the traces of passing time, of decay, and those of a symbolic immobility, an incapacity perhaps to move beyond the fateful events that changed 'everything'. But at any rate none of this is perceptible without a reference to the past – the tenses and verbs chosen for this initial description are plainly linked to the adult Rahel's perception, and recollections:

> The walls, streaked with moss, had grown soft, and bulged a little with dampness that seeped up from the ground. [. . .] The house itself looked empty. The doors and windows were locked. The front verandah bare. Unfurnished. But the skyblue Plymouth with chrome tailfins was still parked outside, and inside, Baby Kochamma was still alive.
>
> [Ch. 1, p. 2]

The diegetic present (the present tense is used a few paragraphs later on the same page to mark Rahel's return, delineating a distinct time zone in the story, even though it does not recur subsequently) is from the start shackled to the traces of the past, and the entire narrative begins under the sign of recollection. The things that have changed – the walls, the general aspect of the house – are contrasted with those that have not – the position of the Plymouth, the presence of Baby Kochamma. It will later be confirmed that indeed Baby Kochamma is all but pickled in time, changeless, at least in mind if not body. From the house, the place where Estha and Rahel have lived united in their childhood, the narrative moves on to the evocation of shared experience, memories and dreams, in order to evoke the rare fusion/confusion of the twins' identities. Within a few lines, the unrolling spool of memory takes us back to the beginning of the twins' existence, and across episodes of their childhood, to their final separation: 'Now' coincides with 'here', the arrival in Ayemenem, the seminal event that enables an initial, geographical circle to be traced in the story, a circle that brings the twins back to their former identity, and provides a model for the spiralling structure of the narrative.

> Now, these years later, Rahel has a memory of waking up one night giggling at Estha's funny dream.
>
> She has other memories too that she has no right to have.
>
> She remembers, for instance (though she hadn't been there), what the Orangedrink Lemondrink Man did to Estha in Abhilash Talkies. She remembers the taste of the tomato sandwiches – Estha's sandwiches, that Estha ate – on the Madras Mail to Madras.
>
> And these are only the small things.
>
> [Ch. 1, pp. 2–3]

Memory is revealingly associated with a sense of transgression, as will be the actual relationship between the twins ('Memories too that she has no right to have'): indeed, memory itself is a transgression of limits and boundaries, those imposed by time and forgetfulness in the 'natural' course of things (cf. Paul Ricœur *La Mémoire, l'histoire, l'oubli*) The 'art of memory' is artful in the literal sense, i.e. artificial and contrived, as the narration seems to demonstrate purposefully. Every one of the character's recollections is a pretext to move forward into another section of the story that is about to be told: in this sense it is an intensely mnemonic process, that gains momentum and energy from every detail seen or remembered by the focalizer. This provokes an almost mimetic integration of 'small things' in the narrative, sown as proleptic hints of future action.

Such a hint is dropped in the depiction of the second important locus evoked, the Ayemenem church: from the diegetic present, Rahel's 'now', the narration spirals back in a few pages to Sophie Mol's funeral, and Rahel as a child pictures the worker who painted the church dome, imagining 'what would happen if the rope snapped. She imagined him dropping like a dark star out of the sky that he had made. Lying broken on the hot church floor, dark blood spilling from his skull like a secret' [Ch. 1, p. 6] Imagination intersects with memory as the image of Velutha's broken body provides the child with the picture of a dreamed-up fallen painter. The projection, at first clearly symbolic (the worker taking pains to perfect the *smallest* details in the *big* church, and literally falling from grace . . .) becomes a link between past and present, through the intercession of place; although at this stage the narrative does not elaborate on the violence of the child's thoughts, the striking imagery suggests a missing link that surfaces and makes sense when the very same detail, the paint streaks in the church 'sky', is evoked in connection with Velutha [Ch. 11, p. 215 and Ch. 21, p. 339].

The image of violence and death conjures up 'the smell. Sicksweet. Like old roses on a breeze' [Ch. 1, p. 6], through which other connections are made later, for instance with Estha's own bottled up memories: 'And a smell. Sicksweet. Like old roses on a breeze' [Ch. 1, p. 32]. These repetitions create a sense of foreboding and apprehension, and their multiplication acts as a signal attracting attention to the patterns that emerge. Furthermore, the recurrence of a sensation (here a smell), described in the exact same terms, but in varying spatial contexts or with different characters, produces the impression of circularity that was mentioned earlier [Ch. 1, p. 8; Ch. 18, p. 310]. If some recurrences can be attributed to the focalizers, their main function is poetic: the narrative is in a way bound to the memories at the core of the main characters' lives, and as a result, all new diegetic elements are organized in the orbit of the central, traumatic event, just as, in the characters' lives, every new experience has to find its place in relation to that traumatic event. Thence the reiterated remark, 'Things can change in one day' [Ch. 7, p. 164; Ch. 9, p. 192; and Ch. 10, p. 202 . . .]: one singular event can colour an entire life, past, present and future, and drastically modify one's perspective.

Smell in particular is an intensely mnemonic sense: it favours sharp but sometimes insignificant recollections, the isolated, inarticulate resurgence of elements of the past. The narrative is precisely the tool through which the inchoate mass of recollections come together to produce a whole, a relation to time, and memory-driven meaning. The recurring smell, therefore, is plainly pointed out to the reader both as a clue to a material, key event, and as a symbol through which wider paradigms are outlined.

They smelled its smell and they never forgot it.[3]
History's smell.
Like old roses on a breeze.
It would lurk for ever in ordinary things. In coat-hangers. Tomatoes.
In the tar on the roads. In certain colours. In the plates at a restaurant. In
the absence of words. And the emptiness in eyes.

[Ch. 2, p. 55]

The smell of death, although rather clearly identified as such through the previous occurrences, is first and foremost symbolic, for the specific circumstances surrounding it have not yet been evoked. The narration is truly circling around this nodal event, the eye of the storm, going through the same semantic fields and symbols, which organize themselves around the core of the story like so many zones of influence, and are recurrently scanned. The reflexivity between the text and one of its key concerns is one of its most powerful attractions, and most skilful contrivances: it is constructed along the lines of mnemonic processes, relying on echoes, associations and imagery to reiterate hints or repeat entire phrases. The 'Sourmetal Smell', first linked to a bus conductor [Ch. 1, p. 8], then to handcuffs [Ch. 1, p. 31], is once again evoked through Rahel's rush of reminiscence in the New York subway [Ch. 2, p. 72], in relation to Ammu's dream of love [Ch. 11, p. 217], and the description of the policemen's action [Ch. 18, p. 310]: this is when the reader finally realizes the web of connections that surround this specific smell, which functions as a mnemonic trigger for the reflector characters. The narration focuses first on the inarticulate sense of recollection and reverses the chronology of the story, so that the characters' olfactory memory in the story becomes a signal of doom, of foreboding, in the narrative.

At the same time, the reader's memory is appealed to for the identification of poetic recurrences, and teased with the absence of that diegetic information which is said to be so crucial to the focalizers' existence and perception. The smell repeatedly evoked, here allegorized as 'history's smell', becomes a structuring force, not only in terms of the novel's poetics, but in the world of the story itself. The characters' incapacity to forget, their haunting by the smell in question, the list of 'ordinary things', all contaminated by a sense that remains mysterious, all this enhances the vacuum surrounding the event in the narrative. By underscoring the memory of the event before approaching the event itself, the narration insists on the role of memory as a structuring process – in the characters' lives, where all their actions gravitate around the incapacity to forget, and in the text, where the aim is not so much to reveal a story as to measure the tensions between individual memory and social heritage, history.

They would grow up grappling with ways of living with what had happened.[4] They would try to tell themselves that in terms of geological time it was an insignificant event. Just a blink of the Earth Woman's eye. That

---

3   In *TGST* this line reads 'They smelled its smell and never forgot it' (Ch. 2, p. 55).
4   In *TGST* this line reads 'They would grow up grappling with ways of living with what happened' (Ch. 2, p. 55).

Worse Things had happened. That Worse Things kept happening. But they would find no comfort in the thought.

[Ch. 2, p. 55]

It is through the first reference to the 'History House' that the narrator comes to broach the subject of what the children do not yet know of their future: that it will be entirely centred on that (for the moment, elusive) single event, 'what happened'. In these few paragraphs, almost all the information delivered by the narrator concerning the twins is organized around the tyranny of memory: the smell, pervasive and invasive; and the identity-shaping struggle to 'live with' what happened. So that the impossibility to forget is put forward as the driving energy in the protagonists' lives and in the narration: retrospective as it is, it constantly reorganizes the events of the past along the spokes of memory. Thus events lose their linear significance to be reshuffled achronologically according to the recollections with which they can be associated; such is the case of the encounter with the woman on the train, in New York [Ch. 2, p. 72]. Or of the 'ghosts of impossible-to-forget toys' [Ch. 3, p. 91] floating around in Ammu's old room: places provoke visions, once again plainly the pictures of memory, the burdens of non-forgetfulness. The room, as the locus of Ammu's dreams, of shared intimacy with her children, of violence from Chacko, and finally of reunion for the twins, offers a typical occasion for explicit, geographical syllepsis[5] (or achronological, thematic, grouping of narrative segments): from pages 220 to 227, the narrative scans all these different moments of the story, binding them together through the unity of place:

The bedroom with blue curtains and yellow wasps that worried the windowpanes. The bedroom whose walls would soon learn their harrowing secrets.

[Ch. 11, p. 224]

The bedroom into which Ammu would first be locked and then lock herself. Whose door, Chacko, crazed by grief, four days after Sophie Mol's funeral, would batter down.

[Ch. 11, p. 225]

The same room in which [. . .] Ammu would pack Estha's little trunk and khaki holdall . . .

[Ch. 11, p. 226]

The room to which, years later, Rahel would return and watch a silent stranger bathe. And wash his clothes with crumbling bright soap.

[Ch. 11, p. 227]

---

5  [Baneth-Nouailhetas's note.] « . . . on pourrait nommer *syllepses* (le fait de prendre ensemble) *temporelles* ces groupements anachroniques commandés par telle ou telle parenté, spatiale, thématique ou autre», *Figures III* (121) ['. . . these anachronistic groupings ordered by a thematic, spatial or other type of analogy may be called temporal syllepses (as in "taking together")'].

The function of space as unifier and prompter of memory is explicitly emphasized in this highly dramatic, almost pathetic passage. The narration moves here, in the space of a few pages, from the evocation of a scene predating the tragedy, to prophetic hints of the events to follow, to the description of the twins' final reunion as adults – but still with the auxiliary 'would', indicating the future *within* the retrospective narration.

Examples of similar reshuffling of events abound, and far from being anarchic, they obey the rules of mnemonic association, although sometimes in antichronological order, as the narration is retrospective, but at the same time intensely proleptic … For instance, in the scene of Margaret and Sophie's arrival at the airport, Rahel is said to be 'hemmed in by humid hips (as she would be once again, at a funeral in a yellow church) and grim eagerness' [Ch. 6, p. 139]. The alliteration ([h]) further attracts the reader's attention to the *sotto voce*, parenthetical comment that allows the intrusion of the adult Rahel's voice, colouring the scene simultaneously in the tones of retrospection and prophecy.

The constant use of prolepsis as a narrational trigger is tinged here by the specificity of a largely retrospective narration: jumps in the time structure are both forward-looking and backward looking, depending on the diegetic time zone. This is what Genette terms proleptic analepsis[6]: the result of a narrative anchored in two time levels, and in which coexist a retrospective vision, and an announcement concerning the story to come. In this novel, most of the time, the 'proleptic', doom-laden pronouncements can be ascribed to the retrospective thoughts of the knowledgeable narrator or reflector character, Rahel. Examples of proleptic-analepsis abound, but here one example is particularly useful: the prophetic references to transgression, rules and punishments, which recur, fitting once again into a Genettian category, that of iterated prolepsis[7]. This type of repetition creates a mounting expectation on the one hand, but it also acts as a goad to memory, from the perspective of the retrospective narration, and it forwards the organization of the narrative as a process of reconstitution of the past, and of understanding:

> Looking back now, to Rahel it seemed as though this difficulty that their family had with classification ran much deeper than the jam-jelly question.

> Perhaps, Ammu, Estha and she were the worst transgressors. But it wasn't just them. It was the others too. They all broke the rules.
> [Ch. 1, pp. 30–1]

This digression is both a moment of rememoration, and a touchstone for the narration: the analytical grid, the result of the character's long reflection on the past, is offered here at the start of the novel as a key for the reader. Thus the

---

6    [Baneth-Nouailhetas's note.] Cf. *Figures III*, 119.
7    [Baneth-Nouailhetas's note.] *Figures III*: «Comme les analepses répétitives remplissent à l'égard du destinataire du récit une fonction de rappel, les prolepses répétitives jouent un rôle d'annonce [. . .]» (111); ['While recurring analepses act as reminders for the narratee, recurring prolepses fulfill the function of announcement [. . .]'].

remark is both analeptic and proleptic, both a reference to past events in terms of chronological time, and a projection in terms of narrational order. Similar announcements recur, reproducing the same structure that superimposes two opposite temporal perspectives: it is truly a spiralling, coiling movement, that constantly changes directions without reversing. 'They didn't know then that soon they would go in. That they would cross the river . . .' [Ch. 2, p. 55]: the narratorial warning given a few pages earlier makes the symbolic value of this prolepsis transparent – here the significance of the narrative's structure relies on the reader's competence, and memory. Then again, a narratorial digression over one of Baby Kochamma's sententious epigrams adds an extra-diegetic sense of foreboding to a family conflict:

'Some things come with their own punishments,' Baby Kochamma said. As though she was explaining a sum that Rahel couldn't understand.

Some things come with their own punishments. Like a bedroom with built-in cupboards. They would all learn more about punishments soon. That they came in different sizes. That some were so big they were like cupboards with built-in bedrooms. You could spend your whole life in them, wandering through dark shelving.

[Ch. 4, p. 115]

The immediate repetition of the phrase signals the narrator's intervention and ironic reappropriation of a terrorizing epigram, which in turn seems to be one of Rahel's memories when her voice emerges with the use of the pronoun 'You'. The paragraph inflates the phrase's prophetic significance by hinting at the tragedy and transgression that are to follow, and picturing its impact on the characters as a projected shadow that will invade their entire existence. The use of the typically psychoanalytical image of rooms in a house as symbols of mental architecture enhances the double effect: the phrase is both an announcement, and a memory, a key to the exploration of the past by the narration.

Pursuing this theme of transgression, another recollection in the diegetic present can be flipped round and transformed into an announcement in terms of the narrative order: one of 'Comrade' Pillai's customers 'remembered vaguely a whiff of scandal. He had forgotten the details, but remembered that it had involved sex and death. It had been in the papers' [Ch. 5, p. 129]. This recollection, although vague, foretells the central tragedy of the novel even though, in terms of the action's chronology, and of the moment in the story where this encounter with the adult Rahel takes place, it is simply an incursion in the past, an attempt at remembrance . . . By the time the story actually unfolds, the symbolic structure into which it falls has been made doubly clear by the (often simultaneous) effect of analeptic recall and commentary, and proleptic announcements.

Finally, the place that most plainly embodies the spatialisation of memory is the 'History House', turned into a hotel where dud Kathakali performances are given. As a counterpoint to this degradation, the temple performance witnessed by the twins is meant to stand for authenticity, 'truth', and as such it sends shock waves into time and space, binding the legendary story to their own. Semantic echoes between the description of the dance and the frame story abound, and they are explicitly made to intersect in an eruption of violence that the twins inevitably connect to their experience:

> There was madness there that morning. Under the rose bowl. It was no performance. Esthappen and Rahel recognized it. They had seen its work before. Another morning. Another stage. Another kind of frenzy (with millipedes on the soles of its shoes). The brutal extravagance of this matched by the savage economy of that.'
>
> [Ch. 12, p. 235]

Space, or the similarity of spaces, binds together the scene of the dance and the memory of the past violence helplessly witnessed by the children. The syllepsis is here based on the symbolic opposition – and therefore, kinship – between the modern 'History House' and the Temple as stages. One artificial and destructive to the legend's coherence, the other, authentic. The Kathakali scene's obvious symbolic relevance (it deals with family duties, treason, love . . .) is doubly highlighted by the memory it connects with for the focalizers, and by its opposite function as a forewarning in the narrative.

Interestingly, in the preceding paragraph, the legendary figure of Bhima is described as he 'hammers' at Dushasana's fallen body, with a violence compared to 'An ironsmith flattening a sheet of recalcitrant metal' [Ch. 12, p. 235]: this is both an echo and an announcement of the deathly scenes to come, associated with metallic smells. The point here is not to link the image with an individual memory, but more to tighten the web of reverberations and resonances in the text so that every expression is potentially oversaturated with multiple meanings.

[. . .]

## Selecting memories

Not only do the actors forward the narrative by adding the pieces of their memories or recollections to the story, but they also characterize themselves through what they recall and forget.

Indeed, memorizing and reciting are valued activities in the little world of Ayemenem. For some, the reasons for this are quite clear-cut, and have already been evoked: 'Comrade' Pillai's mastery of slogans evinces his ideological position; Baby Kochamma's insistence on teaching the twins canonical English texts or prayers, as the one they rehearse for Sophie Mol's ride to Ayemenem – with perfect pronunciation [Ch. 6, p. 154] – reveals a yearning for Englishness. In this instance, as in the case of Comrade Pillai's niece and son's recitations, the English text stands for institutional power and memorization for a subjection to this power. To a certain extent, Chacko shares the same attitude, although he characteristically does not recognize any of his own culture in the wooden, accented recitation of 'Lochinvar' performed for him [Ch. 14, p. 271].

Baby Kochamma's memory, beyond her recollections of 'disconnected snatches' [Ch. 1, p. 28] from soap-opera dialogues, defines her as static and resentful, her mind as closed up as the house she keeps in her old age [Ch. 1, p. 28]: 'In her mind she kept an organized, careful account of Things She'd done For People, and Things People Hadn't Done For Her' [Ch. 4, p. 98]. The (capitalized) contents of this account book, that holds only columns of debit (either what is owed to Baby Kochamma, or what has failed to be delivered ...), are the very essence of the character/type. But just as revealingly, in her case memory and imagination are locked together in her effort to fuel her only love fantasy over Father Mulligan. 'If anything, she possessed him in death in a way that she never had while he was alive. At least her memory of him was hers. Wholly hers. Savagely, fiercely, hers' [Ch. 17, p. 298]. This form of memory spells out the character's phagocytic possessiveness not only towards her alleged love, but towards reality itself; this is confirmed in the way the old woman spins out stories for the benefit of the police, and then of Chacko, bent as she is on her work of destruction. With an utter contempt for others and for reality, Baby Kochamma conflates memory and fantasy in order to devour or destroy whatever escapes her influence in reality: one can note the violence of her imaginary interventions on Father Mulligan's remembered body (she 'stripped' him of 'his ridiculous saffron robes', 'Her senses feasted, between changes, on that lean, concave, Christ-like body', 'She snatched away his begging-bowl' [Ch. 17, p. 298]). This passage is followed by a description of the old woman removing her false teeth, and the image of her dribbling mouth somehow evokes a parodic reflection of the blood-thirsty Hindu goddess Kali, who toys with men and tramples their bodies, and is often pictured with blood staining her savage teeth.

Conversely the twins, naturally at the centre of the narrative's mnemonic mechanisms as it is *their* memory that is being slowly reconstructed, are self-consciously careful, even as children, in their selection of things to remember. Thus a moment of complicity between their uncle and their mother is hoarded away on a rosary of family treasures: 'Moments like these, the twins treasured and threaded like precious beads on a (somewhat scanty) necklace' [Ch. 2, p. 62]. This points out the children's thirst for an 'ideal' family, for unity, in a clearly dysfunctional context, but also reasserts the centrality of all mnemonic processes: memory is both the key and the engine of the story, at the core of the twins' identity. It can divide the family, as in the case of the 'spit-bubbles' Ammu abhors, because ' "It brings back memories" ' [Ch. 2, p. 85] of a detested husband, the twins' father ... Whom they, perhaps, wish to remember by the same token, in a typical fantasy of unity and communion, embodied in a perfect group photograph [Ch. 2, p. 84].

An anecdote, a few pages later, confirms both the urge for unity, and the unceasing work of memory as a fully–fledged actor, when in the cinema toilets, in front of her mother, Rahel watches her grand-aunt urinate: 'Rahel liked all this. Holding the handbag. Everyone pissing in front of everyone. Like friends. She knew nothing then, of how precious a feeling this was. *Like friends*. They would never be together like this again. Ammu, Baby Kochamma and she' [Ch. 4, p. 95] The narrator (whose voice is here indistinguishable from the adult Rahel's) seems to be underscoring the 'precious' moment in the ignorant child's stead, and threading it on the necklace mentioned earlier. But in fact the memory of the moment has been preserved, by Rahel herself, albeit without an immediate awareness of its preciousness. 'Years later during a history lesson being read out in school – *The Emperor Babur had a wheatish complexion and pillar-like thighs* – this scene would flash before her. Baby Kochamma balanced like a big bird over a public pot' [Ch. 4, p. 95]. But the recollection of the scene does not necessarily carry the memory of the feeling, impossible to bring back after the events that follow have cast their own dye over all thoughts of Baby Kochamma. In other words, the narration suggests that the memory of an emotion has to be purposefully selected and concentrated upon for it to survive: it is not the event itself, but the narrative of it, that colours its memory.

Another instance of this deliberate selection is described with the potency of Proustian, childish recollection. If the mechanisms of memory, and the dependence on smell and music, seem familiar enough, the self-awareness with which the child operates her selection is more specific and linked to her consciousness of the present as memory in construction:

> The Torch Man opened the heavy Princess Circle door into the fan-whirring, peanut-crunching darkness. It smelled of breathing people and hairoil. And old carpets. A magical, *Sound of Music* smell that Rahel remembered and treasured. Smells, like music, hold memories. She breathed deep, and bottled it up for posterity.
>
> [Ch. 4, pp. 98–9]

The narrator steps in to spell out the importance of smells as mnemonic vehicles, in a generalizing statement ('Smells, like music . . .') that self-reflexively hints at the significance of all preceding olfactory details. But the impact of the phrase in the present-tense goes beyond the didactic or metatextual: it connects past and present in a palpable way, using the mnemonic device it mentions. The gesture of memorizing is associated with the anticipation of the memory itself, both actions overlapping through the character's awareness. The child's sense of pleasure is doubled up, in a way, by the knowledge that what she saves from oblivion acquires added value. And indeed, every time the children's self-conscious 'memorizing' is detailed, the moments they save are qualified as valuables, as precious treasures.

It is this sense of added value that emerges in the narrational choices, in the anaphoric enhancement of certain details over others, and the ideological, aesthetic enhancement of 'smallness' over 'bigness', that counters the hegemonic discourse of what the narrator terms 'history'.

**Alex Tickell,** 'The Epic Side of Truth: "Storytelling and Performance in *The God of Small Things*" '

This essay revisits and develops some critical ideas from my 2003 essay '*The God of Small Things*: Arundhati Roy's Postcolonial Cosmopolitanism', published in the *Journal of Commonweath Literature*, and has two broad objectives. The first of these is a response to Graham Huggan's reading of the self-reflexive cosmo-politanism of Roy's *TGST* in his book *The Postcolonial Exotic: Marketing the Margins* (which concerns itself with the same politics of cultural consumption that Mongia's essay addresses).[1] While accepting many of Huggan's claims about marketing and the commercial operation of the exotic in *TGST* (see Critical history, **p. 76**), my paper asks whether Roy dramatizes the predicament of her marketability in the novel itself. I explore this possibility in the literal drama of the *kathakali* performances in *TGST*, which are at once integral to the local narrative culture of Kerala and part of a staged show of cultural authen-ticity put on for visiting tourists. In the divergent audiences of the *kathakali* I find a reflection of Roy's own situation as a 'cosmopolitan' Indian novelist who is keenly aware of the cultural politics of her own writing, and anticipates but also undermines the assumptions of her international readership.

As part of this discussion, I develop my earlier analysis of Roy's ambivalent or self-conscious cosmopolitanism by looking closely at the use of pre-modern narrative forms such as the epic in *TGST*. Roy's references to these ancient narrative traditions are wide ranging but centre particularly on the great Hindu religious epics the *Ramayana* and *Mahabharata*, which Roy describes as the 'Great Stories', and which form the basis of the narratives enacted in the *kathakali*. Drawing on Walter Benjamin's essay 'The Storyteller', my essay out-lines Roy's fascination with pre-novelistic 'storytelling' modes and argues that through these older narrative forms she rethinks both the role of the author and the political potential of the Indian English novel.

1    Graham Huggan, *The Postcolonial Exotic: Marketing the Margins*, London: Routledge, 2001.

## From Alex Tickell, 'The Epic Side of Truth: "Storytelling and Performance in *The God of Small Things*"'

In his essay on the nineteenth-century Russian writer Nikolai Leskov, Walter Benjamin recalls the traditional storyteller, a figure who, although once familiar in Western culture, is now 'becoming remote to us'. For Benjamin, the decline of the storyteller and the narratives associated with him [*sic*] – the legend, the fairy tale and the folk epic – is very clearly a consequence of the rise of the novel. Developed in the eighteenth century to meet the literary tastes of a new middle class and produced using new print technologies, the novel not only superseded earlier genres but also irrevocably altered the social circumstances of narrative transmission, because it isolated the author from the immediate community of an audience. Benjamin's argument has some bearing on my discussion of *The God of Small Things*, and is therefore worth quoting at length:

> The storyteller takes what he tells from experience – his own or that reported by others. And he in turn makes it the experience of those who are listening to his tale. The novelist has isolated himself. The birthplace of the novel is the solitary individual, who is no longer able to express himself by giving examples of his most important concerns, is himself uncounselled and cannot counsel others. To write a novel means to carry the incommensurable to extremes in the representation of human life. In the midst of life's fullness, and through the representation of this fullness, the novel gives evidence of the profound perplexity of the living.[2]

Benjamin's eloquent description goes beyond a simple assertion of a historical break between oral narrative forms and the novel, however. His point is that certain novelists such as Leskov retain a sense of the 'craftsmanship' of storytelling within the new medium of the novel, thus maintaining a link with older conventions of narrative. This understanding of the novel's uneasy relationship with its oral predecessors is echoed by Mikhail Bakhtin in his description of the novel as a modern literary genre par excellence that continually returns to draw from, and recycle, its pre-modern past.[3]

A striking parallel to the literary-historical awareness I have traced in Benjamin's essay occurs in *TGST*, when Roy's narrator describes, at some length, the 'Great Stories' of the *Mahabharata*, which are performed as part of the ritualized *kathakali* dance-drama of Kerala. It is necessary, nevertheless, to note the differences between Roy's understanding of storytelling and Benjamin's as we make this comparison. In Roy's novel, the 'Great Stories' have a closer relationship to organized faith (Hinduism) than the stories that Benjamin describes. Today the great Hindu epic of the *Mahabharata* and its later companion narrative, the

---

2   Walter Benjamin, 'The Storyteller: Reflections on the Work of Nikolai Leskov', in *Illuminations*, trans. Harry Zohn, London: Fontana, 1992, pp. 83–107.
3   Mikhail M. Bakhtin, *The Dialogic Imagination*, (ed.) Michael Holquist, trans. Caryl Emerson and Michael Holquist, Austin, Tex.: University of Texas Press, 1981, p. 4. From this perspective, the modern novel can only have a 'negative' parasitic identity, as it constantly remakes itself through and supersedes earlier literary forms, such as the epic (Terry Eagleton, *The English Novel*, Oxford: Blackwell, 2005, p. 6).

*Ramayana* (a shorter, and more self-consciously poetic epic than its predecessor but also a source for *kathakali*) both have a fundamental place in the official religious traditions of Hinduism, and in the iconography of Hindu nationalism. At the same time, these pre-modern narratives also still exist as part of India's local oral-storytelling cultures, where they combine, seamlessly, with tales of local gods and saints, fables, devotional myths and regional folk-narrative traditions. Thus, unlike the modern Western novelist whom Benjamin describes as distanced and 'remote from' earlier storytelling modes, Roy can look to the *Mahabharata* as still adumbrating, in however problematic a manner, a type of narrative tradition.

However, for both Benjamin and Roy, the social and cultural effects of these pre-modern 'storyteller' forms are very much the same. The 'Great Stories', we are told, are 'the ones you have heard and want to hear again. [. . .] They are as familiar as the house you live in. Or the smell of your lover's skin. You know how they end, yet you listen as though you don't' (Ch. 12, p. 229). Elaborating on the history of storytelling, Benjamin remarks that the novel is born out of the 'womb of the epic',[4] and in *TGST*, with its sharp, disarming presentation of inter-generational relationships, the metaphor is particularly apt. Indeed, in her fiction Roy goes beyond a simple relationship of stylistic inheritance or remaking and maintains the oral past of the novel as an enclosed epic sub-drama (the epic as the ancestral past of the novel), in the form of two complete *kathakali* performances – based on episodes from the first two books of the *Mahabharata* and redolent of 'mystery and magic' – in the 'Kochu Thomban' chapter (Ch. 12).

Dating from the fifth century BCE, the *Mahabharata* is defined in Sanskrit as *itihasa*, a term that roughly translates as 'history', while 'making no distinction between what many [. . .] modern readers would regard as "myth" or "legend" '.[5] Thus, as we outline the form of the 'Great Stories' and describe them in English as 'epics', or 'extended religious epics', we should remember that in Hindu culture, historically, the boundary between genres such as epic, legend and myth is rather more porous. In her excellent historical account of the development of the *Ramayana*, Romila Thapar points out that because of the many interpolations and changes in the millennium after they were first recorded, its narratives 'do not belong to a specific period [but] are part of an ongoing tradition', just as 'the epic itself is made to change its function over time when it is converted from bardic to religious literature'.[6] Thapar thus sees the early *Ramayana* as a 'floating' collection of ballads, folk tales and myths, 'threaded together by a bardic poet'[7] that is only later authorized as a sacred religious text. This 'composite' growth and a gradual solidification into religious orthodoxy (and into a more coherent epic

---

4   Benjamin, 'The Storyteller', p. 97.
5   *The Sauptikaparvan of the Mahabharata: The Massacre at Night*, trans. and intro. by W. J. Johnson, Oxford: Oxford University Press, 1998, p. x. Myth is notoriously difficult to define, but can be understood very roughly as a sacred, community-based story that deals with the activities of gods, spirits, imaginary creatures or supernatural events. While myths can be relatively short oral accounts of creation or sacred phenomena, the epic, on the other hand, usually describes a longer story or narrative poem that deals with the legendary exploits of a (super)human hero, often descended from, or guided by, the gods.
6   Romila Thapar, 'A Historical Perspective on the Story of Rama', in Sarvepalli Gopal (ed.), *Anatomy of a Confrontation: Ayodhya and the Rise of Communal Politics in India*, London: Zed, 1990, p. 143.
7   Thapar, 'A Historical Perspective on the Story of Rama', p. 143.

form) is also a feature of the *Mahabharata*, which now enshrines some of the central tenets of Hindu *dharma* (duty) in one of its books, the *Bhagavad Gita*. Keeping these histories in mind, it is important to realize that Roy's definition of the 'Great Stories' actually operates as an umbrella term for various composite or 'threaded' forms of epic and mythical narrative.

This sense of generic fluidity, and an easy exchange between epic and mythic narrative forms is echoed in *TGST* in the juxapositoning of the 'Great [composite epic] Stories' with various godlike figures who generate an informal mythology or mythological pantheon elsewhere in the text: Velutha who is a representative 'god of small things' of the novel, the 'Earth-woman' whom Chacko uses to describe the age of the world, and the jealous river goddess of the Meenachil (discussed in the conclusion of this paper), to whom Sophie Mol is inadvertently sacrificed. In each case, interesting reflections and resonances are set up between the 'incommensurable', highly individualistic and psychologically perplexing *novel* form of *TGST* and the magical, communal and collective storytelling traditions that continually (and almost supernaturally) overshadow it.

Throughout much of the history of the European 'orientalist' scholarly engagement with India, the antiquity of Hinduism's ancient narrative culture operated as the self-justifying negative image of the rationality and progressivism of Western culture.[8] Indeed, the fact that forms of non-European epic such as the *Mahabharata* seemed to evoke both the 'past' and the 'opposite' of Western modernity partly explains the modernist fascination with them. However, this very generalized understanding of European modernism's interest in pre-modern narrative forms is inadequate for our purposes in this essay. This is because it does not register the differences and specificities of the global experience of modernity – amongst them the *contemporary* aesthetic contributions of non-European 'modernist' writers; the unique circumstances surrounding the rise of the novel in India and its ongoing relationship to oral storytelling forms such as the epic and myth. The author and critic Amit Chaudhuri underlines the particularity of an 'Indian' experience of modernity when he emphasizes how, in a relatively short space of time during the nationalist movements of the 1920s and 1930s, Indian political activists introduced Enlightenment concepts of individual choice and democracy to rural communities that believed in the religious and 'the supernatural'. In Chaudhuri's view, this led to a pluralism in twentieth-century Indian literary culture that was not exactly a 'tolerance of different opinions' but rather a 'recognition of the unthinkable, the absurd, and up to a limit, intolerable'.[9]

Possibly the most important difference between European and Indian literary responses to modernity was the growing recognition, amongst Indian writers, of the political significance of their own 'Great Stories'. For colonized peoples, pre-modern narrative genres such as epic and myth were also, crucially, pre-colonial and were therefore vital markers of identity, even though they were associated, problematically, with primitivism in Western thought. While the

---

8    See Nigel Leask, *Curiosity and the Aesthetics of Travel Writing, 1770–1840*, Oxford: Oxford University Press, 2002.
9    Amit Chaudhuri, 'Travels in the Subculture of Modernity', *Times Literary Supplement*, 5 September 2003, p. 13.

modernist interest in India's past in works such as T.S. Eliot's *The Waste Land* was a symptom of a crisis in European (and therefore colonial) identity, for the colonized it represented a positive cultural resource and a way of celebrating and promoting a non-Western sense of self. Dipesh Chakrabarty recognizes the importance of this strategy as a form of cultural resistance when he notes that 'colonial Indian history is replete with instances where Indians arrogated subject-hood to themselves precisely by mobilizing, within the context of "modern" institutions and sometimes on behalf of the modernizing project of nationalism, devices of collective memory [such as the *Ramayana* and the *Mahabharata*] that were antihistorical and antimodern'.[10] Roy's literary transaction with the 'Great Stories' of the *Mahabharata* in *TGST* is thus foreshadowed in some of the earliest nationalist Indian English novels of the 1930s and 1940s, which sought to recre-ate the digressive, spiralling quality of the folktale and ritualized, devotional epic as a way of 'naturalizing' the novel form.[11]

More recently, variations on this hyphenated 'magically' or mythically natural-ized mode have become a feature of what critics such as Tim Brennan have termed the 'cosmopolitan' postcolonial novel.[12] This highly successful international genre, argues Brennan, comprises amongst other things 'an irreverence towards national politics and literatures of national liberation, forms of trans-culturation and dialogic abundance, and an often magic realist combination of epic scope and personal, impressionistic memory'. Brennan goes on to argue that, with the help of cultural priming in Western publishing and academia, literary cosmopolitan-ism (exemplified in the work of writers such as Salman Rushdie) is nothing less than the 'interlocutor' for 'what [now] enters metropolitan literature as "third world literature" ',[13] a development which, in his opinion, encourages a falsely inclusive vision of contemporary global power relations. Brennan's concerns about the 'cosmopolitan' postcolonial novel are echoed by the writer and journal-ist, Pankaj Mishra, who argues that some contemporary Indian novelists (pre-sumably a category from which, as her agent, he exempts Roy) actually exploit their international audience by portraying a 'slickly exilic version of India' which is 'suffused with nostalgia, interwoven with myth, and often weighed down with a kind of intellectual simplicity foreign readers are rarely equipped to notice'.[14]

A more carefully theorized account of literary cosmopolitanism that builds on Brennan's ideas is developed in Graham Huggan's work *The Postcolonial Exotic: Marketing the Margins*, in which he agrees that 'links clearly exist between post-coloniality as a global regime of value and the cosmopolitan alterity industry'.[15] For Huggan, the most distinctive characteristic of cosmopolitan authors such as Rushdie and Roy is the skill with which they manipulate the expectations and 'commercially viable' literary codes of the cosmopolitan alterity industry. This is

10  Dipesh Chakrabarty, 'Postcoloniality and the Artifice of History', in Bill Ashcroft, Gareth Griffiths and Helen Tiffin (eds), *The Postcolonial Studies Reader*, London: Routledge, 1995, p. 383.
11  See Raja Rao's 'foreword' to *Kanthapura*, 2nd edn, New Delhi: Oxford University Press, 1993.
12  Timothy Brennan, *At Home in the World: Cosmopolitanism Now*, Cambridge, Mass.: Harvard University Press, 1997.
13  Brennan, *At Home in the World*, p. 37.
14  Quoted in William Dalrymple, 'The Lost Sub-Continent', *The Guardian*, 13 August 2005, p. 5.
15  Huggan, *The Postcolonial Exotic*, p. 12.

marked in novels such as *TGST* by an ironic display of 'lushly romantic images' and 'transferred Conradian primitivist myths', all of which call attention to the 'continuing presence of an imperial imaginary lurking behind Indian Literature in English'.[16] In Huggan's view, postcolonial authors such as Roy are thus forced to negotiate a double bind, balancing an awareness of their work as a cultural commodity against the counter-hegemonic imperatives of their politics. 'They know that their writing, ostensibly oppositional, is vulnerable to recuperation [. . .] they know that their work might still be used as a means of reconfirming an exoticizing imperial gaze. They are aware of all this, and they draw their readers into that awareness in their writing'.[17]

I have argued elsewhere that certain features of Roy's novel, amongst them forms of stylistic incongruity and troubling meta-fictional reflectors (like the *kathakali* discussed in this essay) complicate readings such as Huggan's, which analyse *TGST* solely in terms of its self-referential cosmopolitanism.[18] It seems to me that while Huggan's insightful reading certainly reveals connections between 'the perceptual mechanisms of the exotic and the metropolitan marketing of Indian literatures in English in the West',[19] it also risks an inadvertent ethnocentrism in which the values of the former colonial centre, although reversed through irony, remain the critical coordinates that guide readings of postcolonial texts. Approaches like this may also fail to take sufficient account of Roy's resistance to the postcolonial 'alterity industry', and the strategies she employs in making her text partially unreadable, 'provincializing', in Dipesh Chakrabarty's phrase, her international audience. What I want to suggest in the rest of this essay is that Roy's presentation of the performed stories from the *Mahabharata* in *TGST* provides an especially interesting site across which these cultural tensions are played out. The political fluidity of the 'Great Stories' (with their tendency to reinforce an 'imperial imaginary' at the same time as they evoke forms of cultural authenticity) means that Roy has to use them, within the structure of her own novel, in particularly careful and ingenious ways. And in doing so, she presents us with some revealing insights into her own literary politics.

In contrast to a number of other Indian English authors who have interwoven Hindu epic narratives into the texture of the contemporary novel, Roy does not merge the former into the latter, even though there are numerous echoes in *TGST* between the various narrative modes. Nor does she indulge in the more fantastic, extended myth-based manipulations of reality that some forms of magic realism entail. Instead, episodes from the *Mahabharata* are bracketed and sealed off from the main plot in the 'Kochu Thomban' chapter (Ch. 12), where they are related as part of a *kathakali* performance watched by the adult twins. This presentation of the 'Great Stories' of the *Mahabharata* as a more or less unified dramatic sub-performance in the novel has important implications for our understanding of the cultural politics of Roy's writing, and if, as Huggan argues, the novel ironically

---

16 Huggan, *The Postcolonial Exotic*, p. 77.
17 Huggan, *The Postcolonial Exotic*, p. 81.
18 Tickell, '*The God of Small Things:* Arundhati Roy's Postcolonial Cosmopolitanism', pp. 73–89.
19 Huggan, *The Postcolonial Exotic*, p. 11.

'dramatizes' the 'material circumstances of its own consumption', the performance of the 'Great Stories' at its heart seems to rehearse the predicament of Roy's
postcolonial cosmopolitanism in rather more searching ways.

Initially, the 'storyteller' form of the *Mahabharata*, brought alive in *kathakali*
dance-drama, seems to present us with a narrative economy that operates in a
broadly thematic mode: Kunti's abandonment of her son Karna (who is cast
adrift in a river because of his illegitimacy) and the vengeful killing of Dushasana
by Bhima both echo Estha's 'return' to his father and Velutha's violent death.
However, Roy makes sure that the textual significance of the *kathakali* watched
by the adult twins in a local temple is also registered at the level of the frame
narrative. In a brief aside, the reader is told 'It was no performance. Esthappen
and Rahel recognized it. They had seen its work before. Another morning.
Another stage [. . .] The brutal extravagance of this matched by the savage economy of that' (Ch. 12, p. 235). We also soon realize that the traditional night-time
performance at the temple, witnessed only by Estha and Rahel, is an adjunct to
more public but less culturally affirming poolside performances which the
*kathakali* men are forced to enact, through economic necessity, at the local hotel
in front of the 'mock[ing . . .] lolling nakedness' of foreign tourists (Ch. 12,
p. 231).

It becomes apparent at this point that the cultural politics of the *kathakali*
performance continues and develops an earlier, highly ironic reference to Kerala's
regional dance-drama made during Ammu's and Chacko's argument over the
relevance of the *kathakali* dancer as a logo for Mammachi's pickle business:
'Ammu said that the kathakali dancer was a Red Herring and had nothing to do
with anything. Chacko said that it gave the products a Regional Flavour and
would stand them in good stead when they entered the Overseas Market' (Ch. 2,
p. 47). The trope is repeated in the souvenir papier-mâché *kathakali* masks displayed at Cochin airport (Ch. 6, p. 137) and, with each instance of *kathakali*
commercialism, Roy draws our attention to the way elements of epic narrative
can be overdetermined as signs of cultural authenticity. In Huggan's reading, a
very similar predicament faces the postcolonial author: 'The globalization of
commodity culture has confronted postcolonial writers/thinkers with the
irresolvable struggle between competing regimes of value. This struggle [. . .]
plays itself out over the value of *cultural difference*.'[20] More than her cosmopolitan literary predecessors, however, Roy builds this internal 'irresolvable'
struggle into her narrative so that the *kathakali* performance itself operates as a
commentary on the politics of cultural commodification.

Like the internationally successful, 'cosmopolitan' Indian-English novel, the
*kathakali* in *TGST* is caught between two culturally distinct constituencies: a
reduced indigenous audience at the temple and a more lucrative foreign tourist
audience at the Heart of Darkness hotel. As I have already indicated, the latter
performances are really little more than acts of staged authenticity: 'six-hour
classics [. . .] shrunk to twenty-minute cameos' (Ch. 5, p. 127) which cater for
'imported attention spans' (Ch. 12, p. 231), and consequently the night-long
drama that Estha and Rahel witness in the deserted grounds of a local temple

---

20  Huggan, *The Postcolonial Exotic*, p.13.

becomes a spiritual compensation, and a way for the actors to 'jettison their humiliation' at their tourist performances.

> On their way back from the Heart of Darkness, [the *kathakali* troupe] stopped at the temple to ask pardon of their gods. To apologize for corrupting their stories. For encashing their identities. Misappropriating their lives.
> On these occasions, a human audience was welcome, but entirely incidental.
>
> [Ch. 12, p. 229]

In the dilemma of its divergent audiences, Roy uses the *kathakali* to throw into relief the fact of her own intrinsically marketable position within 'contending regimes of value'.[21] And although not a direct repudiation of the exoticizing tendencies of cosmopolitanism, at the very least this striking, performed sub-narrative indicates Roy's awareness of the involuntary, assimilative demand which global capital makes in its encounter with local postcolonial cultures.

However, it is not just the split local/global audience of the *kathakali* dance-drama that reveals, and seems to comment on, the cultural politics of a postcolonial 'alterity' industry. In their structure and narrative transmission, the 'Great Stories' which are community based and in which 'you know who lives, who dies, who finds love, who doesn't. And yet you want to know again' (Ch. 12, p. 229) constantly remind the (potentially non-Indian) reader of his/her tourist-like unfamiliarity with, and potentially 'exoticizing' enjoyment of, this colourful sub-drama. Crucially, they also beg further questions of Roy's position as a postcolonial novelist, whose role, as an isolated but potentially wealthier cultural mediator, brings her into uneasy kinship with the *kathakali* performers in her novel. These issues are implicit in Roy's allusion to the 'craftsmanship' of *kathakali* actors, who have been trained in the symbolic moves of the drama from childhood. And yet again, Benjamin's essay on the storyteller provides an apt critical framework. For Benjamin, storytelling is 'an artisan form of communication', and rather than 'conveying the pure essence of the thing, like information or a report' it 'sinks the thing into the life of the storyteller, in order to bring it out of him again'. In other words, the narrative is moulded by the narrator's experiences, allowing 'traces of the storyteller [to] cling to the story the way the handprints of the potter cling to the clay vessel'.[22] A strikingly similar image of mutual shaping occurs in Roy's description of the *kathakali* actors, who surrender even more irrevocably (and non-verbally) to the stories they 'inhabit', and whose bodies have been 'planed and pared down, harnessed wholly to the task of story-telling'. In a subtle reversal of Benjamin's metaphor of shaped pottery, the epic narrative of the *Mahabharata*, we are told, 'shapes' and 'contains' the *kathakali* man:

> This story [. . .] is his colour and his light. It is the vessel into which he pours himself. It gives him shape. Structure. It harnesses him. It contains

21  Huggan, *The Postcolonial Exotic*, p. 28.
22  Benjamin, 'The Storyteller', p. 91.

him. [. . .] his struggle is the reverse of an actor's struggle – he strives not to *enter* a part but to escape it. But this is what he cannot do. In his abject defeat lies his supreme triumph.

[Ch. 12, p. 231]

This degree of meta-fictional or meta-dramatic commentary in any novel draws our attention, by association, to the 'craft' of the novelist, and on the level of the frame narrative Roy recognizes this too, stating that the 'Great Stories' are the ones that 'don't deceive you with thrills and trick endings' (Ch. 12, p. 229, presumably a reference to the cheaper and more meretricious techniques of the cosmopolitan novel). But in spite of these differences in the 'honesty' of their respective narrative crafts, the *kathakali* man's chief predicament becomes, in *TGST*, a recognizably postcolonial literary one of staying true to his material. Roy's narrator worries what the *kathakali* man would become 'if he had a fleet of make-up men [. . .], an agent, a contract, a percentage of the profits' and asks 'would he be too *safe* inside his pod of wealth? Would his money grow like a rind between himself and his story?' (Ch. 12, p. 231). These questions are highly pertinent and could be asked of any socially 'committed' literature, but they are exceptionally prescient in this case, anticipating, as they seem to do, both issues of regional-cultural commercialism and the political predicaments that Roy came to face herself as a 'celebrity' author.

Having examined the significance of the *kathakali* performance in *TGST*, we must not assume that Roy's embedded presentation of the 'Great Stories' is wholly positive or that it represents a simple nostalgia for the cultural coherence of oral storytelling. Earlier in this essay we noted the uneasy political possibilities of a postcolonial return to indigenous narrative traditions and the risk of repeating, through reference to the epic, a colonial tendency to equate non-European cultures and their pre-modern narrative forms with the primitive and the irrational. As well as recognizing this colonial imaginary in her references to the 'Great Stories', Roy's condemnation of untouchability and her awareness of the politics of Hindu nationalism make her choice of episodes from the *Mahabharata* potentially very problematic, since these epic narratives have often been employed to justify gender and caste inequalities. In the past twenty years Hindu nationalists have increasingly used epics such as the *Ramayana* and associated mythical figures to mobilize attacks on non-Hindu communities in India,[23] and although Roy never acknowledges this political use of the Hindu epics in her novel (which is, of course, set before the contemporary 'communalizing' of Indian politics), she is forced to recognize the conservative tendencies of the 'Great Stories', as the basis for forms of cultural nationalism, in other ways.

Thus, Roy adopts a covertly critical approach to the cultural history of the 'Great Stories' in her novel, short-circuiting a potentially nationalist/communalist celebration of Hindu identity by associating the *kathakali* temple performance with the 'love laws' – delineated in the *Manusmriti* or The Laws of Manu – that proscribe Ammu's affair with Velutha and justify Velutha's murder by the police.

---

23  See Peter Morey and Alex Tickell (eds), *Alternative Indias: Writing, Nation and Communalism*, Amsterdam: Rodopi, 2005.

Not only do these laws sanction untouchability, they also reflect the patriarchy of a Brahminical priesthood which always had a vested interest in maintaining the social order. Hence, as the night-long drama in the temple unfolds, Roy points up the routine oppressions of the play world, indicating that, when Dushasana tries publicly to undress Draupadi, the Pandavas' wife, after she has been staked in a game of dice, Draupadi is 'strangely angry only with the men that won her, not the ones that staked her' (Ch. 12, p. 234). The patriarchal violence that characterizes the epic presentation of idealized female figures such as Draupadi is registered again in the sudden jolting bathos at the close of the drama, when dawn arrives and the *kathakali* men take off their make-up and go 'home to beat their wives' (Ch. 12, p. 236). In her presentation of the *kathakali* actors as both victims and victimizers, Roy seems to recognize the inherent conservatism of cultural nationalism, which, as Bart Moore-Gilbert notes, has a 'tendency to relocate its own minorities – women in particular – in a subordinate role in the name of either solidarity or tradition'.[24]

Summing up the relationship between *TGST* and its epic precursor genres is a difficult task because, as much as Roy presents the 'Great Stories' ambivalently or critically within her work, she also seems envious of their cultural integrity and emulates some of their effects. This narrative emulation is not achieved through the use of an actual storyteller figure within the novel (a convention used memorably by a number of other Indian-English novelists), although, as I have suggested, Roy's *kathakali* actors have an ironic correspondence with their author. Instead, Roy's storytelling aspirations are most evident on the level of form. Her description of the 'Great Stories' as 'ones you can enter anywhere' could be applied, equally, to the radical non-linearity of her own fiction, which sets up its own ending as a fateful predetermined conclusion towards which the reader 'knowingly' journeys. And, as it rehearses ancient oppressions, the *kathakali* lends Roy's novel a temporal depth, merging the past with the present in its echo of Velutha's almost ritualized sacrifice. Moreover, Roy's use of memory as a narrative structuring device[25] re-establishes, on the level of personal identity, one of the defining aspects of the epic tradition: that of mnemonic recall and the branching digressions of epic remembrance.[26] Rather than parodying the capaciousness of the national epic, like Rushdie in *Midnight's Children*, Roy constructs an epic in miniature and provides, through a microscopic attention to the details and complexities of personal memories and *petit récits* (small, personal narratives),[27] a sense of epic scope and a mythical transcendence of ordinary time. In *TGST*, 'things can change in a day' (Ch. 1, p. 32), and linear temporality warps into a form of sacred time in the moment that Ammu and Velutha recognize their mutual love: 'The man standing in the shade of the rubber trees [. . .] glanced up and caught Ammu's gaze. Centuries telescoped into one evanescent moment. History was wrong-footed, caught off guard' (Ch. 8, p. 176).

---

24  Bart Moore-Gilbert, 'Postcolonialism: Between Nationalitarianism and Globalisation? A Response to Simon During', *Postcolonial Studies*, 1(1), 1998, pp. 49–65, at p. 56.
25  See Baneth-Nouailhetas, *The God of Small Things: Arundhati Roy.*
26  Benjamin, 'The Storyteller', p. 97.
27  See Boehmer, 'East is East and South is South', p. 70.

Roy's formal investment in the 'Great Stories' must also, in the end, be under-stood in terms of her political commitments and her environmental activism since the publication of *TGST*. Few South-Asian writers working today have articu-lated their political views as clearly as Roy, who claims that the writer's job goes beyond the older political imperative of speaking truth to power; it is also, in an increasingly dispersed world, to 'create links' and to force power to remain accountable. As she states in interview,

> specialists and experts end up severing the links between things, isolat-ing them, actually creating barriers that prevent ordinary people from understanding what's happening to them [. . .] I try to do the opposite: to create links, to join the dots, *to tell politics like a story*, to communi-cate it, to make it real.[28]

In her stress on communication with 'ordinary people', a conviction that informs the title of her recent essay collection *The Ordinary Person's Guide to Empire* (2004), Roy's literary relationship with the narrative conventions of the 'Great Stories' becomes clearer. The holism of her miniaturized epic is, in fact, a way of making the reach of power recognizable and showing how politics enters 'ordin-ary' lives at the most basic level. In this sense, the politics of *TGST* are mirrored in Roy's non-fiction, which also attempts to disclose and demystify the connections 'between power and powerlessness',[29] and draws attention, continually, to 'the absolute, relentless, endless, habitual unfairness of the world'.[30]

In the light of Roy's environmental concerns, the 'storyteller' forms are signifi-cant because, as Walter Benjamin reminds us, they are the product of a time in which the natural world, and the earth and stars, 'were still concerned with the fate of men' whereas today 'both in the heavens and beneath the earth everything has grown indifferent to the fates of the sons of men and no voice speaks to them from anywhere'.[31] In the pollution and squalor that overtakes Ayemenem in *TGST* the mutual indifference of humans and nature is exemplified in the loss of the Meenachil river which is choked by 'pesticides bought with World Bank loans' (Ch. 1, p. 13). It is worth noting that environmental disaster is registered here as the loss of local legend and myth, since the Meenachil is presented throughout Roy's novel as an exacting but sustaining local spirit, the tutelary small river goddess of the communities of fisher people who disappear as their river dies. On these terms, Roy's fascination with the figure of the storyteller and her elabor-ation on the pre-modern genres of the 'Great Stories' must be read, to some extent, as a criticism of the social isolation and cynicism of the cosmopolitan novelist and a protest at his/her 'uncounselled' condition. In Roy's desire to 'tell politics like a story', the integral storytelling role of the writer as counsellor (in Benjamin's definition, a community 'sage' or teacher, or even a type of spiritual visionary) must be maintained. For, as Benjamin states, 'the art of storytelling is

---

28  Roy, *The Chequebook and the Cruise Missile*, p. 10, my italics.
29  Roy, *The Ordinary Person's Guide to Empire*, p. 13.
30  Roy, *The Ordinary Person's Guide to Empire*, p. 20
31  Benjamin, 'The Storyteller', pp. 95–6.

reaching its end because the epic side of truth, wisdom, is dying out',[32] and perhaps in Roy's writing, and in her uncompromising, aphoristic eye for hypocrisy, social inequality and the intimate reach of power, we find a form of political wisdom refashioned as 'the epic side of truth'.[33]

32  Benjamin, 'The Storyteller', p. 86.
33  Benjamin, 'The Storyteller', p. 86.

# 4

# Further reading and web resources

## Critical works on *The God of Small Things*

Existing studies of *TGST* are reviewed at some length in the Critical history section of this guide and therefore will only be discussed briefly here. At present, the most accessible introduction to Roy's novel is Julie Mullaney's *Arundhati Roy's The God of Small Things* (London and New York: Continuum, 2002), but as a comparatively short reader's guide it does not engage fully with secondary criticism on *TGST* or discuss cultural or political contexts at any length. A more focused literary critical study that features some meticulous close readings is Émilienne Baneth-Nouailhetas's *The God of Small Things: Arundhati Roy* (Paris: Armand Colin/VUEF-CNED, 2002). (In my opinion this is a key work for students who are studying *TGST* in any depth, but it is currently difficult to obtain.) A number of essay collections are also available and these include: R. K. Dhawan (ed.), *Arundhati Roy: The Novelist Extraordinary* (New Delhi: Sangam, 1999); Indira Bhatt and Indira Nityanandam (eds), *Explorations: Arundhati Roy's The God of Small Things* (New Delhi: Creative, 1999); J. Dodiya and J. Chakravarty (eds), *The Critical Studies of Arundhati Roy's The God of Small Things* (New Delhi: Atlantic, 2001); R. S. Pathak (ed.), *The Fictional World of Arundhati Roy* (New Delhi: Creative 2001); and Carole Durix and Jean-Pierre Durix (eds), *Reading Arundhati Roy's The God of Small Things* (Dijon: Éditions Universitaires de Dijon, 2002). Most recent is Murari Prasad's 2006 collection *Arundhati Roy: Critical Perspectives* (New Delhi: Pencraft).

Of these, R. K. Dhawan's thematically organized collection is the most comprehensive and features essays from an international range of contributors, some of which are considered individually elsewhere in this guide (see **pp. 72, 92, 93**). Its contents cover Roy's media reception, gender issues, transgression, history and the formal and linguistic aspects of the novel. The contributions are variable in quality, however, and some are too short or poorly referenced. Another major Indian collection, Bhatt and Nityanandam's *Explorations: Arundhati Roy's The God of Small Things*, is similarly uneven, and includes insightful scholarly essays alongside less promising pieces. Pathak's collection features an interesting and informative preliminary discussion of the marketing of *TGST*, but reproduces several essays from Dhawan's publication. Finally, Durix and Durix's collection comprises a selection of illuminating essays by French critics who examine *TGST* from psychoanalytic, post-structuralist or postmodern perspectives, and Murari Prasad's edited collection provides an informative series of essays for readers more interested in Roy's political prose – as well as reproducing two of the essays in this guide and providing an extensive bibliography.

Moving on to critical studies and monographs that examine *TGST* alongside other fictions, Elleke Boehmer's *Stories of Women: Gender and Narrative in the Postcolonial Nation* (Manchester: Manchester University Press, 2005) is a valuable comparative examination of gender and nationalism in postcolonial women's writing, which discusses Roy in two of its chapters and reproduces Boehmer's essay on Sarojini Naidu and Roy. Also taking a comparative view of *TGST*, and concentrating on the marketing of the novel and the politics of Roy's cosmopolitanism, is Bishnupriya Ghosh's *When Borne Across: Literary Cosmopolitics in the Contemporary Indian Novel* (New Brunswick, NJ: Rutgers University Press, 2004). Deepika Bahri devotes a chapter to Roy and analyses *TGST* in terms of the work of the Frankfurt School theorists (see Critical history, **p. 70**) in her monograph *Native Intelligence: Aesthetics, Politics and Postcolonial Literature* (Minneapolis, Minn.: University of Minnesota Press, 2003), and lastly, David Punter compares Roy's novel briefly with the work of postcolonial contemporaries such as Fred D'Aguiar in his *Postcolonial Imaginings: Fictions of a New World Order* (Edinburgh: Edinburgh University Press, 2000).

Contemporary literary reviews of *TGST* are still also worth reading, especially as they are mentioned so frequently in critical essays on Roy's novel. Julie Mullaney summarizes these responses in her reader's guide, and some of the most informative are Shirley Chew's 'The House in Kerala' (*Times Literary Supplement*, 30 May 1997), Michael Gorra's 'Living in the Aftermath' (*London Review of Books*, 19 June 1997), Maya Jaggi's 'An Unsuitable Girl' (*The Guardian Weekend*, 24 May 1997), John Updike's review in the special Indian fiction issue of *The New Yorker* (23 and 30 June 1997) and Alice Traux's 'A Silver Thimble in Her Fist' (*New York Times*, 25 May 1997).

## Theoretical reference points

As a set text, *TGST* usually appears on college courses on Indian writing in English or on modules that deal with a selection of generic 'postcolonial' literary works. In either case, theoretical debates within postcolonial studies are often used as a framework for studying the novel, and some useful introductions to postcolonial literature and theory are outlined below (Further reading and web resources, **p. 171**). Edward W. Said, author of *Orientalism* (New York: Pantheon, 1978), also mentioned below, is a central figure in the development of postcolonial thought, but if we consider potential critical approaches to *TGST*, some other theorists are also highly significant. These include Homi Bhabha whose essays, collected in *The Location of Culture* (London: Routledge, 1994), introduced influential concept terms such as 'mimicry' and 'hybridity' to the critical discussion of colonial and postcolonial fiction. A more historically grounded account of the development of ideas of racial and cultural hybridity (which is particularly useful in thinking about Roy's symbolic use of blurred boundaries and hybrids) can be found in Robert Young's *Colonial Desire: Hybridity in Theory, Culture and Race* (London: Routledge, 1995).

Gayatri Spivak, whose concept of the subaltern is elaborated in her essays 'Can the Subaltern Speak?' (1985; reproduced in Cary Nelson and Larry Grossberg (eds), *Marxism and the Interpretation of Culture*, Urbana, Ill.: University of Illinois Press, 1988, pp. 271–313) and 'Subaltern Studies: Deconstructing Historiography' (1985; reproduced in Ranajit Guha and Gayatri C. Spivak (eds), *Selected Subaltern Studies*, Oxford: Oxford University Press, 1988, pp. 3–32), is an important theoretical reference point in discussions of representation and caste. For further discussion of Spivak's critical formulation of the subaltern, readers should refer to her interview 'Subaltern Talk' in Donna Landry and Gerald MacLean (eds), *The Spivak Reader* (London: Routledge, 1996, pp. 287–308), and for an examination of the wider disciplinary influence of these ideas Vinayak Chaturvedi (ed.), *Mapping Subaltern Studies and the Postcolonial* (London: Verso, 2000) is useful. Readers who find Spivak's famously dense critical style off-putting may also want to refer, initially, to Stephen Morton's lucid and informative guide *Gayatri Chakravorty Spivak* (London: Routledge, 2003).

One of the best general introductions to Said's, Bhabha's and Spivak's work is still Bart Moore-Gilbert's *Postcolonial Theory: Contexts, Practices, Politics* (London: Verso, 1997), which is especially perceptive in its discussion of conceptual instabilities in Spivak's 'subaltern' theorizing. Closely involved in the theorizing of subaltern identity is the issue of gender and women's oppression, and a key introductory essay on the 'location' of Indian feminism is Chandra Talpade Mohanty's 'Under Western Eyes: Feminist Scholarship and Colonial Discourses' (in *Feminist Review*, 30 (autumn), 1988). This essay is reproduced and reconsidered in Mohanty's more recent contribution to the debate over the need to 'decolonize' feminist theory, *Feminism without Borders: Decolonising Theory, Practicing Solidarity* (Durham, NC: Duke University Press, 2003). Another important theoretical work on gender and one that touches on key themes within Indian feminism is Rajeswari Sunder Rajan's *Real and Imagined Women: Gender, Culture and Postcolonialism* (London: Routledge, 1993). For those who are interested in the association between environmentalism and feminism, a significant text is Maria Mies and Vandana Shiva's *Ecofeminism* (London: Zed, 1993), and Cheryll Glotfelty and Harold Fromm, eds, provide a good overview of ecocritical approaches to literature in *The Ecocriticism Reader: Landmarks in Literary Ecology* (Athens, Ga.: University of Georgia Press, 1996).

## The author

Roy gives a number of accounts of her life in interviews and essays, but a more accessible biographical source is Jon Simmons' web site, <http://website.lineone.net/~jon.simmons/roy>, which includes links to relevant related sites and is a good source of reviews and interviews. Possibly the most revealing interview Roy has given about her personal background is 'Knowledge and Power', the first of her conversations with David Barsamian, collected in *The Chequebook and the Cruise Missile* (London: HarperCollins, 2004), and she also reflects on literary celebrity in 'The End of Imagination', in *The Cost of Living* (London: HarperCollins, 1999). Her prosecution for contempt of court in 2001 is detailed in 'On Citizens' Right to Express Dissent' in *Power Politics*, 2nd edn, (Cambridge, Mass.: South End Press, 2001). A number of useful online interviews also exist, including the 1997 *Salon* interview with Reena Jana (<http://www.salonmagazine.com/sept97//00roy.html>), and a talk with Vir Sanghvi for Rediff.com (<http://www.rediff.com/news/apr/05roy2.htm>). For Roy's political views, readers should consult her essay collections, particularly *The Algebra of Infinite Justice* (London: HarperCollins, 2002), which reproduces both 'The Greater Common Good' and 'The End of Imagination', but also includes important essays such as 'The Ladies Have Feelings, So . . .' and 'Power Politics'. Roy's environmentalism and her support for the Narmada Bachao Andolan is the subject of interviews in *The Ecologist*, 30 [6], September 2000 (available online at <http://www.paulkingsnorth.net/guts.html>), and on the Friends of River Narmada web site (<http://www.narmada.org/articles/arinterview.html>); the Narmada Dam projects are also discussed in 'Scimitars in the Sun' (*Frontline*, 18 (1), 6–19 January 2001; available online at <http://www.thehindu.com/fline/fl1801/18010040.htm>). Recently Roy has turned her attention to the cause of global justice, and a new essay collection, *The Ordinary Person's Guide to Empire* (London: HarperCollins, 2004), as well as the Open Media pamphlet *Public Power in the Age of Empire* (New York: Seven Stories Press, 2004) focus on the consequences of contemporary US-led empire-building in Afghanistan and Iraq. Video footage of Roy's speeches can be accessed at <http://www.youtube.com> and <http://www.weroy.org>.

## Postcolonial literary criticism

In order to understand the colonial literary background of *TGST* and gain an awareness of some defining ideas in postcolonial criticism, Edward W. Said's path-breaking works *Orientalism* (New York: Pantheon, 1978) and *Culture and Imperialism* (London: Chatto and Windus, 1993), and Gauri Viswanathan's *Masks of Conquest: Literary Study and British Rule in India* (London: Faber and Faber, 1990) are invaluable. Viswanathan's work is particularly important for its insights on the political role of English literature (and English-teaching) in colonial India. An excellent general introduction to contemporary postcolonial writing and its colonial antecedents remains Elleke Boehmer's *Colonial and Postcolonial Literature: Migrant Metaphors*, 2nd edn (Oxford: Oxford University Press, 2005), which includes new readings of postcolonial women's fiction in its second edition; John McLeod's contribution to the 'Beginnings' series, *Beginning Postcolonialism* (Manchester: Manchester University Press, 2000) is also both readable and informative. Ania Loomba's *Colonialism/Postcolonialism*, 2nd edn (London: Routledge, 2005) is another popular introduction to the field, and a less well-known critical work that deals with the intertextual strategies of postcolonial fiction (and reflects on the creative, and often revisionist relationship between postcolonial works and earlier colonial fictions) is Judie Newman's *The Ballistic Bard: Postcolonial Fictions* (London: Arnold, 1995).

For readers who require a more focused account of Raj literature, a useful starting point is Bart Moore-Gilbert's edited collection of essays *Writing India 1757–1990: The Literature of British India* (Manchester: Manchester University Press, 1996), whilst the most accessible historical introduction to Indian English writing (but one which does not cover women authors in enough depth) is Arvind Krishna Mehrotra's *A History of Indian Literature in English* (London: Hurst, 2003). Mehrotra's *History* features a reprint of Jon Mee's important essay 'After Midnight: The Novel in the 1980s and 1990s' (which is discussed in Text and contexts **p. 46**). The chapter on 'Elite Plotting, Domestic Postcoloniality' in Rosemary George's *The Politics of Home: Postcolonial Relocations and Twentieth-Century Fiction* (Berkeley, Calif.: University of California Press, 1996) is an interesting comparative study of Indian women's writing in the 1980s and 1990s, and readers who require a more general overview of key issues in Indian women's writing – and the history of the genre – should look at the helpful introduction in Susie Tharu and K. Lalita's *Women Writing in India: 600 BC to the Present*, Vol. II (London: Pandora/HarperCollins, 1993).

## Cultural and political contexts

For readers and students who want to know more about modern Indian history, Sunil Khilnani's *The Idea of India* (London: Penguin, 1999), which is organized around the motivating political concepts of the post-independence state (one of which is industrial modernization, symbolized by large dam schemes), is a readable introduction. A more conventional, chronologically structured history of India from the earliest Indus civilizations to the present is Stanley Wolpert's *A New History of India*, 7th edn (Oxford: Oxford University Press, 2004).

The history of the Syrian-Christian community is highly complex and, because of its many theological controversies and internal divisions, readers may find reference works a useful starting point. Two of these, Ken Parry, David J. Melling, Dimitri Brady, Sidney H. Griffith and John Healey (eds), *The Blackwell Dictionary of Eastern Christianity* (Oxford: Blackwell, 1999) and Scott W. Sunquist (ed.), *A Dictionary of Asian Christianity* (Grand Rapids, Mich.: William B. Eerdmans, 2001), have informative summaries of the Syrian-Christian churches in India. The standard historical work on India's Syrian Christianity is Leslie Brown's *The Indian Christians of St. Thomas* (Cambridge: Cambridge University Press, 1956), recent editions of which include an informative updated section on 'The Identity of the St. Thomas Christians' (Brown deals solely with the so-called 'Orthodox' sections of the church). A less scholarly, but more accessible discussion of the Syrian-Christian church occurs in Charlie Pye-Smith's travel account, *Rebels and Outcasts: A Journey Through Christian India* (Harmondsworth: Penguin, 1998) and some of the major Syrian-Christian churches have web sites that provide brief histories (see <http://www.MalankaraChurch.org> and <http://www.marthomasyrianchurch.org/index.htm>).

Readers who are interested in the representation of caste and untouchability in *TGST* should refer to the original teachings of Manu, translated as *The Laws of Manu* by Wendy Doniger and Brian K. Smith (Harmondsworth: Penguin, 1991), and, for an overview of the mythical background of the caste system,

Wendy O'Flaherty's *Hindu Myths: A Sourcebook Translated from the Sanskrit* (Harmondsworth: Penguin, 1975) is also helpful. Probably the most influential work on the Hindu caste system is Louis Dumont's *Homo Hierarchicus: The Caste System and its Implications* (London: Granada Paladin, 1972), which examines caste in terms of hierarchies of purity and pollution and sees Hindu society as an expression of a distinctively 'pre-modern' mode of thought. Dumont's ideas have since been challenged, and Declan Quigley's *The Interpretation of Caste* (Oxford: Oxford University Press, 1993), a key work in the field, covers these debates, while Mary Searle-Chatterjee and Ursula Sharma interrogate Dumont's ideas and provide alternative views in their edited collection *Contextualising Caste: Post-Dumontian Approaches* (Oxford: Blackwell/Sociological Review, 1994). For a discussion of the colonial understanding of caste, Ronald Inden's *Imagining India* (London: Hurst, 1990) has a section on 'India in Asia: The Caste Society', and a chapter in Teresa Hubel's *Whose India? The Independence Struggle in British and Indian Fiction and History* (London: Leicester University Press, 1996) is devoted to the politics of caste and the literary influence and representation of M. K. Gandhi and B. R. Ambedkar.

An essential fictional work on the politics of caste and one which is discussed in Hubel's study, is Mulk Raj Anand's landmark 1935 novel *Untouchable* (Harmondsworth: Penguin, 2005), which features the original preface by E. M. Forster. Anand wrote the novel to draw attention to the plight of India's untouchables, and its uncompromising realism gives readers unfamiliar with the subject a detailed and sometimes shocking sense of the restrictions faced by lower-caste groups in pre-independence India. One of the most comprehensive political histories of the untouchables or *dalits* is Gail Omvedt's *Dalits and the Democratic Revolution* (New Delhi: Sage, 1994), and Eleanor Zelliot's *From Untouchable to Dalit: Essays on the Ambedkar Movement* (New Delhi: Manohar Publications, 1992) is an engaging edited essay collection on the subject. Lastly, intersections between caste and political identities in twentieth-century Kerala are discussed in Dilip Menon's *Caste, Nationalism and Communism in South-India: Malabar, 1900–1948* (Cambridge: Cambridge University Press, 1994).

Readers should seek out Radha Kumar's *The History of Doing: An Illustrated Account of Movements for Women's Rights and Feminism in India, 1800–1990* (New Delhi: Kali for Women, 1993) for an accessible historical account of women's groups and protest movements in India. Another important work of feminist historiography and cultural criticism is Kumkum Sangari and Sudesh Vaid's edited collection *Recasting Women: Essays in Indian Colonial History* (New Brunswick, NJ: Rutgers University Press, 1990), and an earlier study that readers may also find useful for its social breadth is Joanna Liddle and Rama Joshi's *Daughters of Independence: Gender, Caste and Class in India* (London: Zed, 1986). Rajeswari Sunder Rajan provides some relevant contextual material for the study of Roy's fiction and non-fiction in her edited collection *Signposts: Gender Issues in Post-Independence India* (New Brunswick, NJ: Rutgers University Press, 2001) which features discussions of 'caste and desire', and the 'Bandit Queen' controversy. For readers who want to understand the relationship between literacy, gender, and political change in Kerala, an essential work is Robin Jeffrey, *Politics, Women and Well-Being: How Kerala Became 'a Model'* (Basingstoke: Macmillan, 1992).

Among studies of *kathakali*, Phillip Zarrilli's insightful and highly readable *Kathakali Dance-Drama: Where Gods and Demons Come to Play* (London: Routledge, 2000) is one of the best. Zarrilli includes sections on performance contexts and the social history of the drama and also provides translations of actual plays. An older and less scholarly work is David Bolland's *A Guide to Kathakali* (New Delhi: National Book Trust, 1980), which includes useful summaries of thirty-six major *kathakali* plays including *Duryodhana Vadham*. For those who want a brief introduction to the history of *kathakali* dance-drama, a valuable essay is Betty True Jones's 'Kathakali Dance-Drama: An Historical Perspective', in B. C. Wade (ed.), *Performing Arts in India: Essays on Music, Dance and Drama* (Berkeley, Calif.: Center for South and Southeast Asian Studies, 1983, pp. 14–44). *Kathakali* is well covered by web resources and the principal of the Kerala Kalamandalam, M. P. Sankaran Namboodiri, has written an introduction to the form (see <http://www.vvm.com/~pnair/htm/k_kali.htm>).

The standard historical work on Kerala's communist experiment is T. J. Nossiter's *Communism in Kerala: A Study in Political Adaptation* (London: Hurst, 1982), which covers the post-independence period, and wider overviews of the Indian communist movement are provided in Nossiter's *Marxist State Governments in India: Politics, Economics and Society* (London: Pinter, 1988) and in Paul R. Brass and Marcus F. Franda (eds), *Radical Politics in South Asia* (Cambridge, Mass.: MIT Press, 1973). Dilip Menon's *Caste, Nationalism and Communism in South-India*, mentioned earlier, is also useful and, for an incisive discussion of E. M. S. Namboodiripad's political theorizing, readers should consult Menon's essay 'Being a Brahmin the Marxist Way: E. M. S. Nambudiripad and the Pasts of Kerala' in Daud Ali (ed.), *Invoking the Past: The Uses of History in South Asia* (Oxford: Oxford University Press, 1999), pp. 55–87. Namboodiripad himself has written extensively on his political career, and two important works are his two-volume *Selected Writings* (Calcutta: National Book Agency, 1982–5), and his historical work *The Communist Party in Kerala: Six Decades of Struggle and Advance* (New Delhi: National Book Centre, 1994).

On the Naxalbari uprisings, a good starting point is Rabindra Ray's *The Naxalites and Their Ideology* (New Delhi: Oxford University Press, 1988), and a focus on tribal groups in the movement is provided in Edward Duyker's *Tribal Guerrillas: The Santals of West Bengal and the Narcalite Movement* (New Delhi: Oxford University Press, 1987). An accessible historical account of Indian environmental politics in the colonial and postcolonial periods is Madhav Gadgil and Ramachandra Guha's *This Fissured Land: An Ecological History of India* (Berkeley, Calif.: University of California Press, 1993), and Ramachandra Guha has also published an important study of the Chipko movement: *The Unquiet Woods: Ecological Change and Peasant Resistance in the Himalaya*, expanded edn (1989; Berkeley, Calif.: University of California Press, 2000). Roy's own essays, especially 'The Greater Common Good', reproduced in *The Cost of Living*, detail her support for the Narmada Bachoa Andolan. For more information on the NBA's activities, including press releases about Roy, the Friends of River Narmada – a support group and international solidarity network for the NBA – has an excellent web site (<http://www.narmada.org/index.html>). Genetic engineering and the work of multinational pharmaceutical companies in places such as India is the subject of Vandana Shiva and Ingunn Moser's illuminating edited collection *Biopolitics: A Feminist and Ecological Reader on Biotechnology* (London: Zed, 1995), and Vandana Shiva's *Biopiracy: The Plunder of Nature and Knowledge* (Boston, Mass.: South End Press, 1997). Lastly, for a collection of essays that anticipates Roy's focus on 'interconnectedness', see Vandana Shiva (ed.), *Close to Home: Women Reconnect Ecology, Health and Development* (London: Earthscan, 1994).

# Index

Note: Page numbers in **bold** indicate an essay in this book by an author. Page numbers followed by (n) indicate that a quote on the page is attributed to the author in a footnote.